IMITATION TO INNOVATION

The Management of Innovation and Change Series
Michael L. Tushman and
Andrew H. Van de Ven, Series Editors

Emerging Patterns of Innovation: Sources of Japan's Technological Edge
Fumio Kodama, with a Foreword by Lewis M. Branscomb

Crisis & Renewal: Meeting the Challenge of Organizational Change
David K. Hurst

Imitation to Innovation: The Dynamics of Korea's Technological Learning
Linsu Kim

Imitation to Innovation is published in cooperation with the East Asian Institute, Columbia University.

The East Asian Institute is Columbia University's center for research, publication, and teaching on modern East Asia. The Studies of the East Asian Institute were inaugurated in 1962 to bring to a wider public the results of significant new research on modern and contemporary East Asia.

IMITATION TO INNOVATION

The Dynamics of Korea's
Technological Learning

Linsu Kim

Harvard Business School Press
Boston, Massachusetts

Copyright © 1997 by the President and Fellows of Harvard College
All rights reserved
Printed in the United States of America
01 00 99 98 97   5 4 3 2 1

Library of Congress Cataloging-in-Publication Data
Kim, Linsu.
    Imitation to innovation : the dynamics of Korea's technological learning / Linsu Kim.
    p.   cm.—(the management of innovation and change series)
    Includes bibliographical references and index.
    ISBN 0-87584-574-6 (alk. paper)
    1. Technological innovations—Economic aspects—Korea (South)   2. Industries—Korea (South)   3. Korea (South)—Social conditions.
I. Title.   II. Series.
HC470.T4K542 1997
338'.064'095195—dc20   96-28942
                            CIP

The paper used in this publication meets the requirements of the American National Standard for Permanence of Paper for Printed Library Materials Z39.49-1984

CONTENTS

Preface and Acknowledgments — vii

1. Introduction — 1

Part I: Evolution of Public Policy and Sociocultural Environment — 19

2. Government as a Learning Facilitator — 21
3. Hardworking Koreans: Education and Sociocultural Factors — 59

Part II: From Imitation to Innovation in Industries — 83

4. Analytical Frameworks — 85
5. The Automobile Industry: Crisis Construction and Technological Learning — 105
6. The Electronics Industry: From Reverse Engineering to Strategic Alliance — 131
7. The Semiconductor Industry: Leapfrogging into the World Frontier — 149
8. Imitation and Innovation in Small Firms: Two Contrasting Patterns — 171

Part III: Conclusion and Implications — 191

9. Korea's Technological Learning: Conclusion — 193
10. Korea's Technological Learning: Implications — 221

Notes — 245
References — 271
Index — 285
About the Author — 303

PREFACE AND ACKNOWLEDGMENTS

In 1973, as a first-year doctoral student at Indiana University, I was fortunate to attend an R&D management graduate seminar offered by Professor James M. Utterback, (who is now at MIT). While I was struggling to grasp technology and R&D issues in the United States, many questions lingered in my mind. How can science and technology, which seem to be the key to development in advanced countries, be effectively used for economic and social development in catching-up countries? Are theories related to technology management in advanced countries applicable to catching-up countries? If not, how does technology change in catching-up countries and why?

Since then, I have conducted in-depth research of more than 200 Korean firms across many different industrial sectors for more than twenty years. Using Korea as a case in point, I have published in excess of fifty articles internationally to answer these questions. But because each article could cover only one or two narrowly focused subjects, a monograph was needed to synthesize these diverse issues. This book is a fusion of my previous works plus more recent research findings.

This book took longer to pull together than to write. In this process I was assisted by many individuals and institutions. First and foremost, I wish to extend my deepest gratitude to Professor James Utterback, to whom I dedicate this work. His seminar, plus other courses, offered me such solid micro-level training in the field of innovation issues that I switched my academic specialization from managment science to technology management. Professor Jinjoo Lee (Korea Advanced Institute of Science and Technology), coauthor of my first book, *Technology Innovation: Process and Policy*, has been a major source of intellectual stimulation, inspiration, and support since I was a doctoral student.

On completing the doctoral program, I was privileged to work, from 1975 to 1978, at the Center for Policy Alternatives at MIT, which provided me with an opportunity to integrate micro innovation issues with macro policy issues. I owe a great deal to all members of the center, particularly the late Professor Herbert Hollomon, the late Dr. K. N. Rao, Dr. Blair McGugan, and George Heaton for intellectual inspiration and encouragement. I was also fortunate to be involved in the initial stage of Professor Utterback's book *Mastering the Dynamics of Innovation*. Professors Thomas Allen, Edward Roberts, and Eric von Hippel of MIT's Sloan School also encouraged me to approach technology issues from diverse perspectives.

Then a 1981–1985 World Bank project gave me an invaluable opportunity to focus my research on acquiring of technological capability at the firm level. This marked a turning point of my research interest from product and process innovation to technological capability building and organizational learning. I am indebted to the World Bank for financial assistance and to the participants in the project, particularly Professor Larry Westphal (Swarthmore), Dr. Carl Dahlman (World Bank), Professor Alice Amsden (MIT), and Professor Sanjaya Lall (Oxford) for constructive ideas and inspiration.

The World Bank assignment helped me build an important intellectual foundation for participation in a subsequent international undertaking that examined national innovation systems. This enabled me to broaden my outlook even further by considering technology issues in a new light. I benefited a great deal from discussions with other participants, particularly Professors Richard Nelson and Hugh Patrick (Columbia), Giovanni Dosi (Rome), Charles Edquist (Linkoping), Jorge Katz (Economic Commission for Latin American Countries), David Mowery (Berkeley), Keith Pavitt (Sussex), Nathan Rosenberg (Stanford), Jon Sigurdson (Lund), Luc Soete (Limburg), David Teece (Berkeley), and Morris Tuebal (Jerusalem).

In 1993 Columbia University invited me to spend a year as a visiting professor at its business school and to conduct research at its East Asian Institute. This opportunity gave me an intellectually exciting environment, which enabled me to begin writing this book and to test some of my ideas for it on my graduate students. Professors Gerald Curtis, Gari Ledyard, Andrew Nathan, Richard Nelson, and Hugh Patrick at the East Asian Institute, who were instrumental in inviting me to Columbia, encouraged and inspired me. I also thank Margot Landman and Mala Bachus for their administrative help and Madge Huntington for her professional copyediting assistance. At Columbia Business School, Professors Ming-Jer Chen, Donald Hambrick, Katherine Harrigan, Hugh Patrick, and Michael Tushman were sources of inspiration. I am particularly indebted to Professor Patrick and his staff at the Center on Japanese Economy and Business, who made my teaching there most rewarding, and to Professor Tushman, who encouraged me to publish this book through the Harvard Business School Press.

PREFACE AND ACKNOWLEDGMENTS   ix

In 1994 the Institute of New Technology of the United Nations University invited me to spend the summer in Maastricht, the Netherlands, to conduct a seminar and advise Ph.D. interns on their research projects. I extend my gratitude to Professor Charles Cooper, director, and the staff of the institute, particularly Dr. Ludovico Alberto, Dr. Maria Besto, and Professor Shulin Gu, who made my stay most productive. This visit afforded me an opportunity to undertake an extensive literature search and to strengthen the theoretical underpinnings of this book.

Korea University, my home institution for the past ten years, generously gave me a grant to undertake part of the research underlying this book. I am grateful to all the faculty members of its business school, particularly Deans Dong-Ki Kim, Soo-Shik Shin, and Chung Chee and Professor Yoon-Dae Euh, for intellectual as well as personal support. Professor Soo-Young Kwon offered constructive comments on the first several chapters of an earlier draft. I am also indebted to Hyun-Do Seol and Hyun Chin for their able research assistance.

Many people read the entire first draft and offered valuable suggestions. They include Professors Mark Dodgson (Australian National University), Min-Koo Han (Seoul National University), Youngbae Kim (Korea Advanced Institute of Science and Technology), Eleanor Westney (MIT), Danny Miller (École des Hautes Studes Commerciales and Columbia), N.T. Wang (Columbia), Richard Nelson (Columbia), Hugh Patrick (Columbia), Dr. Yooncheol Lim (Science and Technology Policy Institute [STEPI]), Dr. Eul-Yong Park (Korea Development Institute), Dr. Jong-Guk Song (STEPI), and particularly Timothy Wendt (Columbia), who not only made substantive recommendations on the structure and contents but helped me improve the readability of the manuscript. Yoonsun Chung (STEPI) copyedited an earlier draft.

I am also grateful to many at the Harvard Business School Press. Carol Franco, director, strongly believed that a history of Korea's technological learning could be an important book. I was pleased to work with Nicholas Philipson, acquisition editor, whose wise counsel and efficient work style enabled me to write and revise productively. His personal warmth and positive response made my association with the press very enjoyable. Nindy LeRoy, manuscript coordinator, did an excellent job of transforming my manuscript into a book. Thanks also to Gerry Morse for her copyediting skill.

I express my warmest love and appreciation to my wife, Susie, my daughters, Sue and Jean, and my son, Lin, for their unstinting support and prayer throughout the long process of planning and writing this volume. Finally, any glory associated with my work should redound to the loving Almighty God, who has paved my path from many years before the beginning of my academic life until the completion of this work.

IMITATION TO INNOVATION

1 Introduction

"In ten years, even the mountains move," says a Korean proverb. This is true in economy, business, technology, society, and even in Korean politics. Few economies in the world have matched the phenomenal economic development of South Korea—hereinafter Korea—in terms of industrialization and technological progress.

RADICAL TRANSFORMATION

Korea has indeed been transformed from a subsistent agricultural economy into a newly industrialized one during the past three decades. As late as 1961, Korea suffered from almost all the difficulties facing most poor countries today. Korea's per capita gross national product (GNP) was less than that of Sudan and less than one-third that of Mexico in 1961.

But beginning in 1962, the Korean economy grew at an average annual rate of almost 9 percent, raising GNP per capita in current prices from $87 in 1962 to $8,483 in 1994 (Table 1-1),[1] which was more than 18 times that of Sudan and 2.3 times that of Mexico.[2] With GNP per capita passing $10,000 and total GNP of $440 billion in 1995,

Table 1-1 Major Economic Indicators
         (in current price)

	1953	1960	1965
Population (in millions)	21.5	25.0	28.7
GNP ($ billions)	1.4	1.9	3.0
GNP/per Capita ($)	67.0	79.0	3.0
Exports ($ millions)	39.6	32.8	175.1
Structure of GDP			
Percent of Primary	47.3	36.8	38.0
Percent of Mining	1.1	2.1	2.0
Percent of Manufacturing	9.0	13.8	18.0
Percent of Utilities	2.6	4.1	4.7
Percent of Service	40.0	43.2	32.1
Structure of Manufacturing			
Percent of Light Industry	78.9	76.6	68.6
Percent of Heavy Industry	21.1	23.4	31.4

SOURCE: Office of Statistics, *Tong-gyero bon Hankukeo Baljachi* (Korea's Progress in Statistics) (Seoul: Office of Statistics, Republic of Korea, August 1995).

[a]Tentative figure.

Korea ranks eleventh among the world's top economic powers in terms of GNP and seventh in terms of manufacturing value-added.

Korea has also achieved phenomenal growth in its exports, which increased from a mere $40 million in 1963 to $96 billion in 1994. The share of manufactured goods in exports increased from 14.3 percent to more than 92 percent during the same period. As an exporter of manufactures, Korea moved from number 101 in the world in 1962 to number 13 in 1994. Thanks to a flourishing middle class, income distribution in Korea nears that of the Organization for Economic Cooperation and Development (OECD) countries.[3] Ezra Vogel concludes, "No nation has tried harder and come so far so quickly, from handicrafts to heavy industry, from poverty to prosperity, from inexperienced leaders to modern planners, managers, and engineers."[4] Some project that Korea could well become the first country to establish itself as an advanced industrial power since the emergence of Japan.[5]

	1970	1975	1980	1985	1990	1994[a]
	32.2	35.3	38.1	40.8	43.4	44.5
	8.1	20.9	60.6	91.1	251.8	376.9
	253	594	1,597	2,242	5,883	8,483
	835.2	5,081.0	17,504.9	30,283.1	65,015.7	96,013.2
	26.6	24.9	14.7	12.5	8.7	7.0
	1.5	1.6	1.5	1.2	0.5	0.3
	21.0	25.9	28.2	29.3	29.2	26.9
	6.6	5.9	10.1	10.6	13.7	15.8
	42.2	41.7	45.5	46.5	47.9	50.0
	60.8	52.1	46.4	41.5	34.1	26.9
	39.2	47.9	53.6	58.5	65.9	73.1

How have Korea and Korean firms managed to achieve such a phenomenal growth in industrialization in only three decades? What are major factors behind the growth? Most developing countries have tried to industrialize their economies. Yet the great majority of them have made little progress; only a few have managed to make a significant stride in catching up. Under what conditions, then, is catching-up possible? What are the implications for other catching-up countries? What are the implications for advanced countries? More specific questions related to the catching-up process are raised later in this chapter. This book is aimed at answering these questions by explaining Korea's rapid technological learning.

Technological change has been a major determinant of national economic development. In industrialized economies, many studies have shown that more than 50 percent of long-term economic growth stems from technological changes that improve productivity and lead to new products, processes, or industries.⁶ For this reason, the question often raised is how science and technology, which appear to be the key to industrial development in advanced countries, can be effectively used for economic and social development in the less developed regions of the world.⁷

TECHNOLOGICAL CAPABILITY AND LEARNING

Korea's rapid industrialization may be attributed to many factors. The most important of all may be the technological change in its industries, which flowed from the accumulation of technological capability over time.⁸ The term "technology" refers to both a collection of physical processes that transforms inputs into outputs and knowledge and skills that structure the activities involved in carrying out these transformations. That is, technology is the practical application of knowledge and skills to the establishment, operation, improvement, and expansion of facilities for such transformation and to the designing and improving of outputs therefrom.

The term "technological capability" refers to the ability to make effective use of technological knowledge in efforts to assimilate, use, adapt, and change existing technologies. It also enables one to create new technologies and to develop new products and processes in response to changing economic environment. It denotes operational command over knowledge. It is manifested not merely by the knowledge possessed, but, more important, by the uses to which that knowledge can be put and by the proficiency with which it is used in the activities of investment and production and in the creation of new knowledge. For this reason, the term "technological capability" is used interchangeably with the term "absorptive capacity": a capacity to absorb existing knowledge and in turn generate new knowledge.⁹

Technological capability has three elements: production, investment, including duplication and expansion, and innovation. "Production capability," defined in Table 1-2, refers to numerous technological capabilities required to operate and maintain production facilities. These may be divided into two broad subsets. The first subset includes those capabilities required to achieve efficient operation within the parameters of the original technology and the capability to repair and maintain existing physical capital according to a regular schedule or as needed. The second subset encompasses capabilities needed to adapt and improve the existing production technology, still within the origi-

Table 1-2 Elements of Technological Capabilities

Production Capability

Production management to oversee operation of established facilities

Production engineering to provide information required to optimize operation of established facilities, including raw material control, production scheduling, quality control, troubleshooting, and adaptations of processes and products to changing circumstances

Repair and maintenance of physical capital according to regular schedule and as needed

Investment Capability

Manpower training to impart skills and abilities of all kinds

Investment feasibility studies to identify possible projects and ascertain prospects for viability under alternative design concepts

Project execution to establish or expand facilities, including project management, project engineering (detailed studies, basic engineering, and detailed engineering), procurement, embodiment in physical capital, and start-up

Innovation Capability

Basic research to gain knowledge for its own sake

Applied research to obtain knowledge with specific commercial implications

Development to translate technical and scientific knowledge into concrete new products, processes, and services

SOURCE: Adapted from Larry E. Westphal, Linsu Kim, and Carl J. Dahlman, "Reflections on the Republic of Korea's Acquisition of Technological Capability," in Nathan Rosenberg and Claudio Frischtak, eds., *International Transfer of Technology: Concepts, Measures, and Comparisons* (New York: Praeger Press, 1985), 167–221.

nal design parameters, in response to changing circumstances and to increase productivity. Adaptation and improvement start almost simultaneously with the operation of technology.

"Investment capability" refers to abilities required for expanding capacity and establishing new production facilities. It includes investment feasibility analysis and project execution. The former involves ability to undertake the initial analysis of its profitability, detailed specifications of the project, and ability to ascertain prospects for viability under alternative design concepts. The latter involves abilities in project engineering—both basic and detailed engineering—project management that organizes and oversees the activities involved in project execution, procurement to choose, coordinate, and supervise hardware suppliers and construction contractors, embodiment in physical capital to accomplish site preparation and construction of plants, and start-up operations to attain predetermined norms of manufacturing facilities.

"Innovation capability" consists of abilities to create and carry new technological possibilities through to economic practice. The term covers a wide range of activities from capability to invent to capability to innovate and to capability to improve existing technology beyond the original design parameters. Invention and innovation are the product of both formal and informal activities. The term "innovation" is often associated by many with technological change at international frontiers. Most innovations in advanced countries generally denote a change of the frontier. Major technological innovations, however, are neither the only, nor perhaps the main, sources of productivity improvement in the history of industrial development in advanced countries. Minor changes to given technologies are a vital and continuous source of productivity gain in practically every industry in both advanced and catching-up countries.

The term "technological capability" is used here to indicate the level of organizational capability at a point in time, while the term "technological learning" is used to depict the dynamic process of acquiring technological capability. Thus, I use technological learning and the acquisition of technological capability interchangeably.

This book attempts to shed light on this dynamic process of technological learning in Korea from 1960 to 1995. To this end, it is necessary to understand Korea's economic and social conditions before 1960, which set the stage for the subsequent technological development.

INITIAL SETTING

Possessing one of the world's longest histories as an independent nation, Korea has a long tradition of its own civilization and scientific achievements. Korean astronomy, printing, and ceramics, though many originally based on technologies imported from China, were in some sense more advanced than their Chinese counterparts. The earliest Korean educational institution, *T'aehak* (Great Learning), which was modeled after similar Chinese institutions, was established in A.D. 372 to train prospective government officials, and it continued through succeeding kingdoms until the late nineteenth century. The adoption of Chinese government and educational institutions, though in highly modified form, stimulated the growth of Confucian scholarship among the upper classes. Koreans were good imitators of Chinese institutions.

Sang-Woon Jeon documented hundreds of nineteenth-century Korean scientific and technological achievements ranging from astronomy, meteorology, physics, physical technology, and chemical technology to geography.[10] To mention a few, Korea built the world's earliest known extant observatory in A.D. 647. Subsequently, Korea invented armillary clocks, automatic clepsydras, and sundials, leading to the development of a much more accurate calendar. Another well-known relic of seventh-century high scientific achievements is the artificial cave temple, *Sokkuram*, which required a high degree of mathematical and engineering knowledge. Korea also invented a movable metal type some 200 years before Johannes Gutenberg. Although many basic ideas came from China, attempts were always made to fit foreign inventions to local needs and conditions, leading to significantly important new inventions and discoveries. That is, Koreans also appear to have been good innovators.

Unlike the great majority of developing nations first formed by Western colonial powers, Korea had been a unified, independent state for more than 1,200 years since the Silla dynasty with its own splendid cultural heritage. But surrounded by big powers—China in the west, Mongolia and Russia in the north, and Japan in the east—Korea was frequently subject to foreign invasion. The most recent was by the Japanese, a thirty-six-year colonialization lasting from 1910 to 1945. Prior to that time, Koreans were far better civilized and their society was far better organized than their counterparts in other colonies.

Under Japanese colonial rule, the manufacturing sector averaged an annual growth rate of 9.7 percent between 1910 and 1941.[11] However, the Japanese accounted for 94 percent of the authorized capital of manufacturing establishments in Korea. Such key sectors as metals, chemicals, and electrical appliances were almost wholly owned by the Japanese. Korean firms were much smaller and financially and technologically weaker than those of the Japanese. According to one estimate, there were some 1,600 Korean technicians in the manufacturing sector, but this accounted for only 19 percent of all technicians in Korea. The proportion was much smaller (11 percent) in the key manufacturing sectors mentioned above.

It should also be noted that nearly 300,000 Koreans were experienced in mining and manufacturing when Korea gained independence in 1945.¹² This means that Koreans enjoyed greater participation in these sectors than indigenous populations in colonies under Western rule. This number, however, is small compared with the total population of 25 million, and most of these workers had menial jobs, which explains why imported foreign technology in the postwar years often took the form of turnkey plants.

From 1945 to 1953, unprecedented events significantly disrupted Korean economic development: (1) the political and economic vacuum and chaos caused by the Japanese withdrawal from the Korean Peninsula when Japan surrendered to the Allied forces in 1945; (2) the arbitrary division of the nation into North Korea and South Korea in 1945 and the consequent loss of mining, metal fabrication, and chemical manufacturing and power sectors to the North; and (3) destruction of industry and infrastructure in the 1950–1953 Korean War.

First, when the Japanese withdrew from Korea, much of the physical capital was un- or underutilized owing mainly to the lack of technical and managerial capability. For example, the number of manufacturing and construction establishments had fallen more than 50 percent by 1948; employment declined 41 percent.¹³ The shipbuilding industry provides an interesting illustration of the lack of Korean technological capability in 1945. The Japanese left a steel shipyard with four small-steel ships under construction. It took several years for the Koreans to discover the blueprints for the ships, which had lain untouched for almost a decade. By the time the Koreans acquired enough experience to figure out what to do with the half-finished vessels, the ships were so rusted that they had to be scrapped. This is an example of the minimal skill formation achieved by Koreans involved in modern enterprises under Japanese domination.¹⁴

Second, the division of the nation resulted in disaster by splitting in two an economy that had been built as an integrated whole. South Korea retained nearly two-thirds of the population and agricultural output, but lost more than 90 percent of electric power and more than 75 percent of coal and iron ore production to North Korea. In manufacturing, South Korea had little industry aside from textiles; North Korea kept most of metal fabrication and chemicals. By 1948 the unexpected partition of the nation, together with the sudden evacuation of Japanese entrepreneurs, managers, and technicians, and the disruption of supplies of intermediate products and separation from their markets, had caused a radical drop in manufacturing output to about 15 percent of South Korea's 1939 level.¹⁵

Third, the Korean War was much more detrimental to the economy and the society as a whole than the division of the nation. It destroyed the majority of industrial and infrastructure facilities Korea had inherited from the Japanese and caused more than a million civilian casualties. Nonmilitary damage to buildings, structures, equipment, and other movable assets amounted to $3.07 billion at the implicit exchange rate for 1953, or between 86 and 200 percent of estimated Korean GNP for 1953, depending on which GNP estimate one uses. In the manufacturing sector, the government estimated that approximately 44 percent of prewar facilities was destroyed during the war. Damage was heavier in relatively large-scale textile and cement facilities of industrial areas.

When the armistice was signed in 1953, the net commodity product (no consistent pre-1953 national income account data are available for comparison) decreased by 26 percent compared with the 1940 figure, and net commodity product per capita declined by 44 percent.[16] Agriculture, forestry, and fishery accounted for 48.6 percent of GNP and manufacturing for less than 7.7 percent in 1953. Total fixed investment in those days was so insignificant that it barely covered the depreciation on existing capital stock. Yet 88 percent of this modest amount had to be financed out of foreign aid.[17]

Korea emerged from the war with a subsistent rural economy. The share of GNP provided by agriculture and forestry was 45.5 percent in constant 1970 prices, and more than 64 percent of employment was still involved in it in 1960. Mechanization of some of the most onerous and labor-consuming tasks, such as the milling of grain, had begun in the 1930s and 1940s. But given the labor-surplus condition, farm mechanization was at a minimum level. The two notable exceptions to the backward rural development were the land reform measures undertaken in the late 1940s and the wide use of chemical fertilizers. First, land reform led to a major redistribution of both land and income from landlords to the new owner-cultivators. Through the land reform, the proportion of tenant farmers declined from 81 percent to 5.7 percent of all cultivators, and the amount of rented land fell from 60 to 15 percent of total cultivated land, eliminating a powerful landowning class that could be a major obstacle to the development of dynamic capitalism.[18] Second, Korean farmers used more than 20 kilograms of plant nutrient per hectare in the 1930s and about 100 kilograms per hectare by the late 1940s.[19]

The Japanese developed both the fiscal and financial systems in Korea to relatively high levels of sophistication during their colonial reign. Financial institutions were predominantly owned and managed by the Japanese. After the Japanese withdrew in 1945, these institutions were taken over by Koreans, but the volume of banking activity declined drastically. According to a study that described the 1950 financial system, there were no money or capital markets in the accepted sense of the term and no adequate facilities for mobilizing savings. The use of checks was highly underdeveloped and the bulk of the country's monetary transactions was carried out in cash. A large fraction of the aggregate turnover of goods and services did not even involve the use of money, but took the form of payments in kind and barter transactions.[20]

Modern education, first introduced to Korea by American missionaries, was expanded by the Japanese colonial government. The Japanese, however, limited Koreans mainly to the primary grades simply to convert Korean youth into loyal subjects and to train them for subordinate roles in agriculture and industry. Some Koreans were able to go beyond these limits, but they were few. At the end of Japanese rule, only 2 percent of the Korean population older than fourteen had completed secondary school, and the illiteracy rate stood at 78 percent.

The emergence of the United States as the guardian of the free world against communist aggression after World War II led to the Asian version of the Marshall Plan, providing economic and military aid to Korea at the front line of that global struggle. The United States pumped almost $6 billion to Korea through the 1960s. U.S. economic aid financed more than 80 percent of Korea's capital formation and import surplus until the mid-1960s. U.S. military aid built Korea's military machines, providing disciplined training to every male in Korea, leading to the formation of many bureaucrats and managers for both the public and the private sectors.[21] The U.S. military presence also provided opportunities for some Korean firms to learn Western technologies by engaging, for instance, in small construction projects.

In short, the vacuum and chaos caused by the fall of Japanese colonial rule, arbitrary division of the nation into North Korea and South Korea, and the ensuing civil war, all of which occurred between 1945 and 1953, flattened Korea as "a nation with little left of its past and facing a bleak future."[22] In spite of U.S. aid, which brought Korea back to its prewar economic level, Korea still suffered from almost all the problems facing most resource-poor, low-income countries today. Korea, beginning with a far lower technical base than and as the poorest of the newly industrializing countries (NICs),[23] has achieved phenomenal industrial development in a generation.

FROM IMITATION . . .

Such rapid industrialization in Korea stemmed largely from imitation, which does not necessarily imply illegal counterfeits or clones of foreign goods; it can also be legal, involving neither patent infringement nor pirating proprietary know-how. A study shows that 60 percent of patented innovations were imitated legally within four years of their introduction.[24] Imitation ranges from illegal duplicates of popular products to truly innovative products that are merely inspired by a pioneering brand. Steven Schnaars categorizes several distinct imitations: counterfeits or product pirates, knockoffs or clones, design copies, creative adaptations, technological leapfrogging, and adaptation to another industry.[25]

First, counterfeits and knockoffs are duplicative imitations, but one is illegal and the other legal. Counterfeits are copies that resemble the same premium brand name as the original but of low quality, illegally robbing the innovator of due profits, for example, a Rolex watch sold at a fraction of its regular price. In contrast, most knockoffs or clones are legal products in their own right, closely copying the pioneering products in the absence or expiration of patents, copyrights, and trademarks but marketed with their own brand names at far lower prices. IBM PC clones are good examples. Clones often surpass the original in quality.

Duplicative imitation does not require specialized investment in R&D and information channels. Only a low level of learning is necessary since the firms cannot and are not required to generate new knowledge. Nevertheless, duplicative imitation can rarely occur in a vacuum. Unlike replication within the same firm, in duplicating another firm's products or processes, target routine is not substantially available as a template. Therefore, it is not possible to resolve all the problems arising in the imitation by closer scrutiny of the prototype's production system. At one extreme, the production in question may be a novel combination of highly standardized technological elements. In this case, reverse engineering may result in the identification of those elements and the nature of their combination, leading to an economically successful imitation. At the other extreme, the target routine may involve so much idiosyncratic and firm-specific knowledge that imitation is highly problematic, requiring substantial help by means of formal technology transfer from the originator.

In the wide range of intermediate cases, the imitator has to obtain as much understanding of the technological elements and the nature of their combination as possible and fill in remaining gaps by independent efforts.[26] Or the imitator must rely substantially on technical assistance in various forms from the forerunner. For this reason, it requires considerable internal capability to identify the nature and source of relevant technology, to negotiate its transfer or reverse-engineer, and to assimilate so as to be able to apply it to the specific market needs and material availabilities facing the firm. Duplicative imitation conveys no sustainable competitive advantage to the imitator technologically, but it supports competitive edge in price if the imitator's wage cost is significantly lower than the imitatee's.

For this reason, when it is legal, duplicative imitation is an astute strategy in the early industrialization of low-wage, catching-up countries, as such technology is generally mature and readily available and duplicative imitation of mature technology is relatively easy to undertake.

Second, design copies, creative adaptations, technological leapfrogging, and adaptation to another industry are creative imitations. Design copies mimic the style of the market leader but carry their own brand name and unique engineering specifications. Japanese luxury cars, for instance, emulate German models but possess their own engineering features. Creative adaptations are innovative in the sense that creative improvements are inspired by existing products. Technological leapfrogging depicts a late entrant's advantage in getting access to newer technology in the wake of more accurate understanding of a growing market, enabling the imitator to leapfrog the innovator. Adaptation to another industry illustrates the application of innovations in one industry for use in another.

Creative imitations aim at generating facsimile products but with new performance features. They involve not only such activities as benchmarking and strategic alliances but also notable learning through substantial investment in R&D activities in order to create imitative products, the performance of which may be significantly better or production cost considerably lower than the original. Michele Bolton argues that Japanese strategy represents these features and calls it reflective imitation.[27]

Korea's 1960s and 1970s strategy was largely associated with duplicative imitations, producing on a large scale knockoffs or clones of mature foreign products, imitative goods with their own or original equipment manufacturers' brand names at significantly lower prices.

Korea's 1980s and 1990s industrialization increasingly involves creative imitations.

TO INNOVATION

Imitation alone is insufficient for Korea to realize its dream of becoming a highly industrialized country. Both creative Japanese-style imitation and American-style innovation are required not only to catch up in existing industries but also to challenge advanced countries in new industries.

Innovation is defined as a pioneering activity, rooted primarily in a firm's internal competencies, to develop and introduce a new product to the market. Distinction between innovation and creative imitation is, however, blurred. Joseph Schumpeter distinguished the two by saying that innovation involves commercialization of invention, which is the purely physical set of creation and discovery, while imitation refers to the diffusion of innovation.[28] Most innovations do not, however, involve breakthrough inventions but are deeply rooted in existing ideas. As Nelson and Winter note, imitators working with an extremely sparse set of clues might claim the title of innovator, since most of the problem is really solved independently.[29]

As the first firm to establish itself in its market, an innovator benefits from first-mover advantages that are unavailable to imitators. They include, among other things, image and reputation, brand loyalty, an opportunity to pick the best market, technological leadership, an opportunity to set product standards, access to distribution, experience effects, and an opportunity to establish an entry barrier of patents and switching costs.

Several industries in Korea, such as semiconductors, electronics, and biotechnology, are stretching their R&D activities to transform themselves into innovators as well as effectively creative imitators. Korea's 1990s innovation drive in selective industries is marked by intensified in-house R&D activities and participation in global alliances and reflects Korea's aspiration to become a member of the industrially advanced community.

Many skills and activities required in reverse engineering have easily been transformed into activities called R&D, as Korea approached the technological frontier. Reverse engineering involved activities that sensed the potential needs in a market, activities that located knowledge or products which would meet the market needs, and activities that would infuse these two elements into a new project. Reverse engineering also involved purposive search of relevant information, effective interactions among technical members within a project team and with marketing and production departments within the firm, effective interactions with other organizations such as suppliers, customers, local R&D institutes, and universities, and trial and error in developing a satisfactory result. Skills and activities required in these processes are in fact the same in innovation process in R&D.

The above discussions lead to two questions: How did Korea acquire the technological capability to undertake duplicative imitations—reverse engineering—in the 1960s and 1970s? How has Korea accumulated enough capability to conduct creative imitations and innovations in the 1980s and 1990s? Part II of this book answers these questions.

DRIVING FORCES

In the evolution from duplicative imitation to creative imitation and innovation, the configuration of Korea's production and exports has changed significantly. In the mid-1960s, Korea began exporting textiles, apparel, toys, wigs, plywood, and other labor-intensive mature products. Ten years later, ships, steel, consumer electronics, and construction services challenged established suppliers from industrially advanced countries. By the mid-1980s, computers, semiconductor memory chips, videocassette recorders, electronic switching systems, automobiles, industrial plants, and other technology-intensive products were added to the list of Korea's major export items, with the semiconductor chip topping the list in terms of export value. In the mid-1990s, Korea is working on such next-generation products as multimedia technology, high-density television, personal communication systems, and a new type of nuclear breeder. By 1994 Korea ranked second in the world in shipbuilding and consumer electronics, third in semiconductor memory chips, fifth in textiles, chemical fibers, petrochemicals, and electronics, and sixth in automobiles and iron and steel.[30]

What are the driving forces underlying the dynamic process from imitation to innovation in Korea? There appear to be several conspicuous major characteristics, some idiosyncratic to the country: the Korean War, which transformed Korean society; strong government, which directed industrial development; large conglomerates—*chaebols*, the Korean version of the Japanese family enterprise *zaibatsu*—which served as engines; hardworking Koreans who empowered these engines; an export-oriented strategy, which imposed competitive pressure on Korean firms; and crisis construction as a major means of expeditious technological learning.

First, the 1950–1953 Korean War set the Korean economy twenty years back but made a major impact on Korean society, drastically transforming a rigid class society into a flexible, classless society. What was the impact of the war on the formation of Korean mental attitude and organizational life? How did the war impact technological learning in subsequent decades?

Second, one of the most conspicuous characteristics of the industrialization of Korea is the strong government and its orchestrating role. The government held the wheel and supplied the fuel, while private firms, particularly chaebols, functioned as the engines. This prompts several questions: What made it possible for the government to become so strong in Korea? What made Korean technocrats so smart as to make their intervention relatively effective amid widespread and generally inefficient state intervention in most of the Third World? How has Korean government learned relatively effectively from Japanese experience? What policy mechanisms has the government used in facilitating technological learning in industry?

Third, behind the remarkable industrial growth are big businesses, which have emerged as powerful engines in the past decades. Korea's four chaebols—Samsung, Daewoo, Ssangyong, and Sunkyong—were on *Fortune* magazine's list of the world's 100 largest industrial corporations in 1992. Hyundai and LG, formerly Lucky-Goldstar, two of the three largest *chaebols* in Korea, coyly resisted revealing their group revenues, but if they did, they would probably rank just above or below Samsung. That is, Korea's six largest chaebols all rank among the top 100 global industrial enterprises.[31] How has the government helped chaebols form and prosper? What role have the *chaebols* played in acquiring technological capability for labor-intensive industries in the 1960s and 1970s and for technology-intensive industries and the globalization of Korean businesses in the 1980s and 1990s?

Fourth, these *chaebols* employ well-trained, hardworking Koreans who have empowered the Korean engines. Deprived of natural resources, Korea finds its greatest resource in its human resources. Commitment to education by Korea was the strongest among the eight industrialized nations—Denmark, Germany, Italy, Japan, Sweden,

Switzerland, the United Kingdom, and the United States—and two semi-industrialized countries—Singapore and Korea—studied by Michael Porter.[32] These well-educated Koreans worked long and hard for Korea's success. The average Korean manufacturing worker, for instance, worked 53.8 hours each week in 1985 compared with 33.1 to 42.9 hours in OECD countries, including Japan, 44 to 48 hours in other Asian NICs, and 46 hours in Mexico.[33] Even in 1994, Koreans worked longest among these countries. How has Korea invested for human resource development? What made Koreans work so long and hard?

Fifth, Korea pursued an export-oriented industrialization strategy from the very beginning, when import substitution was still in its early stage. The Korean government made exports a life-or-death struggle in order to achieve economic growth goals. The government pushed and pulled firms with threats and promises. How has the export-oriented strategy affected Korean firms in technological learning?

Finally, the government and *chaebols* used crises as a major means of technological transformation. The government deliberately imposed a series of crises on firms by demanding that they achieve overly ambitious goals. Top management also constructed a series of crises as a strategic means to expedite technological learning. How have *chaebols* turned these crises into creative opportunities for expeditious learning? Why is crisis construction a useful means of technological transformation?

APPROACH AND ORGANIZATION OF THE BOOK

This book attempts to answer these questions and shed light on the dynamics of technological learning in transformation from imitation to innovation. Understanding the dynamic process of technological learning calls for a multilevel, multidisciplinary approach. It requires one to examine interactions among actors at the macro, meso, and micro levels.[34] It also requires one to analyze the process from several perspectives—technology, economics, management and organization, sociology, and cultural anthropology.

There are numerous books about Korea's economic development. Many authors have treated the subject from a macro perspective, focusing primarily on government and its macroeconomic performance.[35] Several have discussed Korean firms at the micro level, focusing mainly on their cultural, anthropological, managerial, or technological aspect, but few have looked at the interactions between actors at different levels and from a multidisciplinary perspective.[36] One exception is Alice Amsden's work on Korea's late industrialization, which analyzes the role of the state and its interaction with big businesses primarily from a macro perspective. But Amsden also examines the process of imitative learning of two selected industries at the micro level.[37]

In contrast, the primary focus of this book is the dynamic process of technological learning at the microeconomic level—the firm as the unit of analysis—examining how firms learn and unlearn in response to changes in market and technology. It is the firm that brings about product and process changes in order to survive and grow in the competitive market, and that in turn enhances international competitiveness of the economy. This book also examines the dynamic workings from macro and meso perspectives in attempts to understand the mechanism of technological learning at the firm level holistically.

Part I examines the state role and sociocultural factors under which Korean firms have accumulated technological capability. Chapter 2 discusses industrial and technological policies that to a great extent shape the external environment of firms. Chapter 3 examines the educational system and sociocultural factors that mold the characteristics of well-educated, hardworking Koreans.

Part II analyzes industry cases, depicting the transformation from imitation to innovation. Chapter 4 provides several analytical frameworks to help readers deepen their understanding of industry case studies. Chapter 5 discusses the automobile industry, an interesting case that illustrates most vividly how crisis construction facilitates technological learning. Chapter 6 examines the electronics industry, which has made significant strides from reverse engineering to strategic alliances. Chapter 7 treats the growth of the semiconductor industry, which has leapfrogged into the world's frontier in memory chips. Chapter 8 presents the case of small and medium-size firms, showing two contrasting patterns.

In Part III, Chapter 9 draws conclusions on Korea's technological learning. Chapter 10 outlines the implications of Korea's technological learning for public policymaking and corporate management and addresses implications for other catching-up countries as well as technology suppliers in advanced countries.

Evolution of Public Policy And Sociocultural Environment

PART I

2 Government as a Learning Facilitator

"Here comes the Korean," once heralded *Newsweek* in its cover story on Korea's economic miracle and Korea's stampede into the international market. Many economists attribute Korea's success to the Korean government's developmental role,[1] concluding that the economic miracle stemmed from a policy miracle.[2] The government envisioned a miracle and provided a policy environment, but it was industry that made it reality.

The role of the government in industrialization is so complex and multifaceted that it cannot be adequately covered in a single chapter. Therefore, this chapter limits its discussions only to those facets directly or indirectly related to technological learning in Korea at the microeconomic level. Other writers have covered the government's developmental role in Korea more extensively, though mostly at the macroeconomic level.[3]

What can the government do to facilitate technological learning at individual firms under a dynamically changing global technology environment? Over the years, the Korean government has adopted an array of policy instruments designed to facilitate technological learning in industry and in turn strengthen the international competitiveness of the economy. This history can be better understood by analyzing it from three perspectives: market mechanism, technology flow, and time.

Market mechanism perspective includes both the demand side of technology development that creates market needs for technological change and the supply side of technology development that strengthens technological capability. The former is often referred to as industrial policy in a narrow sense of the term, while the latter can be thought of as science and technology (S&T) policy.

In other words, this perspective organizes policies related to technological development into three major components: policies designed to strengthen the demand side, creating market needs for technology, policies designed to strengthen the supply side, increasing S&T capabilities, and policies designed to provide effective linkages between the demand and supply sides, attempting to ensure that innovation activities are both technically and commercially successful.[4]

Unless there is a competitive market in which firms believe that innovation in products and processes is necessary to sustaining and raising market competitiveness, there is little investment in innovation activities, as innovation is usually uncertain and risky. Also, strong links to the market are needed to make sure public R&D efforts are effective and efficient. In this sense, science and technology policies should be an integral part of the overall industrial policies that shape market structure and industrial development.

However, even though the market calls for the introduction of new products and processes, countries without indigenous technological capabilities cannot be expected to grow industrially. Some economies have indigenous technological capabilities but still don't grow. To be commercially exploited, technological capabilities must be coupled with the right business capabilities.

Finally, despite the presence of both demand for innovation and supply of capabilities, few innovations can be realized unless there is good management of the R&D system, effectively linking demand with supply. The absence of this linkage explains why in some industrialized countries there is little innovation despite a strong demand for it and an adequate supply of technical capabilities. Some linkage instruments such as institutions to bridge the demand and supply sides of technology and tax and financial incentives for R&D efforts in developing countries are not effective in stimulating technological activities in the absence of demand and supply of technology.

Government policies related to technology development may also be assessed by the technology flow perspective. This perspective is mainly concerned with three key sequences in the flow of technology from abroad to catching-up countries: transfer of foreign technology, diffusion of imported technology, and indigenous R&D to assimilate and improve imported technology and to generate its own technology. The first sequence involves technology transfer from abroad through such formal mechanisms as foreign direct investment, the purchase of turnkey plants and machinery, foreign licenses, and technical services. Such transfer can facilitate the acquisition of technological capability in catching-up countries.

The effective diffusion of imported technology within an industry and across industries is a second sequence in upgrading technological capability of an economy. If a technology is transferred to a firm and its use is limited only to its original importer, it may give the firm monopoly power over other firms for a period of time; however, the broader economic effect of the technology may be considerably limited. To maximize its benefits, imported technology has to be diffused throughout its economy.

The third sequence involves local efforts to assimilate, adapt, and improve imported technology and eventually to develop one's own technology. These efforts are crucial to augmenting technology transfer and expediting the acquisition of technological capability. Technology may be transferred to a firm from abroad or through local diffusion, but the ability to use it effectively cannot. This ability can only be acquired through indigenous technological effort. Local endeavors can include self-directed attempts to copy or reverse-engineer foreign products and processes, those aimed at improving and adapting previously acquired technology, and one's own research and development. Such efforts become increasingly important as industrialization progresses. These activities are necessary to strengthen international competitiveness in the face of increasing pressure from other catching-up countries.

The two perspectives outlined here, market mechanisms and technology flow, may be combined as illustrated in Figure 2-1. The dynamic perspective dimension is added as the third dimension to indicate time, which is very important. The relative impact of the individual sequences of technology flow and the impact of different types of market mechanisms—demand, supply, and linkage—change as an industry advances through different stages of development over time

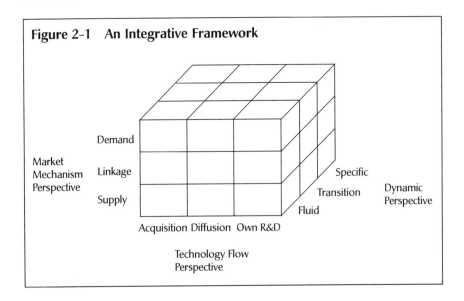

Figure 2-1 An Integrative Framework

(see Chapter 4 for detailed discussions). This integrative framework is used below to analyze and evaluate Korea's industrial and S&T policies.

GENERAL BACKGROUND

One of the most conspicuous characteristics of the industrialization of Korea is the strong government and its orchestrating role. The government steered the wheel and supplied fuel. It set ambitious goals and directed the private sector with sticks and carrots, and private firms, particularly *chaebols*, functioned as engines. What then made it possible for the government to become so strong in Korea? What made Korean technocrats smart enough to make their intervention relatively effective amid widespread and generally inefficient government intervention in most of the Third World? How has Korean government learned relatively effectively from Japanese experience?

First, when Park Chung Hee seized power in 1961, he was single-minded in his goal to industrialize Korea and transform its subsistent agricultural economy into an industrialized one in spite of the odds against it. Toward this end, he created a highly centralized, strong government to plan and implement ambitious economic development programs. The government was vested with power to license important business projects to private firms and set the direction of industrialization. Commercial banks were nationalized to allocate resources for industrial projects according to national priority. To push industrialization at the fastest possible speed, Park borrowed heavily from abroad rather than waiting patiently for domestic savings to be formed. This mechanism of channelling low-cost foreign finance to private firms further strengthened his centralized power. Then, with a small group of competent economists to advise him, he made all important decisions himself.[5] As a former army general, he was literally a field commanding general of Korea's industrialization drive.

Another important government means to consolidate its power over the private sector was in the handling of illicit wealth accumulation charges. The Park regime arrested thirteen leaders of large business conglomerates charging that they had engaged in illicit and illegal behavior in accumulating wealth during the corrupt Rhee years, 1948–1960, demonstrating that the government was in a powerful position to prosecute them. The government soon released most of the accused businessmen who promised to comply with the government in undertaking some of the major industrial projects, laying a ground rule of government dominance over the private sector during the Park regime through the 1970s.

Second, the centralized decision making by the president was relatively effective and efficient, compared with other developing countries, owing to competent technocrats who formulated and implemented development programs. Cultural values plus a selection process enabled the Korean government to staff its ministries in charge of industrialization programs with the most talented and best-educated young people. Confucian tradition, which imbued respect for scholars over farmers, craftsmen, and merchants and the civil service over all others, attracted well-educated young people to public service despite its low wages.[6] Except for political appointments at the cabinet level, examinations are used in selecting and in many cases promoting civil servants. Together with merit-based personnel evaluation, the system produced "meritocratic elites."[7] Successfully passing the highly competitive examination for the middle-level civil service is one of the most prestigious achievements for a young man in Korea. Such prestige enabled the government to recruit the cream of the leading universities.

Third, Korea had the broadest base from which to learn the Japanese experience effectively. Both Korea and Taiwan had been occupied by the Japanese, but Taiwanese leaders came from the mainland after 1949. In contrast, Korean political leaders and technocrats in the 1960s and 1970s not only mastered the Japanese language but also acquired a significant understanding of Japan's culture and social system during the 1910–1945 Japanese occupation of Korea. President Park, for example, was one of a few who had been trained at the Japanese Military Academy. Many of his advisers and technocrats had also been educated in Japan or in Korea by Japanese during the occupation, studying the Japanese experience in detail. Even in 1990, 250,000 South Korean high school students were learning the Japanese language, accounting for about 70 percent of all non-Japanese high school students around the world studying Japanese.[8] A survey showed that the number of persons studying Japanese outside Japan had more than tripled in ten years to 1.62 million in 1993, and Koreans account for more than half of them.[9]

Although Alice Amsden concludes that on average American-trained Korean economists tend to accept the Anglo-Saxon model as the best solution to Korea,[10] no nation could profit more from an understanding of Japanese industrial success than Korea, given the geographical and cultural proximity and historical relations.[11]

Given the background, what policy mechanisms has the government used in facilitating technological learning in industry? How has the government role evolved in response to the rapidly changing economic environment?

INDUSTRIAL POLICY: DEMAND SIDE OF TECHNOLOGY

Korea's "developmental state" was at the wheel of its industrialization drive, at least through the 1970s.[12] In its efforts to create conditions for industrial growth and to ensure the transition from one stage to the next, the government used a complex web of direct and indirect policy instruments to define growth targets and discipline businesses to reach them. These instruments have largely been employed toward the following objectives: (1) the deliberate promotion of big business as an engine of technological learning, achieved through a systematic and comprehensive array of subsidies and incentives, (2) ambitious export-oriented industrialization, achieved by pushing the private sector into crises to reach imposed targets while providing incentives to make the crises creative rather than destructive, (3) the promotion of technologically advanced heavy and chemical industries, accomplished through even more critical crises, and (4) the repression of labor to maintain industrial peace, providing a conducive environment for learning.

Big Business

To overcome the disadvantage of a small domestic market and to exploit the stable nature of mature technologies on which initial industrialization strategy was to be built, the Korean government intentionally created large firms, *chaebols*. These organizations were deemed necessary to marshal the scale economies inherent in mature technologies, which would be used to attack government-designated strategic industries, producing export growth to fuel an advancing economy. A *chaebol* is a business group consisting of varied corporate enterprises engaged in diversified business areas and typically owned and managed by one or two interrelated family groups.[13]

The government helped the capital formation as well as the subsequent diversification of the *chaebols*. It sold Japanese colonial properties and state-owned enterprises to selected local entrepreneurs on favorable terms during the inflationary period, handing the local entrepreneurs windfalls. Owning all commercial banks in the early years, the government then provided these firms with scarce foreign currency and preferential financing at the official rates, both of which were only half the real market rate. The government also gave them large import-substitution projects and guaranteed the foreign loans. Foreign debt burdens resulting from currency devaluation were compensated with increased low-interest loans, further reducing the risks for these businesses.[14]

Their resulting huge growth enabled the *chaebols* to dominate Korea's industrial scene and stand out as world-class multinational corporations. Samsung, Daewoo, Ssangyong, and Sunkyong, as mentioned earlier, were among *Fortune* magazine's 100 largest industrial corporations in 1993. Including the two *chaebols*, Hyundai and LG, that did not reveal their group revenues all six rank in the top 100 global industrial enterprises.[15] Korea, sixth in the rank of firms included in the global 100, was preceded only by the United States, Japan, Germany, the United Kingdom, and France. This is especially noteworthy when Korea is compared with other Third World countries; only one state-owned petroleum corporation in each of Brazil, Venezuela, and Mexico made the list. Only Korea among these nations places private, nonpetroleum industrial corporations on it.[16] Six other *chaebols*, also among the global 500, have been powerhouses for Korea's industrialization.

The Korean government managed the *chaebols* relatively effectively compared with similar conditions in other catching-up countries. The government effectively disciplined the *chaebols* by penalizing poor performers and rewarding only good ones, a marked difference from big-business promotion efforts in other developing countries. Good performers were rewarded with further licenses to expand. The government rewarded entrants to risky enterprises with industrial licenses in more lucrative sectors, thus leading them to further diversification. In contrast, the government refused to bail out relatively large-scale, badly managed, bankrupt firms in otherwise healthy industries, appointing better managed *chaebols* to take them over.[17]

> President Park believed that even private projects in the First Economic Development Plan should be completed as scheduled so as not to make them turn into a burden to the government, because the government fully guaranteed the foreign loans. Personally, President Park checked and reviewed the development of all important projects, both public and private.[18]

In addition, *chaebols* that relied entirely on political collusion rather than on performance could not survive long, as they lost political support when power shifted from one hand to another. In contrast, better managed *chaebols* have endured and survived in a series of political power shifts.[19] As a result, only three of the ten largest *chaebols* in 1965—Samsung, LG, and Ssangyong—made the list in 1975. Similarly, seven of the ten largest in 1975 made the list in 1985. In fact, few of the original *chaebols* have survived. Most of them have evolved dynamically from small businesses in the midst of political turmoil, largely through rapid learning under effective strategic and organizational management.[20]

The *chaebols'* rapid growth and diversification have enormously affected industrial structure and market concentration in Korea. By 1977, 93 percent of all commodities and 62 percent of all shipments were produced under monopoly, duopoly, or oligopoly conditions in which the top three producers accounted for more than 60 percent of market share. The ten largest *chaebols* accounted for 48.1 percent of GNP in 1980, making Korean industry even more highly concentrated than that of Taiwan or Japan. Total factor productivity as well as output, however, grew faster in Korea's highly concentrated economy than in that of almost any other country.[21]

Chaebols played a crucial role in the rapid acquisition of technological capability in Korea. They were in the most advantageous position to attract the cream of the best universities. They had organizational and technical resources to identify, negotiate, and finance foreign technology transfer and assimilate and improve imported technologies. They also played a major role in drastically expanding and deepening R&D activities in Korea in the 1980s and 1990s. As a result, by the end of the 1970s, Korea had the largest textile plant, the largest plywood plant, the largest shipyard, the largest cement plant, and the largest heavy machinery plant in the world.

Export Promotion

The import-substitution policy played an important role in creating demand for foreign technology transfer.[22] Since there was no local capability to establish and operate production systems, local entrepreneurs had to rely completely on foreign sources for production processes, product specifications, production know-how, technical personnel, and components and parts. Studies in the electronics, machinery, steel, computer, and pharmaceutical industries demonstrate that import substitution under protection was one of the most powerful instruments that facilitated technology transfer from abroad, leading to the emergence of new industries and the introduction of more sophisticated products in existing industries.[23]

The export drive was a more important policy. The Korean government made exports a life-or-death struggle in order to achieve economic growth goals. The Korean government designated so-called strategic industries for import substitution and export promotion. Plywood, textiles, consumer electronics, and automobiles in the 1960s and steel, shipbuilding, construction services, and machinery in the 1970s are examples.

The strategic industries, which were created in violation of their static comparative advantage, had to suffer from high costs in addition to infant-industry growing pains. To help the industries overcome these problems, the government sheltered the domestic market from foreign competition. The average effective rate of protection was atypically high for the strategic industries. In some, protection was quickly lifted as firms accomplished a rapid rite of passage from infant to exporter. But in others, where technology was complex and marketing more elaborate, protection lasted relatively long, providing a lengthier period of incubation.[24] The United States benignly overlooked Korea's protected market well into the 1970s.

The government pushed firms with ambitious goals. It instituted the export-targeting system in the 1960s as a regular instrument to assess industrial success. Annual targets were assigned to major commodity groups, which were allocated to related industrial associations. They were also assigned by destinations, which were allocated to Korean embassies in respective countries. The Ministry of Trade and Industry maintained a situation room to monitor export performance. The data were then reported to the Monthly Trade Promotion Conference attended by the president of the nation, cabinet members, heads of major financial institutions, business association leaders, and representatives of major export firms. The conference served to solve many problems encountered by exporting firms through guidance and the president's final decisions.[25]

"Sticks" in the form of administrative guidance (a euphemism for Korean government orders) forced firms to reach its goals. If a firm did not respond as expected to particular goals, programs, or incentives, its tax returns were subject to careful examination or its application for bank credit was studiously ignored, or its outstanding bank loans were not renewed. Government agencies often showed no hesitation in resorting to command backed by compulsion. It usually did not take long for a Korean firm to learn that it would be better to get along by going along.[26] In other words, the role of the government was much stronger in Korea than in Japan and Taiwan, especially during the 1960s and 1970s. And it worked.

The government also cajoled firms with incentives, borrowing heavily from abroad and channeling the funds into export-oriented investments at below-market interest rates. Firms were granted unrestricted and tariff-free access to imported intermediate inputs and automatic access to bank loans for working capital for all export activities, even when the domestic money supply was being tightened. These firms also had unrestricted access to foreign capital goods and were encouraged to integrate vertically in order to sustain international competitiveness. These incentives operated automatically and constituted the crux of the Korean system of export promotion. Furthermore, the rationing of longer-term bank loans was used as a carrot to draw firms to new paths of exporting, encouraging diversification, and to export more than ever. These incentives, offered to all exporting firms, were particularly effective when combined with the greater organizational, financial, and political leverage of the *chaebols*, which grew even larger.[27] Exporters also benefited from a variety of tariff exemptions, accelerated depreciation, exemptions from value-added taxes, and duty-free imports of raw materials and spare parts. Tax holidays and reduced rates on public utilities further boosted corporate profitability. Assignment of lucrative import licenses was linked to export performance.[28]

With the government's sticks and carrots, Korea's total exports increased from a mere $175 million, or 5.8 percent of GNP, in 1965 to $1,132 million, or 12 percent of GNP, by 1971. With an average annual growth rate of 36.5 percent, Korea rose from number 101 in the rank of exporters in 1962 to fourteenth by 1986.[29]

How has the import-substitution and export-promotion policy affected technological learning in industry? While it created new business opportunities, it also created crises for firms to invest heavily in technological learning to acquire foreign technologies and assimilate and improve them in order to survive in the highly competitive international market.

As a result, firms in export-oriented industries (EOI) learned significantly more rapidly and in turn grew faster than firms in import-substituting industries (ISI). Likewise, countries with export-oriented industrialization grew faster than those with import-substituting industrialization. The average annual economic growth rate for EOI countries was 9.5 and 7.7 percent, respectively, for 1963–1973 and 1973–1985 compared with 4.1 and 2.5 percent for ISI countries. The real per capita income growth rate was 6.9 and 5.9 percent for the same periods for the former as compared with 1.6 and −0.1 for the latter, as the ISI group had a higher population growth rate.

Heavy and Chemical Industry Promotion

By the late 1960s, Korean government policymakers recognized the necessity of gradually restructuring the economy from labor-intensive light industries to more technology-intensive heavy industries. They understood the importance of developing the technological capability to do so, as Korea's competitive advantage in light industries was shifting to second tier catching-up countries, such as Thailand, Malaysia, China, and Indonesia.

A major change in international political conditions, however, prompted the Korean government to invest for the heavy and chemical industry program ahead of schedule. Frustrated by its protracted war in Vietnam, the U.S. government announced the Nixon doctrine in 1969, signaling its decision not to commit its ground forces in Asian future conflicts, and the Nixon administration withdrew one of two

U.S. Army divisions from Korea in 1971. President Park became obsessed with acquiring a self-reliant national defense capability by developing heavy and chemical industries (HCIs) at a far greater intensity and in a far shorter time than previously envisioned. $12.7 billion was poured into HCIs, accounting for more than 75 percent of total manufacturing investment in 1973–1979.[30] Steel, shipbuilding, heavy machinery, petrochemical, industrial electronics, and nonferrous metal industries were created by the HCI promotion. As a result, it took only fifteen years for the ratio of value added in light industries over HCI to fall from 4 to 1 in Korea, whereas the same shift took twenty-five years in Japan and fifty years in the United States.[31]

This hasty creation of HCIs on a gigantic scale without adequate preparation in technological capability, more for military purposes than for economic rationality, resulted in a rapid rise in foreign debt from $2.2 billion in 1970 to $27.1 billion in 1980.[32] It also bred misallocation of resources, rapid inflation, wage increases far in excess of productivity gains, and further concentration of economic powers in several *chaebols* involved in HCIs.

The most significant effect of the hasty HCI promotion, however, was a major crisis in technological learning. Lacking capability, the *chaebols* had to rely almost entirely on foreign sources for technology. Tasks required to assimilate imported technology were so far beyond the capability available at these firms that the HCI program imposed a major crisis in setting up and starting up plants, let alone mastering them. Firms were forced to assimilate technology very rapidly and upgrade capacity utilization by expediting learning in order to survive. Later chapters present more detailed discussions of how firms in these industries expedited their technological learning to turn the crisis into an opportunity.

Industrial Peace

"Economy is a tender flower. It does not flourish in the soil of war or social unrest," said Paul Samuelson.[33] Likewise, the multinational firm as a buyer, supplier, and investor considers industrial peace, among other things, one of the most important factors in developing and expanding businesses with firms in catching-up countries.

In attempting to create a conducive environment, in which government's development goals could be achieved without interruptions, the Korean government, as the central orchestrator for economic development and exports, also emerged as the responsible agency to control labor movements and maintain industrial peace. The government's leading role in repressing labor was a consistent policy through the late 1980s. Although the formal ban on unions had been lifted in the early 1960s, the legal framework in which unions could function was so restrictive that it virtually eliminated the possibility of organizing any genuine independent unions.[34] Furthermore, the government used the Korean Central Intelligence Agency (CIA) to spy on and repress labor as part of a broader economic strategy through the 1970s.[35] As a result, workers became exceedingly docile. For example, between 1979 and 1984, average lost workdays per 100 workers per year was only half a day in Korea compared with two in Japan and fifty in the United States.[36] A drastic shift toward political democratization in the late 1980s, however, triggered the explosion of labor unrest, which is discussed in Chapter 3.

Many intellectuals, in Korea and abroad, criticized the dreadful negative side of many of the government's practices to suppress labor movements, but it at least provided Korean firms with uninterrupted opportunities to learn cumulatively and discontinuously, making undoubtedly significant contributions to rapid industrialization. Such a repressive policy retarded the growth of trade unions and workers taking part in industrial democracy. Scandinavian and German experiences show that industrial democracy supports and encourages innovation.

In short, the government had been at the core of Korea's industrialization in the 1960s and 1970s. Some say that the government played the role of chairman in Korea, Inc., while *chaebols* functioned as its production units.[37] The government role included not only policy formulation but also the techniques of policy implementation, using an array of direct and indirect incentives and sanctions to harness the private sector in achieving rapid technological learning and, in turn, high growth.

Shift of Economic Environment and Public Policy

The economic environment for Korea, however, changed significantly in the 1980s, for several reasons. First, the world economy generally slowed down in the 1980s, particularly affecting outward-looking economies like Korea. Second, in the wake of rising trade imbalance, North America and Europe moved toward protectionist policies, making it increasingly difficult for Korea to sustain export growth in industries that led its export-oriented strategy in the past. Third, Korea lost its competitiveness in low-wage-based labor-intensive industries, as its real wage rose at an average annual growth rate of 5.8 percent in the

1960s and 7.5 percent in the 1970s. Concomitantly, other developing countries with much lower wage rates were rapidly catching up with Korea in these industries. Fourth, advanced countries, particularly Japan, were increasingly reluctant to transfer technology to Korea as it attempted to enter industries that they dominated. Fifth, Korea was forced to change its copyright and patent laws, preempting the imitative reverse-engineering of foreign products.

In the face of an increasingly unfavorable environment in the 1980s and 1990s, the Korean government set out on a major policy shift. It attempted to reduce government intervention and introduce market mechanisms and to undertake structural change toward the development of more technology-based industries. The policy shift included, among other things, antitrust legislation, trade liberalization, financial liberalization, promotion of small and medium-size enterprises, foreign investment liberalization, and shifting emphasis on innovation-related activities.

Antitrust and Fair Trade

The *chaebols'* increasing economic power gave rise to monopolistic abuses such as creating scarcities, price gouging, and predatory behavior in the domestic market. In response, the government shifted its policy on *chaebols* from promotion in the 1960s and 1970s to the regulation of their growth in the 1980s by adopting a policy of economic democratization. The Fair Trade Act of 1980, along the lines of American antitrust legislation, included, among other things, the prohibition of unfair cartel practices and mutual investment among the *chaebols'* affiliated companies, a ceiling on investment by and credit to large *chaebols*, and restrictions on their vertical and horizontal integration. The government also directed the thirty largest *chaebols* to restructure their sprawling businesses around three or fewer core sectors.

However, the *chaebols* continued to grow, with economic concentration increasing further until the mid-1980s and declining slightly thereafter; the number of affiliated companies of the ten largest chaebols increased from 77 in 1974 to 667 including 365 abroad in 1994,[38] and the combined sales of the five largest *chaebols* as a percentage of GNP increased from 12.8 percent in 1975 to 52.4 percent in 1984 and decreased slightly to 46.5 in 1993.[39] The number of *chaebols* designated by the government as dominating their respective markets increased from 105 in 1981 to 216 in 1985, but only ten were accused of having abused their economic power. Of 1,172 applications for vertical and horizontal integration, only two were rejected by the government.

Why? Although the antitrust policy made a small dent in the mid-1980s, the economic power of *chaebols* and their collusion with political power were so strong that the government could not implement some announced policy programs, showing a significant gap between what it intended to do and what it actually could do. In addition, the government bailed out insolvent enterprises to mitigate their impact on downstream sectors, not to tarnish the credibility of *chaebols* in the international market. As a result, some of them, anticipating a government rescue, expanded well beyond their evident financial capability and some postponed adjustments to market changes. In many cases, the government was under pressure to accept economic reality rather than fulfill economic justice.

Then, facing accelerating globalization in the 1990s, the government once again shifted its policy on *chaebols* from regulation to liberalization by revising the Antitrust and Fair Trade Act. Restrictions on the credit controls of the thirty largest *chaebols* were lifted, provided that their firms reduced internal ownership to less than 20 percent, raised capital-to-assets ratio above 20 percent, and offered more than 69 percent of its shares to the public. Such a liberalization policy was designed to enable *chaebols* to compete freely in the expanding global market. Although those firms' ownership and management structures have changed significantly in the past decade,[40] the new policy is expected to make significant progress in the separation of management and ownership in *chaebols*. LG Business Group, for instance, announced a plan to reduce its internal ownership (interfirm and family ownership combined) from 39 percent in 1995 to 19.5 percent by 1999 and family ownership from 5 percent to 3 percent during the same period.

In short, after promoting the formation and growth of *chaebols* during the first two decades and attempting unsuccessfully to regulate them in the 1980s, the government decided to limit protection and intervention and rely more on market mechanisms. *Chaebols* have been and will be the dominant factor in Korea's industrialization and globalization.

Trade Liberalization

In drastic contrast to the government's export-targeting system, the situation room, and heavy export subsidy programs in the 1960s, Korea's export trade was significantly liberalized during the 1970s.

Most of the ad hoc incentive measures used in the 1960s were abolished, and Korea's export trade was almost completely liberalized by 1982. The ratio of net export subsidies to the exchange rate dropped, for instance, from 36.6 in 1963 to 6.7 in 1970 to 0.4 in 1982.[41] In other words, although export-oriented industrialization continued in the 1980s and 1990s, Korean firms have been able to compete in the international market without government subsidies in these decades.

Import policies were also liberalized in the 1980s. The government promulgated the Tariff Reform Act in 1984, which was aimed to phase in general reductions in tariff levels. As a result, the import liberalization ratio—defined as the ratio of the number of unrestricted items to the total—rose from 51 percent in 1973 to 95.2 percent by 1988 and to 98.6 percent in 1994. The government also brought down the average tariff rate from 26.7 percent in 1984 to 7.9 percent by 1994. Nontariff barriers such as delay in custom clearance and tax examination of foreign car purchasers were also largely eliminated in recent years. As a result, imports increased, for instance, by 20.1 percent in 1989 compared with a 2.8 percent increase in exports, forcing Korean firms to compete, with little government assistance, against multinational firms not only in the export market but also in the domestic market.[42]

Financial Liberalization

In contrast to its monopoly of the financial sector in the 1960s and 1970s, the government has also taken major steps to liberalize the financial market. For example, the government reduced the regulation of nonbank financial intermediaries, many of which had long been controlled by *chaebols*, resulting in a significant rise in their share of total deposit liabilities in the 1980s. The denationalization of commercial banks led to a shift of significant share from government hands to the *chaebols*. The conversion of local short-term financing firms to either securities firms or commercial banks in 1990 marked another important step forward in restructuring the financial sector, thus allowing increased participation of private firms.

Although the government exercised its influence on financial institutions through its power to authorize the opening of new branch offices, it lost its teeth in allocating financial resources. Nevertheless, the protection of the local market from foreign financial institutions resulted in gross inefficiencies; Korean banks are loaded with nonperforming loans—8.8 percent of total credits in 1992.[43] The timetable has been set to completely liberalize the financial sector by 1997 in preparing to join the OECD, which requires Korea to make obligatory adjustments including complete financial liberalization.[44]

SME Promotion

A major government mistake in the 1960s and 1970s was neglecting to encourage balanced growth between large firms and small firms. It was the late 1970s when the government belatedly realized the importance of small and medium-size enterprises (SMEs) in healthy economic growth. The government began promoting SMEs, particularly technology-based small firms, to remedy the imbalance between the large- and small-business sectors. The government established sanctuaries for SMEs, designating 205 business territories where neither large corporations nor their affiliates can intrude. The Compulsory Lending Ratio program stipulates that the nationwide commercial banks should extend more than 35 percent of total loans and that regional banks offer more than 80 percent of their total loans to SMEs.

The government also took the initiative in establishing the venture capital industry as a means to advancing the emergence of technology-based small firms in which the private sector had no interest. Specifically, the government enacted a special law to establish the first venture capital firm, which was jointly funded by the government and a group of private firms. The government took a further step by enacting the Small and Medium Enterprise Formation Act in 1986, leading to the emergence of more than thirty venture capital firms, all jointly vested by the government and the private sector.

Preoccupied with *chaebols*, the government failed to learn from Japanese experience in developing an institutional framework for technology diffusion to SMEs. Only in 1979 did the government begin establishing several important institutions, such as Small and Medium Industries Promotion Corporations, Korea Trade Promotion Corporation, and SME-related R&D centers, as a way to support SMEs in developing technological capability and promoting their exports. The government also earmarked a significant portion of its investment fund, W (won) 2.5 trillion ($3.1 billion) in 1994, to promote SME modernization. Despite various support schemes, the number of SMEs that went bankrupt increased steadily over the years—6,156 in 1991 to 10,488 in 1994—due mainly to increasing imports from low-waged China and other Asian countries. The severe competitive rules set by the World Trade Organization will make it even more difficult for SMEs to survive.

Intellectual Property Rights

In Korea, as in other catching-up countries, imitative reverse engineering of existing foreign products was a backbone of industrialization through the mid-1980s. Even advanced countries today rely heavily on copying foreign products and refuse to honor copyrights until they develop enough capability to stand on their own. The United States, for instance, refused to join the Bern Convention on copyrights for more than 100 years, saying that as a developing country it needed to retain easy access to advanced foreign works, an argument still used by many developing countries.[45] Japan and Switzerland refused to recognize product patents until 1976 and 1978, respectively, when they developed enough capability to innovate their own new materials. For instance, they invented ninety-three and eighty-seven new materials, respectively, in the year they introduced product patent systems.[46] Now the United States is the world's international property rights (IPR) policeman, forcing ill-prepared catching-up countries to respect IPR.

Under U.S. pressure, Korea introduced new legislation in 1986 to maintain IPR, preempting the reverse engineering of foreign products. This hit all industries hard, particularly pharmaceuticals and chemicals. The new statute also introduced an arbitration system for compulsory licensing and increased penalties for infringement.

Enforcement of the law was not easy in Korea, where, as in other Asian countries, people don't believe in owning an idea or thought and consequently in paying for it. Frequent police raids in major cities and lawsuits have, however, resulted in a rapid disappearance of pirated products in the local market. The number of cases brought to court by police and lawyers almost quintupled in four years, from 2,254 in 1989 to 10,423 in 1993.[47] Although Seoul's Itaewon Street still draws foreign tourists for counterfeit goods produced by small underground shops, a tide swept through major industries, eliminating duplicative reverse-engineering practices to a large extent. Such forced adoption of IPR resulted in significant upward pressure on costs of Korean products because of increased royalties. On the other hand, it forced Korean firms to intensify their technological efforts to innovate on their own.

Shifting Emphasis

The focus of industrial policy has shifted from the promotion of strategic sectors to promotion of innovation-related activities. In the 1960s and 1970s, special incentives—tax concessions, custom rebates, access to foreign exchange, and other forms of protection or enhancement—were granted to strategic industries to make them competitive at a world level. In contrast, the government abolished all industry-specific promotion acts introduced in the 1960s and 1970s and instead legislated a new Industrial Promotion Act in 1986 that ties all incentives to special industrial activities such as R&D and human resource development. In the late 1980s, however, the government again designated several high-technology industries, including information technology and aircraft, for support, but its role in these industries is much more limited than that in labor-intensive industries in the previous two decades.

In short, the focus of industrial policy related to creating the demand for technological learning has shifted significantly. The earlier policy period was marked by heavy government intervention. The new period focuses on the introduction of market principles such as enhancing competition through the control of *chaebols'* growth, trade liberalization, financial liberalization, investment liberalization, and support for innovation-related activities. In other words, government's developmental role has substantially weakened over the years, but some claim that the government still remains relatively powerful in Korea compared with other countries.[48]

TECHNOLOGY POLICY: SUPPLY SIDE OF TECHNOLOGY

The government not only stimulates the demand side of technological learning through industrial policy instruments but also gives rise to the supply of technological capability through technology policy instruments.[49] The technology flow perspective—technology transfer, technology diffusion, and indigenous R&D—provides insight into understanding how developing countries catch up with advanced countries.

Technology Transfer

Lacking technological capability at the outset of its economic development, Korea had to rely on foreign technology imports. However, Korea's policies on foreign licenses (FLs) was quite restrictive in the 1960s. In the case of manufacturing, general guidelines issued in 1968 gave priority to technology that promoted exports, developed intermediate products for capital goods industries, or brought a diffusion effect to other sectors. The guidelines also set a ceiling for royalties at 3 percent and duration at five years. This restrictive policy on licensing strengthened local licensees' bargaining power on generally available mature technologies, leading to lower prices for technologies than would otherwise have been the case.[50]

The 1970s, however, saw a significant change in national policy. In an attempt to attract sophisticated technologies in response to the changing international environment, restrictions on foreign licensing were relaxed in 1970 and 1978, allowing, for one, a higher royalty rate. As a result, royalty payments for FLs increased significantly, as shown in Table 2-1, from $0.8 million during the first five-year economic development plan (1962–1966) to $451.4 million in the fourth one (1977–1981). This increase is insignificant compared with FLs in the 1980s. Most foreign licensing in the early years was associated with technical assistance needed to train local engineers to run turnkey plants.

Table 2-1 Foreign Technology Transfer to Korea, 1962–1993 (in millions of dollars)

Source	1962–1966	1967–1971	1972–1976
1. Foreign Direct Investment			
Japan	8.3	89.7	627.1
United States	25.0	95.3	135.0
All others	12.1	33.6	117.3
Total	45.4	218.6	879.4
2. Foreign Licensing			
Japan	—	5.0	58.7
United States	0.6	7.8	21.3
All others	0.2	3.5	16.6
Total	0.8	16.3	96.6
3. Capital-Goods Imports			
Japan	148	1,292	4,423
United States	75	472	1,973
All others	93	777	2,445
Total	316	2,541	8,841

SOURCES: Korea Industrial Technology Association for foreign direct investment and foreign licensing data; Korean Society for Advancement of Machinery Industry for capital-goods import data.

In contrast to the gradual relaxation of government control on foreign licensing, the government policy on foreign direct investment (FDI) saw a complete swing in the 1960s and 1970s. The FDI policy was quite free in the 1960s, permitting any form of bona fide foreign capital, including fully owned subsidiaries. But few foreign investments were made during the 1960s, primarily owing to questions about Korea's political stability and its uncertain economic outlook.

The government reversed its FDI policy in the 1970s, tightening its control. Joint ventures received higher priority than wholly owned subsidiaries. A general guideline was adopted setting three criteria: first, competition with domestic firms was seldom allowed in both domestic and international markets; second, export requirements were forced on FDIs; and third, foreign participation ratios were basically limited to 50 percent. Korea was one of the few countries with restric-

1977–1981	1982–1986	1987–1991	1992–1993	Total
300.9	876.2	2,122.3	441.1	4,465.5
235.7	581.6	1,477.7	719.9	3,270.1
184.0	309.6	2,035.9	777.8	3,472.9
720.6	1,767.7	5,635.9	1,938.8	11,208.5
139.8	323.7	1,383.6	619.1	2,529.9
159.2	602.7	2,121.9	870.9	3,784.4
152.4	258.5	853.9	307.0	1,592.1
451.4	1,184.9	4,359.4	1,797.0	7,906.4
14,269	20,673	54,641	25,337	120,783
6,219	12,434	33,098	18,832	73,103
7,490	17,871	33,213	22,983	84,872
27,978	50,978	120,952	67,152	278,758

tive regulations on FDI when technology was not a critical element and necessary mature technologies could be easily acquired through mechanisms other than FLs or FDI, for example, reverse-engineering. Under this restrictive policy environment, Korea induced the FDIs, as shown in Table 2-1.

Consequently, the size of FDI and its proportion to total external borrowing were significantly lower in Korea than in other newly industrializing countries (NICs). For example, Korea's stock of FDI in 1983 was only 7 percent that of Brazil, 23 percent that of Singapore, and less than half that of Taiwan and Hong Kong. The proportion of FDI to total external borrowing was only 6.1 percent in Korea compared with 91.9 percent in Singapore, 45 percent in Taiwan, and 21.8 percent in Brazil.[51] The comparative figure reflects Korea's explicit policy of promoting its independence from multinationals in management control.

As a result, unlike these other countries, FDI had a minimal effect on the Korean economy. For example, FDI's contribution to the growth of Korean GNP in 1972–1980 amounted only to 1.3 percent, while its contribution to total and manufacturing value-added was only 1.1 percent and 4.8 percent, respectively, in 1971 and 4.5 percent and 14.2 percent, respectively, in 1980.[52]

Instead, Korea promoted technology transfer in the early years through the procurement of turnkey plants and capital goods. The rapid growth of the Korean economy required commensurate growth in investment for production facilities. However, government policy had been biased in favor of the importation of turnkey plants and foreign capital goods as a way to strengthen international competitiveness of industries using capital goods. Such a policy led to massive imports of foreign capital goods at the cost of retarding the development of the local capital goods industry. Protection of the machinery industry was relatively low until the first half of 1971, giving capital goods users almost free access to foreign capital goods. For example, chemical, cement, steel, and paper industries, established in the 1960s and early 1970s, all resorted to the purchase of turnkey plants and foreign capital goods for their initial setup. But Korean firms assimilated imported technologies so rapidly that they managed to undertake subsequent expansions and improvements with little assistance from foreigners.

The massive imports of foreign capital goods became a major source of learning through reverse-engineering by Korean firms.[53] Of the three categories of technology transfer listed in Table 2-1, capital goods imports far surpassed other means of technology transfer in terms of value through 1981. Capital goods imports were worth twenty-one times the value of FDI and seventy times the value of FLs. The total value of capital goods imports was sixteen times that of the other two categories combined. Although the values of different modes of technology transfer are not strictly comparable since they measure different things, they are useful indicators when compared with other countries. Among NICs, the proportion of capital goods imports to total technology transfer was highest in Korea, suggesting that Korea had acquired more technology from advanced countries through the importation of capital goods than through any other means when compared with such NICs as Argentina, Brazil, India, and Mexico.[54]

Various instruments also played an important role in lubricating the inflow of foreign capital goods to Korea. For example, the slight overvaluation of the local currency, tariff exemptions on imported capital goods, and the financing of purchases by suppliers' credits, which carried low rates of interest relative to those on the domestic market, all worked to increase the attractiveness of capital goods imports.

In short, Korea restricted FDI but promoted technology transfer through other means such as capital goods imports in the early years. Capital was acquired in the form of foreign loans. Such a policy, designed to maintain Korea's management independence from foreign multinationals, was effective in forcing Korean firms to take the initiative and a central role in learning, that is, acquiring, assimilating, and improving imported technologies, rather than relying entirely on foreign sources.

After two decades of restrictive policy toward foreign direct investment and foreign licensing, Korea liberalized its technology transfer policies in the 1980s and 1990s. Progressively more sophisticated foreign technologies were needed to sustain its international competitiveness in high value-added industries. The proportion of Korea's 999 industrial subsectors open to FDI rose from 44 percent in the 1970s to 66 percent in 1984 and to 90.6 percent by 1994. In response to complaints from foreign investors about extremely cumbersome bureaucratic redtape, in 1995 the government introduced the automatic approval system, the expansion of tax and other incentives for investment in strategic high technology sectors, and a one-stop service center.[55]

New FDI in manufacturing has, however, declined steadily in recent years from $1,069 million in 1991 to $527 million in 1993. In contrast, foreign investment in service sectors has significantly increased, accounting for 27.4 percent of the total investment in 1992 and 72.8 percent in the first seven months of 1994.[56] In the 1960s and 1970s, foreign companies invested in Korea to reap cheap labor costs. Now foreign companies are not so willing to collaborate with Korean companies in relatively more technology-intensive areas.

Foreign licensing has been completely open for all industries and for all terms and conditions. The approval system—obtaining prior consent from the government—changed to the reporting system—simply informing the government.[57] The government plans to abolish the reporting system in the near future, except for technologies related to the defense industry.[58] As a result, technology transfer through licensing has soared recently. FLs increased from 247 in 1981 to 707 in 1993, reflecting the liberalized public policy as well as the private sector's aggressiveness in acquiring more sophisticated foreign technologies. Slight drops in the early 1980s and 1990s reflect economic recessions in Korea.

Table 2-1 also reveals that Korea relied heavily on both Japan and the United States for technology. These two countries accounted for more than 80 percent of FDI and more than 70 percent of FLs and capital goods imports during the first two decades of Korea's industrialization. Japan in particular had been the major source of technology for Korea in those years. Korea acquired its mature technologies mainly from Japan and exported its products to the United States in the early years. But the U.S. share of technology transfer has increased significantly in the 1990s. The proportion of foreign licensing cases from the United States increased from 28.4 percent in 1991 to 42.8 percent in 1994. In contrast, FLs from Japan decreased from 47.6 percent to 28.9 percent during the same period, indicating Japanese reluctance to transfer sophisticated technologies to Korea and Korea's preference for U.S. technologies in emerging areas.[59]

Technology Diffusion

In upgrading the overall technological capability of the economy, the effective diffusion of imported technology across firms within an industry and across industries within an economy is as, if not more, important as the acquisition of foreign technology. If technology is transferred successfully to a firm and its use is limited only to its original importer, it may give the firm monopoly power over other firms for a time; however, the economic effect of the technology may be considerably limited. Government interventions that create necessary institutions would give rise to the firm's learning from the domestic community, resulting in the effective acquisition of knowledge available elsewhere in the economy.

There may be many specialized diffusion agents, such as capital goods producers, consulting engineering firms, and public research institutes, which the government could promote for the diffusion of technology within the economy. But these agents were not effective in Korea in diffusing technology in the 1960s and 1970s.

The government's plan to develop the capital goods sector was initiated in 1968 but not seriously implemented until the mid-1970s. The development of local consulting engineering firms was promoted by the Engineering Service Promotion Law of 1973, which stipulated that, if possible, all engineering projects should be given to local firms as major contractors with foreign partners as minor participants. Such a scheme was aimed mainly at stimulating the emergence of local engineering firms and providing local firms with opportunities to learn from experienced foreigners. But local infant engineering service firms were not capable of playing the role of diffusion agent in the early years of industrialization.

In 1962 the government established a scientific and technological information center as a linking mechanism for disseminating technical information, but its use by industry was quite limited in the early years because mature products were easily imitated through reverse-engineering without the need to consult technical literature. In 1966 the government established a public research institute as a diffusion agent. But Korean researchers, mostly from academic fields or R&D centers in advanced countries, lacked the manufacturing know-how that was in greatest demand during the early years and failed to serve as diffusion agents. The most important diffusion agents the government unintentionally created were the government enterprises established in the 1950s and 1960s. Engineers who accumulated modern production experience in state-owned fertilizer and machinery plants spun off later to head engineering and production departments of private enterprises.

Only in the 1980s did the Korean government introduce an extensive network of government, public, and nonprofit (private) technical support systems to promote technology diffusion within the economy, particularly among SMEs.[60] Some of the support systems dated back to the 1970s but flourished in the 1980s with the growing importance of technology. Figure 2-2 presents a schematic diagram of institutional arrangements related to technology diffusion systems.

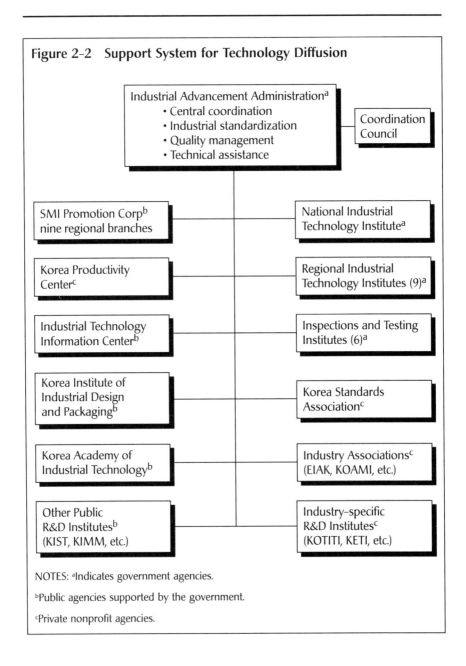

Figure 2-2 Support System for Technology Diffusion

NOTES: [a] Indicates government agencies.
[b] Public agencies supported by the government.
[c] Private nonprofit agencies.

The Industrial Advancement Administration, a government agency, coordinates the functions of different technical support agencies for both large and small firms. The National Industrial Technology Institute and eleven regional industrial technology institutes, together with the Small and Medium Industry Promotion Corporation, constitute a national network of technical extension services, while the Korea Academy of Industrial Technology, together with other government R&D institutes (GRIs) and industry-specific R&D institutes under trade associations, comprise a core of an R&D network for technology diffusion. Several private, nonprofit technical support systems also play an important role in technology diffusion among SMEs. The Korea Standard Association with its national network and Korea Productivity Center promote technology diffusion among firms mainly through their educational and training programs on quality control, value engineering, physical distribution, and factory automation. In addition, the government introduced a scientific and technical information dissemination system by developing a data base in ten member institutions and integrating them through an on-line network.

In short, Korea developed, in the 1980s, an elaborate network of technical support systems for technology diffusion, which have evolved dynamically in response to changes in industries.

INDIGENOUS RESEARCH AND DEVELOPMENT

Korean firms acquired and assimilated foreign technology primarily through imitative engineering in the 1960s and 1970s, when relevant technology was readily available in a machine-embodied form and learning by doing was relatively easy. Consequently, none of the policy instruments to stimulate the country's own R&D were effective.

As Korea underwent structural adjustments and entered progressively more technology-intensive industries, the government focused more attention on indigenous R&D activities, primarily through two major mechanisms: direct R&D investment and indirect incentive packages. The government's direct investment is to develop the science and technology (S&T) infrastructure and to promote R&D at universities and GRIs. Its indirect incentive packages, including preferential finance and tax concessions, are aimed at stimulating increased industry R&D. Table 2-2 summarizes the foregoing discussions of industrial and science and technology policies as well as R&D policies discussed below.

Table 2-2 Industrial and Science and Technology Policies

Policies	1960s and 1970s	1980s and 1990s
Industrial Policies	Deliberate promotion of big businesses	Promotion of SMEs
	Export orientation	Export orientation
	Promotion of heavy and chemical industries	Antitrust and fair trade
		Trade liberalization
	Repression of labor to maintain industrial peace	Financial liberalization
		Intellectual property rights protection
		Shifting emphasis on R&D, manpower development
Science and Technology Policies	Restriction on FDI and FLs	Promotion of FDI and FLs
	Promotion of capital-goods import	Extensive diffusion networks
	Promotion of GRIs in lieu of university research	Promotion of university research
	Promotion of GRIs	Promotion of corporate R&D activities
		Promotion of national R&D projects

Science and Technology Infrastructure Development

Anticipating increasing demands for science and technology, the government established the Korea Institute of Science and Technology (KIST) in 1966 as an integrated technical center to support the industry's technological learning. As Korea's first multidisciplinary research institute, KIST covered a broad spectrum of activities in applied research ranging from project feasibility studies to R&D for new products and processes. KIST spent a large proportion of the nation's total R&D expenditure in its early years.

To keep pace with increasing sophistication and diversity, the government established several GRIs as spin-offs from KIST. Each was designed to develop in-depth capabilities in an area of high industrial priority: shipbuilding, marine resource, electronics, telecommunications, energy, machinery, and chemicals.

The government also created two science centers; Seoul Science

Park started in 1966 with three R&D institutes and three economic research institutes, but it failed to attract private R&D centers to the vicinity. Two of the three R&D institutes have been relocated. In contrast, Taedok Science Town, established in 1978 in an area 200 kilometers south of Seoul, boasts fourteen GRIs and three tertiary educational institutions and has attracted more than eleven corporate R&D laboratories. Eighteen more firms plan to establish their R&D laboratories in the town within a few years, making it the first high-technology valley in the country. But despite almost twenty years of existence, it has neither built a reputation for attracting world-class scientists, as Tsukuba has in Japan, nor become a bustling industrial park with technology-based SMEs that have large shares of world markets for personal computers and peripherals, as Hsinchu has in Taiwan.

The government also created an important milestone in 1975 by establishing a research-oriented graduate school of applied science and engineering, the Korea Advanced Institute of Science, offering both master's and Ph.D. programs, adding another in 1995. These schools draw the most highly qualified entrants by offering extraordinary incentives for students (e.g., full fellowships covering tuition, room, and board and exemption from military obligation).[61] These schools produce almost half of all Ph.D.s in science and engineering in Korea.

University R&D

Research endeavors in universities have been relatively underdeveloped. Their R&D expenditures increased significantly from W 572 million ($1.5 million) in 1971 to W 608 billion ($790 million) in 1994. While those institutions accounted for only 7.7 percent of the nation's R&D spending in 1994, they provided 33 percent of the nation's R&D manpower and 73.7 percent of its Ph.D.-level R&D personnel.

Government statistics indicate that basic research accounted for 14.4 percent, applied research for 23.8 percent, and development for the remaining 61.8 percent of the nation's total R&D expenditures in 1994. The statistics also show that the private sector accounted for 45.1 percent of the nation's basic research and 64.5 percent of applied research, while universities accounted for only 29.1 percent and 6.3 percent, respectively.[62] There is reason to doubt these figures for basic and applied research, particularly the share commanded by the private sector. Only fairly recently have the leading *chaebols* begun rather limited investment in applied research in their largest technology businesses such as semiconductors and information science. Basic research has been even less developed.

The Korean government's attempts to promote university R&D

activities began in the mid-1970s. Frustrated in its efforts to reform the undergraduate teaching-oriented tradition in education, the government conceived a dual system: since almost all universities under the Ministry of Education, public or private, were essentially teaching-oriented, the Ministry of Science and Technology (MOST) founded a research-oriented S&T school in 1975 and another in 1995, establishing a new research tradition in university education.[63]

The government also enacted the Basic Research Promotion Law in 1989, explicitly targeting basic research as one of the nation's top technological priorities. Emulating the U.S. experience, in 1989 the government introduced a scheme to organize science research centers (SRCs) and engineering research centers (ERCs) in the nation's universities. By 1993, fourteen SRCs and sixteen ERCs had been established, receiving government R&D subsidies of almost W 20 billion ($24.2 million) in 1993.

The lack of development in university research has been a major bottleneck in producing well-trained researchers. The government's recent efforts should result in significant reform in university R&D.

GRI R&D

Given the inadequacy of university research, GRIs have served as the backbone of advanced R&D in Korea. The government has made these institutes the major instruments in its Industrial Generic Technology Development Project (IGTDP), National R&D Project (NRP), and Highly Advanced National R&D Project. They have been the recipients of more than 90 percent of the research grants awarded by the government in new technology areas. GRIs undertake most of these projects in conjunction with private firms.

IGTDP concentrates mainly on current problems in existing technology areas with high economic externalities. Each year the Ministry of Trade, Industry, and Energy undertakes a survey to identify urgent R&D projects in industrial firms and offers financial support to GRIs and university laboratories to take on the projects jointly with private firms. Most of them are related to import substitution of Japanese components in the electronics and machinery industries. In 1989, for instance, 174 technologies were identified, 146 of which were designated as projects to be funded. For IGTDPs, the government earmarked W 11.5 billion ($17.2 million) in 1989, W 88.7 billion ($110.8 million) in 1993, about $118,000 per project in 1987 and $388,000 in 1993. These amounts are not substantial enough to solve critical problems.

In contrast, NRP projects focus primarily on future problems in new (to Korea) technology areas with a high risk of failure or with high economic externalities, thus warranting public support. MOST identified several target areas: localization of machinery parts and components, new materials development, semiconductor design, super-mini computer development, energy conservation technology, localization of nuclear energy fuel, new chemical development, biotechnology development, and basic research in universities. The government's total investment in NRPs increased significantly, from W 13.3 billion ($17.7 million) in 1982 to W 98.8 billion ($123.5 million) in 1993.

The most ambitious government vision is the Highly Advanced National R&D Project, also known as the G-7 Project, which is aimed at lifting Korea's technological capability to the level of G-7 countries by 2020.[64] The G-7 project has two parts: product technology development projects and fundamental technology development projects. The former includes new drugs and chemicals, broadband integrated services digital network, next-generation vehicle technology, and high-definition television (HDTV). The latter contains ultra-large-scale integrated circuit, advanced manufacturing systems, new materials for information, electronics, and energy industries, environmental technology, new functional biomaterials, alternative energy technology, and next-generation nuclear reactor. Jointly, the government, universities, and industries will invest $5.7 billion, about half of which will come from the private sector.

The $1.3 billion invested during the first three years involved more than 13,000 researchers and resulted in 2,542 patent applications, almost 2,000 academic articles, and three cases of technology export valued at $6 million. Notable outcomes include quinolon-based antibiotics, liver disease treatment medication, HDTV, and the completion of 256-mega dynamic random-access memory (DRAM) chip development.[65]

In the face of the rapid expansion of private R&D activities and increasing intensity in university R&D, reform of GRIs to redefine their roles has been discussed for some time. But inertia and the labor union of GRI members have made it difficult to implement the reform.

Military R&D

Given the threat of hostilities from North Korea, national security has been one of the major concerns in Korea. As a result, the home market for military technology is unusually sophisticated and demanding.

Seeking to lessen reliance on foreign weapon suppliers and to ensure military independence, the Korean government launched an ambitious program in the late 1970s to build local capability to develop modern weaponry, particularly nuclear warheads and missiles. Startled by Korea's bold move to develop its own defense capability, the U.S. government used carrots and sticks to persuade Korea to abandon the military R&D program.

As a result, the ambitious program was scaled back in the 1980s. Its budget dropped to $114 million in 1988, only 0.2 percent of that of the United States and 4 percent of that of France. The ratio of military R&D budget to total military expenditures was only 1.5 percent in Korea, compared with more than 10 percent in France and the United States. The nature of the R&D is confidential, and the R&D endeavors have been conducted almost strictly within the military: only 1.48 percent of the military R&D budget was allotted to universities in 1988.[66]

The isolated military R&D efforts have had little impact on the development of technological capability in the wider economy. The private sector is involved in manufacturing some traditional weaponry, but the spillover effects of such operations on industrial innovation appear to be negligible, except for improving the degree of precision in the machinery industry.

Indirect Support for Industry R&D

The government offered various tax incentives and preferential financing for R&D activities in the 1960s and 1970s, but during the 1970s the interest rate for R&D loans was one of the highest, reflecting the low priority of R&D in government policies. At the same time, these mechanisms were largely ignored by industry owing to the absence of a clearly felt need to invest in R&D and the relatively easy means of acquiring and assimilating foreign technologies then available from many sources. Only in the early 1980s did preferential R&D loans become the most important means for financing private R&D activities. Preferential financing amounted to W 671.6 billion ($848 million) in 1987, accounting for 94.3 percent of total corporate R&D financing funded by the government. In contrast, direct R&D investment by the government through NRPs and IGTDPs accounted for only 4 percent of the total and direct investment through venture capital firms accounted for 1.7 percent of the total.

Public financing (W 712.4 billion), mostly in the form of preferential loans, accounted for 64 percent of the nation's total R&D expenditure in manufacturing in 1987. In short, the government plays a major role in funding corporate R&D in Korea, primarily through allocation of preferential financing. The impact of this financing, however, may be overstated. With rates of preferential loans ranging between 6.5 percent and 15 percent, they conferred little advantage over financing terms available in markets outside Korea.[67]

Tax incentives are another indirect mechanism to make funds available for corporate R&D. In Korea, tax incentives may be classified into five categories, according to objectives to be served. Most important are tax incentives aimed at promoting corporate R&D investment, reduced tariffs on import of R&D equipment and supplies, deduction of annual noncapital R&D expenditures and human resource development costs from taxable income, and exemption from real estate tax on R&D related properties. The incentives also include a tax reduction scheme, Technology Development Reserve Fund, whereby an enterprise can set aside up to 3 percent (4 percent for high-technology industries) of sales in any one year to be used for its R&D work in the following three years. The private sector did not take advantage of this scheme in its early years, in the absence of the need for technological activities, but now considers it an important way to finance its R&D. Other tax incentives are aimed at reducing the cost of acquiring foreign technology, promoting technology-based small firms, reducing the cost of commercializing locally generated technologies, reducing the cost of introducing new products, and promoting the venture-capital industry.

In addition, the government introduced various indirect support programs for specific industrial R&D activities. For instance, the World Class Korean Products program, first instituted in 1986, is a government scheme to make selected Korean products world class. The government selected twenty-seven products involving fifty-nine manufacturers in the existing industries and offered preferential financing and other supports to improve the quality of the products, to develop innovative ideas for future development, and to energize overseas marketing strategies. Sports shoes, fishing rods, pianos, tires, bicycles, compact disc players, ultrasonic scanners, VCRs, and videotapes are examples.[68]

In 1993 the government introduced the New Technology Commercialization Program, in which the government offers preferential financing for activities related to R&D and commercialization of new (to Korea) technologies developed locally and designated by the government. The government certifies them as KT (Korea technology) or NT (new technology).

Realizing the importance of new technology venture firms, the government introduced in 1992 the Spin-off Support program to encourage researchers in GRIs to spin off and establish new technology-based small firms. Financial, managerial, and technical assistance are offered to such prospective technical entrepreneurs.

R&D Investment

Facing the imperative to shift to higher value technology-intensive products, R&D investment has seen a quantum jump in the past decades. Table 2-3 shows that total R&D investment increased from W 10.6 billion ($28.6 million) in 1971 to W 7.89 trillion ($10.25 billion) in 1994. Though the Korean economy recorded one of the world's

Table 2-3 Research and Development Expenditures, 1965–1993 (in billions of won)

	1965	1970
R&D expenditures	2.1	10.5
Government	1.9	9.2
Private Sector	0.2	1.3
Government vs. Private	61:39	97:03
R&D/GNP	0.26	0.38
Manufacturing Sector		
R&D Expenditures	NA	NA
Percent of Sales	NA	NA
Number of Researchers (total)[b]	2,135	5,628
Government/Public Institution	1,671	2,458
Universities	352	2,011
Private Sector	112	1,159
R&D Expenditure/Researcher (W 1,000)	967	1,874
Researcher/10,000 Population	0.7	1.7
Number of Corporate R&D Centers	0	1[c]

SOURCE: Ministry of Science and Technology (Korea), *1994 Report on the Survey of Research and Development in Science and Technology* (Seoul: MOST, December 1994).

NOTES: [a] For 1976.
[b] The figures do not include research assistants, technicians, and other supporting personnel.
[c] For 1971.

fastest growth rates, R&D expenditure rose even faster than GNP. R&D increased its share of GNP (R&D/GNP) from 0.32 percent to 2.61 percent during the same period, surpassing that of the United Kingdom (2.12 percent in 1992). It should, however, be pointed out that there are many reasons to suspect bubbles in the R&D statistics, particularly those of the private sector.

The government has launched various programs to induce the private sector to establish formal R&D laboratories. These include tax incentives and preferential financing for setting up new laboratories and exemption from military service obligations for key R&D personnel. Owing partly to these programs and partly to increasing competi-

1975	1980	1985	1990	1994
42.7	282.5	1,237.1	3,349.9	7,894.7
30.3	180.0	306.8	651.0	1,257.1
12.3	102.5	930.3	2,698.9	6,634.5
71:29	64:36	25:75	19:81	16:84
0.42	0.77	1.58	1.95	2.61
16.70[a]	75.97	688.59	2,134.70	4,854.1
0.36[a]	0.50	1.51	1.96	2.55
10,275	18,434	41,473	70,503	117,446
3,086	4,598	7,542	10,434	15,465
4,534	8,695	14,935	21,332	42,700
2,655	5,141	18,996	38,737	59,281
4,152	15,325	27,853	47,514	67,220
2.9	4.8	10.1	16.4	26.4
12	54	183	966	1,980

tion in the international market, the number of corporate R&D laboratories increased from one in 1970 to 2,272 in 1995, reflecting the seriousness with which Korean firms are pursuing high-technology development. Although small and medium-size firms account for more than 50 percent of corporate R&D centers, *chaebols* dominate R&D activities. R&D spending in the manufacturing sector has grown faster than sales. The machinery and electronics industry spent more than 4 percent of sales on R&D activities beginning in the mid-1980s.

Consequently, there has been significant structural change in R&D investment. The government played a major role in R&D activities in early years, when the private sector faltered in R&D investment despite the government's encouragement. More recently, the private sector has assumed an increasingly larger role in the country's R&D efforts in response partly to increasing international competition and partly to a policy environment supportive of private R&D activities. For example, while the private sector accounted for only 2 percent of the nation's total R&D expenditure in 1963, the figure had risen to 84 percent by 1994, which is the highest among both advanced and newly industrialized countries.

TOTAL GLOBALIZATION POLICY

A report by International Management Development (IMD) in Switzerland ranked Korea low in international competitiveness indicators.[69] Its 1994 study shows that of forty-one advanced and newly industrializing countries included in the survey, Korea ranked thirty-ninth in globalization, thirty-ninth in finance, thirty-first in business management, thirtieth in government, twenty-ninth in infrastructure, twentieth in human resources, eighteenth in science and technology, and seventh in domestic competitiveness. Korea ranked near the bottom in many more indicators, including trade policy support for firms' globalization, domestic market liberalization, foreign investment liberalization, openness toward foreign culture, government's price control, balance in fiscal policy, financial support for firms, ease of overseas financing, and autonomy of financial institutions.[70]

Even among eighteen newly industrializing countries Korea slid from the top in 1991 to fifth in 1994 in domestic competitiveness, from fourth to ninth in infrastructure, from fourth to thirteenth in globalization, from third to ninth in business management, from fourth to tenth in government, from top to third in science and technology, and from seventh to tenth in finance during the same period. Korea's incredibly low ranking in the IMD study prompted several local institutes to undertake comparable studies just to find similar results.[71]

Shocked by these reports, the government launched another ambitious scheme, *segyehwa*, "total globalization policy," with a goal to raise various activities in Korea to international standards. The *segyehwa* committee is manned by cabinet members and twenty-three representatives from the private sector and cochaired by the prime minister representing the government and a university president representing the private sector. This committee delineated twelve major tasks including the reform of educational system and foreign language training, human resource development for "future" industries, and the acceleration of information to society. *Segyehwa* manifested Korea's belated determination to make major reforms in human resource development and government bureaucracy. Its efficacy, however, remains to be seen.

SUMMARY

The government played a developmental role in Korea's early industrialization. On the demand side of technological learning, the government created and fostered the growth of large *chaebols* as a vehicle for effective technological learning. The government then sanctioned them to accommodate technologically challenging, government-imposed new industrial projects and overly ambitious export goals and to accomplish them within the planned time frame, inducing a series of challenging crises for the private sector. These crises pushed the private sector into something of a life-or-death struggle and forced them to exert all efforts toward accelerating technological learning. But at the same time, the government provided necessary supports through various incentives to make the crises creative rather than destructive.

On the supply side of technological learning, the government restricted foreign direct investment and foreign licensing, instead promoting technology transfer through such other means as capital-goods imports in the early decades. Such a policy was effective in forcing Korean firms to acquire and assimilate foreign technology primarily through imitative reverse engineering of imported foreign goods in the early decades, when learning by doing was relatively easy. Consequently, none of the policy instruments to stimulate the country's own

R&D were effective. But anticipating increasing demands for S&T, the government established S&T infrastructure and GRIs when the private sector faltered in R&D investment.

Significant changes in Korea's economic environment in recent decades have, however, forced the Korean government to make a major policy shift from protection of the local market, regulation of foreign investment, and direct support of exports and R&D to liberalization of trade, foreign investment and financial market, antitrust legislation to enhance competition, and indirect support for R&D activities. This policy shift was designed to introduce market mechanisms and to undertake a structural change toward relatively more technology-based industries. Despite efforts in the 1980s, several indicators show that Korea's international competitiveness has dwindled mainly as a result of inertia in bureaucracy.

One encouraging sign is rapid growth in indigenous industrial R&D activities, an important indicator of learning in industry. The private sector has assumed a major role in Korea's R&D efforts in response partly to increasing international competition and partly to a policy environment supportive of private R&D activities. The private sector accounted for more than 80 percent of the nation's total R&D expenditures in the 1990s. Korea is, however, far behind advanced countries in R&D activities.

The policy environment described in this chapter, together with education and sociocultural environment, discussed in the following chapter, shaped the way firms have developed technological capability.

3 Hardworking Koreans: Education and Sociocultural Factors

No nation has tried harder and come so far so quickly from agrarian poverty to industrial prosperity as Korea.[1] At center stage of its successful rapid industrialization are dynamic manufacturing firms that responded to the changing market and technology environment. In these firms, committed individuals acquired technological capability rapidly.

Technological capability has two important elements. The first, an existing knowledge base, is essential in technological learning, as knowledge today influences learning processes and the nature of accumulated experience tomorrow. A firm's history determines the rate and direction of the technological efforts it pursues, which connect its past with its present.[2] The second is the intensity of effort or commitment. It is insufficient merely to expose individuals or firms to knowledge. Without the conscious efforts of individuals within a firm to internalize such knowledge, learning cannot take place.

The foregoing prompts two questions: (1) How have Koreans acquired knowledge so quickly (prior knowledge base)? (2) Why have Koreans worked so hard (high intensity of effort)? This chapter examines Korea's education and training system to answer the first question and identifies sociocultural factors in an attempt to answer the second.

EDUCATION AND TRAINING

Lack of valuable natural resources has been both a curse and a blessing to Korea, which is almost completely dependent on foreign resources. This is a serious curse because Korea is highly vulnerable to fluctuations in the availability and price of natural resources in the international market. On the other hand, it is a blessing because it has forced Korea to develop its abundant human resources, whose entrepreneurship and capability enable the country to prosper in a hostile environment. The lack of natural resources has been turned into a blessing in building competitive capability through the development of human resources.

There is little agreement among specialists on the degree of development of human resources under Japanese rule. But, as discussed in Chapter 1, the fact that the illiteracy rate at the end of Japanese colonial rule in 1945 was 78 percent and that only 2 percent of the Korean population over fourteen years of age had completed secondary school indicates that Korea was forced to start its modernization drive with a low level of human resource development.

General Education

Korea's first move toward modernization was in education, which can be seen in the growth of government investment. The share of education in the total government budget, for instance, rose from 2.5 percent in 1951 to more than 17 percent by 1966. Government disbursement, however, accounted for only one-third of the total expenditures in education, the remainder being borne by the private sector and parents, reflecting the high commitment to education within Korean society. This commitment, as pointed out earlier, was strongest in Korea among eight industrialized and two catching-up countries Michael Porter studied.[3] The returns on education were greater and more direct in Korea than in societies in which upward mobility depended more on vested social interests; hence the private demand for education was greater in Korea.

Enrollment at the various levels of the formal education system has increased rapidly since 1953. Elementary school enrollment has grown more than five times. Even faster growth is seen in the secondary and tertiary education levels. Table 3-1 shows that school enrollment as a percentage of the corresponding age group rose to more than 100 percent by 1970 for the elementary school level. Although secondary and tertiary education was not free, the enrollment ratio rose from 21 percent in 1953 to almost 99 percent in 1994 for the

Table 3-1 Indicators of Human Resource Development in Korea

	1953	1960	1970	1980	1990	1994
Illiteracy Rate (%)	78.0	27.9	10.6	NA	NA	NA
Enrollment as a Percentage of the Corresponding Age Group						
Elementary School[a] (ages 6–11)	59.6	86.2	102.8	101.0	100.7	100.5
Middle School (ages 12–14)	21.1	33.3	53.3	94.6	98.7	99.0
High School (ages 15–17)	12.4	19.9	29.3	68.5	86.9	88.7
Tertiary schools[b]	3.1	5.0	8.7	16.0	37.7	48.8
Graduates of Vocational Training Centers (1,000)	NA	NA	28.2	104.5	67.7	184.4
Number of Junior College Graduates (1,000)	NA	NA	7.8	51.5	87.1	128.4
Number of University Graduates (1,000)	NA	18.0[c]	28.2	52.2	170.9	183.4
Number of Graduates from Tertiary Schools[d] (per 10,000 population)	NA	6.6[c]	11.4	27.7	59.4	69.5

SOURCES: Ministry of Education, Korea; Noel F. McGinn, Donald R. Snodgrass, Yung Bong Kim, Shin-Bok Kim, and Quee-Young Kim, *Education and Development in Korea* (Cambridge, Mass.: Council on East Asian Studies, Harvard University, 1980); and Office of Statistics, Korea, 1995.

NOTES: The illiteracy rate after the mid-1970s was so insignificant that the government ceased to collect data on it.
[a] Students older than eleven years were enrolled in elementary schools.
[b] The government controlled the quota for tertiary-level schools. The demand for that educational level was far greater than its quota. Tertiary schools include two- and three-year junior colleges.
[c] For 1963.
[d] The figures include both junior colleges and university graduates.

middle school level and from 12 percent to almost 89 percent for the high school level during the same period. As a result, the illiteracy rate dropped to 27.9 percent by 1960, to 10.6 percent by 1970,[4] and to an insignificant level by 1980.

Several other catching-up countries attained an equally rapid growth in elementary education. But what was unique in Korea was the well-balanced expansion in all levels of education early enough to support its economic development. Using data from the late 1950s for seventy-three developing countries, Frederick Harbison and Charles Myers found three nations—Korea, Taiwan, and Yugoslavia—with levels of educational achievements far above what one would expect, given their levels of economic development. That is, with Korean per capita income of $90, Korea's educational achievement stood fairly close to the level expected for a country twice as wealthy. When the per capita GNP of Korea reached $107, its educational level was equivalent to that of countries with a per capita gross national product (GNP) of $380.[5]

The number of high school students, for example, increased rapidly, as shown in Table 3-2, from 160,000 in 1953 to more than 2 million in 1994. Also noteworthy in secondary school education are the on-site vocational secondary schools established by large private firms for their teenage workers as an incentive to retain those skilled workers. Teenage workers spend their lives on the premises for many years, going to in-plant training centers for their initial skill, working in the plant, staying at in-plant dormitories, and attending school within the premises. This scheme benefited both employers and employees. Productivity improvement from low turnover, a higher self-image for the workers, loyalty to the company, and its value in

Table 3-2 Number of Secondary and Tertiary School Students (in thousands)

	1953	1960	1979	1980	1990	1994
Middle Schools	324	529	1,319	2,472	2,276	2,509
High Schools	160	273	590	1,697	2,284	2,061
Junior Colleges	NA	4.9	33.4	165.1	323.8	506.8
Universities	38.4	90.9	158.6	413.4	1,056.1	1,150.7

SOURCE: Office of Statistics, 1995.

attracting to the firm achievement-oriented workers who were willing to pursue further education during off-hours more than offset the costs of operating such a program. Employees' benefits included subsidized room and board, security, and free secondary education. Many large companies also provided students with free textbooks and notebooks.

The number of such secondary schools founded and operated by firms increased from five in 1977 to forty-two in 1980. At the outset, three of the five were middle schools, but in 1983 thirty-six of forty-six schools were high schools, indicating that firms upgraded educational opportunities as the workers completed the middle school program. Also, 5,889 smaller firms sent their teenage workers, at company expense, to evening classes at nearby secondary schools to gain the same benefits. By the early 1980s, more than 70,000 teenage workers completed their secondary education while on the job.

Vocational Training

Vocational training also made a significant contribution to the formation of a skilled manpower base in Korea. Although a few public vocational centers were established with foreign aid in the early years, systematic planning for vocational training essentially began when the Vocational Training Law of 1966 was enacted to complement the formal education system. In 1974 the government enacted a law that made in-plant training compulsory for all industrial enterprises with 300 or more workers. Under this law, many firms either established their own vocational training institutes to train at least 10 percent of their skilled workforce every year or paid levies. Unlike the Latin American experience, the Korean system required in-plant training as a matter of principle and accepted payment of levies only as an exception. The number of graduates from these vocational training centers more than tripled from 31,621 in 1970 to 104,504 in 1980.

Tertiary Education

As shown in Table 3-2, enrollment at two-year junior colleges expanded from 4,900 students in 1960 to 506,800 in 1994. Technical programs were particularly emphasized at this level, accounting for 30 to 40 percent of the total through the early 1970s and up to 70 percent of the total in 1980. The expansion of such junior college programs reflects efforts to upgrade technicians in response to increasing technical complexity in industry.

University enrollment also expanded rapidly, from 38,400 in 1953 to 1.15 million in 1994. The enrollment at junior colleges and universities as a percentage of corresponding age groups grew from 3.1 in 1953 to 48.8 in 1994.[6] The expansion of science and engineering education at the tertiary level was even more pronounced. The number of science and engineering students at four-year colleges increased from 37,000 in 1965 to 493,000 in 1994, accounting for 35.1 percent and 43.5 percent of all university students, respectively, making Korea's one of the highest tertiary enrollment ratios in the world.[7]

Consequently, Korea, one of only four developing countries that double-jumped from low- to medium- and to high-level groups in terms of the human development index between 1960 and 1992, had the largest absolute increase and the highest score among the four in 1992.[8] The number of R&D scientists and engineers has risen more than fivefold, from 18,434 in 1980 to 98,764 in 1993 with an average annual growth rate of 14 percent, which is the highest in the world. The number of scientists and engineers per 10,000 population increased from 4.8 to 22 during the same period. The latter figure is the highest among developing countries[9] and closer to that of France (23) and the United Kingdom (21.3).[10]

Fed by a rich base of educated human resources, the manufacturing sector has significantly increased its engineering manpower relative to production or managerial manpower. The number of engineers increased tenfold in twenty years from 4,425 in 1960 to 44,999 in 1980, while that of production workers and managers increased by a factor of only 5.4 and 2.2, respectively.[11] These engineers have played a pivotal role in Korea's imitative learning along the technology trajectory.

The more rapid expansion of education compared with that of economic development, however, created a short-term unemployment problem; the number of graduates in most fields exceeded demand. Consequently, unemployment among the educated was regarded as a serious social problem in the 1960s. But the formation of educated human resources laid an important foundation for the subsequent development of the economy, which soon absorbed the surplus.

Progress has been very impressive in terms of quantity but dreadful in terms of quality. Recent decades have seen underinvestment in education (relative to national needs to upgrade quality) and the consequent short supply of highly trained human resources, creating a major bottleneck in Korea's innovation drive.

One of the Korean government's major mistakes in developing a nationwide system for innovation has been its underinvestment at all educational levels since 1970. So preoccupied with achieving its short-term production and export targets, the government has long neglected upgrading the quality of education, which has long-term effects. Its sluggish commitment to education is well reflected in the government budget; the share of education in the budget has stalled at 23 percent in the past decades. In fact, its share decreased slightly from 23.4 percent in 1993 to 22.78 percent in 1995. The ratio of education budget to GNP (3.71 percent in Korea) is far below the average rate (5.2 percent) of advanced countries and even lower than that (3.9 percent) of developing countries.[12]

The problem of underinvestment in education is most critical in higher education. The government tightly controlled student quotas and tuition and fees at both state and private universities. Despite the fact that 76 percent of university students attend private schools, government subsidies in both education and research, particularly for private universities, has been scarce, stifling their growth.

The consequence of underinvestment is especially acute in university education. The environment for quality education and research has significantly deteriorated over this period, a result of lagging investment in expanding and modernizing physical facilities and recruiting new faculty members. Lifelong tenure is granted to university faculty members on recruitment, but there are no incentives for quality teaching and research, no publish or perish principle in Korea. Consequently, all universities have remained primarily undergraduate-teaching-oriented rather than research-oriented institutions.

There are a few exceptions. The Korea Advanced Institute of Science and Technology emulated MIT. Other exceptions include Seoul National University and Pohang University of Science and Technology, a new research-oriented school established by the Pohang Iron and Steel Company.

Recognizing the seriousness of poor quality university education, which is viewed as a major bottleneck in the future development of the Korean economy, the government contemplates a major reform to upgrade at least a dozen universities to a globally competitive level in research. Its implementation and effects remain to be seen.

U.S. Influence and Study Abroad

Overseas training and observation have been characteristic of human resource development in Korea. Due to the geopolitics of the cold war,

Korea was one of the biggest recipients of U.S. economic and military aid in the 1950s. The degree to which such assistance aided Korea's economic buildup, however, is controversial because the era of massive aid ended in the mid-1960s, when Korea's ultra-high growth performance began.[13] However, in the process of implementing aid programs, American tutors provided Koreans with ample opportunities to accumulate invaluable experience in modern technology and management in government, the military, and industry. The U.S. military forces, particularly, played a major role in organizing and training the Korean military. Most young men performed compulsory military service for two to three years, obtaining various technical skills and experience in military bureaucracy.

In addition, a high proportion of senior personnel in government, business, and academia have been exposed to foreign training, mainly in the United States, under economic assistance programs.[14] The tradition of overseas training continues to this day. The ratio of third-level students training abroad to all third-level students is twice as great in Korea as in Argentina, Brazil, and India and higher than in Mexico.[15] The 31,076 Koreans studying in American universities in 1993 ranked fifth after China, Japan, Taiwan, and India. The ratio of Koreans studying in the United States per population is the second highest after Taiwan among these countries.[16] The 13,000 Korean students studying in Japan comprise the second largest foreign student group in Japanese universities, trailing only China.[17]

The number of Koreans who received Ph.D.'s from foreign institutions reached 12,088 by 1995, more than 62 percent from American universities. More than 70 percent of them received their degree in 1991–1995, indicating a drastic increase in recent years. Science and engineering account for 57 percent of the total.[18]

The large number of students studying abroad resulted in a serious brain-drain problem for Korea, at least through the 1960s. What characterized the situation was the refusal of overseas graduates to return home, not the emigration of high-level manpower educated locally. As of 1967, 96.7 percent of Korean scientists and 87.7 percent of Korean engineers educated abroad remained there, primarily in the United States, compared with the corresponding world figures of 35 and 30.2 percent for all countries.[19]

The first systematic government efforts to repatriate Korean scientists and engineers abroad began in 1966 when the government established the Korea Institute of Science and Technology (KIST) as the first government R&D institute (GRI). The nature of state involvement was directive rather than promotional in orientation. The government vigorously pursued the repatriation of experienced scientists and engineers with a highly attractive compensation package, a significant departure from the administrative culture of Korea, where the literati-bureaucrats historically exerted power over technicians.[20] Eighteen were recruited in 1966 as the founding members of the Korea Institute of Science and Technology. By 1975, the number reached 68. The total of permanent repatriates through 1980 reached 276. The state-led repatriation program was quite successful, as few repatriates went back to the advanced countries.

The program also set a model for the private sector, which assertively recruited high-caliber scientists and engineers in the 1980s and 1990s to leapfrog into state-of-the-art technologies. The United States is populated with thousands of top-notch Korean-American scientists and engineers. Leading *chaebols* have lured away some of the best. Many left Korea more than a decade ago, earned Ph.D.'s in America's best universities, and rose through the ranks of such leading U.S. concerns as IBM, Fairchild, Intel, and National Semiconductor. The well-financed Korean *chaebols* gave them challenging jobs and attractive compensation packages with considerable independence. Government statistics show that the number of scientists and engineers recruited by corporate R&D centers from abroad was 427 in 1992 alone. Some came back for short-term assignments, indicating that many Korean scientists and engineers abroad maintain close technical ties with Korean firms.[21]

Another program instituted by the government is a scheme called Brain Pool, in which the government offers subsidies to GRIs and universities, which recruit scientists and engineers abroad for particular R&D projects for six months to two years. Both Koreans and foreigners are eligible for the program.[22]

These Koreans have worked extremely hard, enabling Korea to achieve phenomenal economic development. The commitment and energy of these individuals are as, if not more, important as their educational attainment in technological learning. Their commitment and energy strengthen not only work activities (i.e., using their existing knowledge) but also learning activities (i.e., acquiring and generating new knowledge). The following section presents several sociocultural characteristics of Korean individuals and their society in an attempt to shed light on their high energy.

SOCIOCULTURAL CHARACTERISTICS

Many Western scholars have attributed the rapid industrial progress of Korea and other East Asian tigers (e.g., Taiwan, Singapore, Hong Kong, and Japan) to their Confucian tradition.[23] This argument not only contradicts the 1950s arguments that Confucian heritage retarded modernization in East Asian nations, but also fails to explain rapid industrialization in non-Confucian countries such as Chile, Brazil, Mexico, Malaysia, Thailand, and Indonesia.[24]

Neo-Confucianism

Confucian heritage is still readily visible in Korea. Confucian teachings are said to have been more strictly observed in Korea than in China, where they originated. The five cardinal virtues—filial piety and respect, the submission of wife to husband, strict seniority in social order, mutual trust in human relations, and absolute loyalty to the ruler—still permeate Korean society. The traditional Confucian values have, however, been significantly altered by Christianity, which came to Korea in 1884 and introduced, among other things, modern education, Western civilization, and Protestant ethics. Protestants are the largest and most active religious group in Korea, accounting for more than 25 percent of its population.[25]

Tu Wei-Ming argues that traditional Confucian ethics have been combined and significantly modified by Western Christian ethics to form "new Confucian ethics."[26] The new Confucian ethics, according to him, is an amalgam of the family or collectively oriented values of the East with the pragmatic, economic-goal-oriented values of the West.[27] Such a modification has significantly altered the traditional Confucian view of an occupational hierarchy of scholars and civil servants at the top, farmers second, artisans third, and merchants last, making it possible for businessmen and engineers to prosper in the new industrial society.

The new Confucian ethics include five key characteristics.[28] First, education is greatly emphasized, which is why Korean parents and their counterparts in other East Asian newly industrializing countries (NICs) sacrifice their lives for the education of their children. According to a study, Korea's total—public and private—expenditure for education amounted to 13.3 percent of GNP in 1984 compared with 5.7 percent in Japan in 1982 and 6.7 percent in the United States in 1981.[29] The majority of private expenditure for education, however, is to send children to informal institutions for exam preparation rather than to channel them to formal educational institutions.

Second, the clan plays an important role in social and economic relations. It is not uncommon for a core of Korean firms to be staffed by family members, distant relatives, people from the hometown, or graduates of the owner's alma mater, and to be managed like a quasi-family unit. It is also common for some Korean firms to undertake economic transactions with members of the clan. In this way, clan ties and the system of reciprocal obligation provide the social sinews and help manage conflicts.

Third, harmonious interpersonal relations are emphasized. Cooperation, consensus, and social solidarity among members of the organization are important in decision making and organizational life, creating distinctive organizational dynamism in Korean firms. Collectivism is not, however, as strong in Korea as in Japan, but it contrasts with Western emphasis on individualism and competition.[30]

Fourth, the new Confucian ethics stress the pursuit of the highest good in this world with harmony and the adaptation of oneself through self-cultivation and active participation therein. As a result, Koreans are action and future-oriented.

Fifth, discipline is also emphasized in the new Confucian ethics. Discipline in the family, in the school, and in the organizational life is the basic element in social power.

Situational Factors

Neither traditional Confucianism nor new Confucianism alone, however, explains the dynamic energy of Korean people and society. Socioculture is determined more by situational factors than by religious and moral teachings. Korea's rapid learning at the national level may be attributed to (1) individual commitment and entrepreneurship, (2) discipline at the organizational level, (3) effective mobility and networking at the societal level, and (4) particular cultural traits at the national level. Most of these characteristics are determined by situational factors.[31] This chapter examines the effect of situational factors on rapid learning at the four different levels.

Hardworking Koreans at the Individual Level. "Koreans work incredibly long hours, from morning to night, like robots," some Japanese say. Their comments echo American complaints about Japanese.[32] What made Koreans work so hard? There appear to be at least five situational factors: (1) the national trait of tenacity, (2) *han* psyche, (3) conditioning during school days, (4) physical environment, (5) "beat Japan" spirit, and (6) experience of deprivation.

First, tenacity to endure hardship is deeply rooted in Korean characteristics. "Koreans have made many splendid achievements in the past but you should be most proud of your country as a nation with distinct language and culture for thousands of years amid frequent foreign invasions from big powers around you," Professor Glenn Page said to a group of Korean students at the East West Center in Honolulu.[33] As a small country surrounded by big powers—China, Mongolia, Russia, and Japan—Korea has a history of foreign invasions, almost one every two years. Koreans had often been ruled by foreign invaders for extended periods of time. They, however, refused to succumb to the invaders and endured suffering, turmoil, and associated hardships inflicted on them for thousands of years. Yet Koreans have maintained their unique language and culture to this day. Tenacity to endure hardship appears to be a factor in forming *han* psyche among Koreans.

Second, the Korean word *han*, which means "resentment or grudges," is a common psyche among Koreans. This is an aspect of the Korean mind that developed as a result of permanent feelings of frustration, repressed anger, regret, remorse, grief, deprivation, and inability to change events in the family and society and under foreign rule. Culturally, fathers require their sons to be filial; employers require their employees to be compliant; rulers, local or foreign, require the ruled to be obedient. Thus, children in the family, employees in the organization, and people in the society are required not only to repress feelings of anger and frustration toward their fathers, superiors, and rulers, but also to maintain a properly respectful attitude toward them regardless of provocation.[34]

On the other hand, like codependents in Western society, Koreans with *han* psyche have an intense need to excel in all aspects of life to win approval from their superiors. That is, *han* is a source of energy that drives Koreans to work with a kind of frenzy, to be tenacious, to sacrifice themselves for the betterment of their families and country.[35]

Third, most Koreans are also conditioned to work hard during their school days. Like those from other East Asian countries (Japan, Taiwan, Singapore, and Hong Kong), most Korean students undergo "examination hell" from kindergarten on to win a competitive entrance examination at an upper-level school. To mitigate examination hell, the government eliminated the entrance examination to middle school and made high school entry merely a procedural process, but that failed to cool the competitive heat. Preparation still begins in kindergarten for admission to leading universities. The entrance exams are so difficult that both teachers and parents discipline students to acquire the habit of hard work.

Students commonly spend many after-school hours each day in tutorial programs to develop a solid foundation for these examinations years later. Acquiring the discipline to study ten to twelve hours a day is not uncommon for them. In short, Koreans, like other East Asians, are conditioned to work hard for long hours.

Fourth, Korea's physical environment fosters a respect for hard work. Korea's land area (99,000 square kilometers) is scarcely larger than Indiana or Hungary, but it houses more than 44 million people. In terms of population density, Korea ranks second after Bangladesh.[36] But Korea's situation is significantly more severe than that of other countries. Korea is crossed by mountains with only one-third of the land inhabitable or arable and that yields only one crop a year owing to severe winter weather. The scarcity of natural resources, the cramped conditions, and the severe winters, combined with competitive spirit in the society, appear to have forced Koreans to work hard and long whenever possible to survive in the unfavorable environment.

Fifth, while Koreans admire and attempt to emulate Japanese economic success, the old generation has a vivid memory of a brutal and exploitive Japanese occupation. A sense of "beat Japan"—to settle old scores in all fields—is a major force energizing Koreans. This spirit has been ingrained in the new generation through indoctrination in school. All streets, for instance, are virtually deserted in Korea when there is any type of match against Japan.

Sixth, with their memories of deprivation during Japanese occupation and the Korean War, Koreans were grateful to find employment, working as many hours as necessary at low wages when the high unemployment rate was common through the mid-1970s.[37]

This hardworking trait is well reflected in the Korean language. The first Korean word foreigners learn, *pali pali*, meaning "hurry-up, hurry-up," is the word most frequently spoken by Koreans. They use it to mean not only "speed-up" but also "don't be lazy."

As a result, it is common for Koreans to work ten to twelve hours per day. Managers work even longer, averaging seventy to eighty hours a week.[38] However, the price Koreans seem to be paying for their hard work is staggering. The 1989 death rate attributable to stress-related illness among Korean males forty to fifty years old was 2.3 times higher than that of their Japanese counterparts[39] and three times higher than that of their Korean female counterparts.[40] The ratio of their 1989 death rate over that of the total population in Korea was 1.3 compared with between 0.3 and 0.5 in other countries.[41]

Entrepreneurship. "This is the most entrepreneurial country I have ever visited," said Professor Herbert Hollomon of MIT after visiting Seoul and its Eastgate market in 1979. His remark was verified by a recent study of sixty-one ethnic groups in the United States by Robert Fairlie and Bruce Meyer.[42] After controlling for such factors as age and education, they found that Israelis and Koreans had the highest self-employment rate, nearly 30 percent for men, while Korean women top the list at 19 percent, followed by Russians with 12 percent.[43]

The government played a significant role in nurturing *chaebol* entrepreneurs, as noted in Chapter 2. The government selected relatively successful firms with proven entrepreneurs and provided resources to strengthen them into diversified *chaebols*.[44] These entrepreneurs were bolder in exploring risky businesses than their counterparts in most other countries because the government stood behind them, ready to help.[45]

Entrepreneurship can also be seen among smaller firms, which received far less help from the government. For example, the number of firms producing electronic products increased from 231 in 1971 to 1,026 in 1983, small firms accounting for 74 percent of the total. Most founders of these subsequent entrants spun off from existing firms, exploring entrepreneurial opportunities in the growing industry.[46]

Dislocated northerners who migrated to the South during the Korean War were more entrepreneurial than their southern counterparts.[47] A 1980 study shows that about 3.3 percent of male population cohorts of the northerners were entrepreneurs compared with less than 1.0 percent of the southerners.[48] The entrepreneurs who came from North Korea are better educated, wealthier, and more heavily influenced by Christianity than their southern counterparts and have industrial and commercial backgrounds, because the communist regime in North Korea was hard on the educated, learned, and religious.

The tendency toward hard work and entrepreneurship, together with self-cultivating characteristics of both Confucian culture and the Protestant work ethic, strengthen the personal drive for achievement. Initial success in international competition gave Koreans (i.e., policymakers, managers, and workers) confidence in their own abilities, further fueling their determination to continue their efforts and strengthening their can-do spirit in the face of series of economic and managerial crises. This spirit was, for example, well demonstrated in two oil crises. With Korea relying 100 percent on foreign oil, the manufacturing sector was extremely vulnerable to the fluctuation of the available quantity and its price. When the crises hit, Korea entered the Middle Eastern countries to exploit the rapidly rising construction-service market to earn enough foreign currency to pay for increasing oil prices and to secure oil from the region. Thus, Koreans turned the crises into opportunities, which is the coherent story in the process of Korea's industrialization.

Discipline at the Organizational Level. The Saudi government once suspected that the more than 60,000 Koreans working in Saudi Arabia, reportedly a larger force than Saudi's own military and police combined, were military rather than construction workers, because they were so well organized and disciplined. Where did this discipline come from?

The importance of the group over the individual and Confucian attitudes toward groups have undergone significant modification. The importance of ascriptive groups such as the family and local community has declined, but new solidarities such as the place of employment and occupational specialty have grown, allowing less room for the individual to behave idiosyncratically in organizations. Group leaders not only teach these values to members but also accept responsibility for members who abide by the values and apply social pressure on those who do not.[49]

In addition, the 1950–1953 Korean War brought in U.S. military forces and forces from fifteen other countries under the United Nations flag. The U.S. forces helped organize the Korean military, transferring military technology and military organization management to Koreans. Then in 1961, the Korean military leaders took over the government and introduced military bureaucracy to its system.[50] Retired officers have involved themselves extensively in the management of government organizations and subsequently private firms.

The influence of military culture and discipline was often direct since all young Korean males were and are subject to compulsory military service for two to three years during an important stage of life. These young men underwent military training, received the strictest discipline, experienced tightly intertwined organizational life; enlisted men and noncommissioned officers learned to manage small groups, and officers learned to handle large organizations and sophisticated military technology. They also learned to manage complex logistical support systems using modern transport and communications. Such military discipline became the foundation of *chaebol* growth.

Mobility and Networking at the Societal Level. The prevailing social organization has undergone great and rapid change, but the underlying strains of Korean identity have endured. This has fostered both continuity in basic attitudes and social flexibility in Korean society.

Hermit Kingdom Korea was a culture highly segregated by social class and family with low geographical and occupational mobility. Villages were predominantly family-oriented and tightly closed, with a single family name commonly accounting for more than 90 percent of the resident population, making it difficult for others to move in.

The Korean War radically transformed Korean society, making a lasting impact on it. The major exodus from communist-occupied North Korea to South Korea and social turmoil during the Korean War resulted in the amalgamation of people not only from different geographical areas but also from different families and classes. This made Korean society significantly more flexible and mobile than it had been in the prewar period. Furthermore, compulsory military service brought together young men from diverse geographical, social, and family backgrounds to undergo the same experience for an extended period of time, breaking long-standing social barriers. The new social order established out of chaos during and after the Korean War created a tradition of social flexibility for subsequent industrial development.

Industrialization brought rapid urbanization. A study estimates that 12.5 million, or almost one in three Koreans migrated from rural to urban areas in the twenty years from 1962 to 1983, let alone intercity moves. Cities became a melting pot of people from diverse social, cultural, and geographical backgrounds.[51]

Rapid industrialization also gave rise to high occupational mobility. As in Japan, Korean firms implicitly guaranteed lifetime employment. But unlike the Japanese, Korean workers enjoyed individualistic freedom to hop from one firm to another as opportunities opened up in industrial expansion. As a result, the average turnover rate of a Korean manufacturing firm exceeded 5 percent, even higher than that of the United States (4 percent) and more than double the rate of Japan (2 percent) in 1979.[52] Such high job mobility resulted in a rapid diffusion of imported technology throughout the economy.

As noted earlier, the clan plays an important role in economic and social relations. Networking is exceptionally active among extended family members, among people from the same hometown, and among cohorts from the same school. Since one cannot choose the first two networks, becoming a member of a leading school network is practically a guarantee of social advancement, making the entrance examination to leading universities all the more competitive. Such networks also play an important, informal role in bringing about lateral coordination across organizations.

Nationalism at the Country Level. Korea is also a geographically small country, making it easy to integrate people into a single culture. The relatively small size of the country—all parts are reachable within a half-day trip—with nearly the same climate and natural environment, enables Koreans to maintain close relationships and a similar lifestyle. As a result, Korea is a homogeneous country in terms of its race, language, and culture. Koreans belong to the Altaic family, speak one language, using an indigenously developed *hangul*—an alphabet invented by King Sejong the Great in 1443—and have a homogeneous culture. Uniformity in education in terms of textbooks, school rituals, and centralized administration has been a major tool in shaping the national uniformity that bred a nationalistic character among the people.[53]

Frequent foreign invasions and Japanese occupation for thirty-six years further reinforced Korean nationalism, as foreign invaders were targeted as a common enemy for Korea to strengthen the cohesiveness among its people. "Compared with the Taiwanese, who responded to colonialism with subservience, Korean hostility remained nearer the surface. Koreans resisted more vigorously than the Taiwanese, and when the Japanese responded with tougher military repression, Korean nationalism grew still more determined."[54]

National identity among Koreans is so strong that despite their strong animosity toward North Korea, South Koreans side with North Koreans in sports matches against Japan. Such strong nationalism may be a factor in the pursuit of independent strategy by Korean *chaebols*.

Nationalism is also evident in employment. No foreign companies are on the list of best employers selected by university graduates. Few graduates of leading universities join foreign companies in Korea.[55] Even among Koreans educated abroad, nationalism prevails. According to a survey, the majority of Korean students in the United States plan to return to Korea on completing their education. Of the students surveyed, 67.5 percent want to work for Korean companies compared with only 15.7 percent who wish to join foreign companies, which is a significant contrast with other Asians.⁵⁶ Such cultural homogeneity and nationalism may, however, be a liability for Korean firms in globalizing their business operations.

Labor Unrest

The government controlled the labor movement tightly to keep industrial peace, but sporadic labor strikes began to emerge in the 1970s in the textile and garment industries; still, the number of labor disputes averaged only 100 per year through 1984 and the number of workdays lost per 100 workers was a quarter that of Japan and one-hundredth of that in the United States, indicating how submissive Korean workers were.

Then, political events precipitated the explosion of labor disputes. Following the democratization decree in the summer of 1987, the labor movement launched an offensive; unionists' demands suddenly exploded in disorderly, violent, and in many cases unlawful actions. Tear gas, beatings, and the loss of life drastically changed Korea's political and social climate virtually overnight. The movement shifted the center of gravity from small and medium-size firms in the textile and garment industries to *chaebols* in the heavy industries, and from young female rural migrants to militant male workers with an urban and higher educational background. The number of labor unions rose from 2,725 in June 1987 to 7,358 by the end of 1989. "Korea was swept with an unprecedented wave of strikes—more than 3,600 in a half year, with 2,552 disputes in August 1987 alone—affecting 70 percent of all corporations with more than 1,000 employees."⁵⁷ Between the summer of 1987 and late 1989 more than 7,100 labor disputes erupted throughout Korea.⁵⁸

These disputes resulted in work stoppages, missed export delivery deadlines, lowered product quality, wage hikes exceeding increases in productivity, and a significant drop in worker morale. In the half year after liberalization was announced in 1987, 8.2 million workdays were lost in labor disputes.⁵⁹ In 1989 alone, labor disputes cost a total of about $6.2 billion in production as well as $1.36 billion in reduced exports. At the demand of militant unions, Korea's real wages increased a cumulative 62.5 percent between 1987 and 1989. With currency appreciation, the increase amounted to 91.1 percent in terms of U.S. dollars, which was 2.8 times that of productivity.⁶⁰ Once released, the pendulum, which had been held at one extreme, swung all the way to the other extreme.

Experiencing rapidly deteriorating social and economic climates, both unions and management came to share the view that there was a need to revive the nation's slumping economy. The once militant and dogmatic unions matured and evolved into more responsible and pragmatic forces. The days were gone when simple differences of opinion quickly led to emotionally charged strikes, leading to workplace lockouts by management, police raids, and subsequent clashes between riot police and striking workers. As a result, labor disputes declined from 1,616 cases in 1989 to 121 in 1994 (see Figure 3-1). The number of workdays lost through labor disputes also declined from 6.35 million days to 183,000 and to 34,000 during the same period.[61]

However, democratization and the labor movement have resulted in significant change in social and organizational climate; there have been shifts in the power structure and workers have become far less submissive than previously. A study shows that the proportion of workers who agreed to comply with seniors' opinions dropped from 77.3 percent in 1979 to 40.6 percent in 1991, and those who agreed

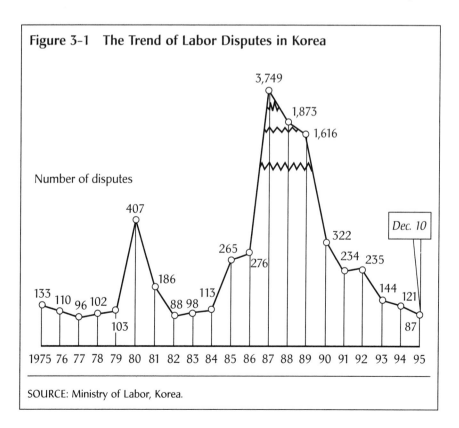

Figure 3-1 The Trend of Labor Disputes in Korea

SOURCE: Ministry of Labor, Korea.

to obey to superiors' directions went from 90.6 percent to 65.3 percent during the same period (see Table 3-3). Attitudes have also changed. Those who agreed to view their company as second family slid from 94.3 percent in 1979 to 59.2 percent in 1991.[62] In an international comparative study of forty-seven advanced and newly industrialized countries, Korea's work attitude, in terms of labor dispute days and absentee ratio, fell from third in 1985 to 24th in 1994.[63]

But some argue that the changes have been limited, and those which remain—cultural traits and physical environment—are probably undiminished. "Despite persistent problems, the values and cultural traits that have supported Korea in the past will continue to make it a force to be reckoned with."[64] That is, the cultural characteristics of Koreans still endure. For instance, neo-Confucianism, *han* psyche, "can-do spirit," and nationalism still permeate Korean society. The conditioning in schools, mobility and networking, and physical environment have changed little. The new generation brought up in affluence is less willing to work hard compared with the older generation, but their dedication and economic patriotism are unquestionable. Korean workers still exhibit a strong can-do spirit.[65] Koreans still work the longest hours with the shortest vacation among hardworking Asians. Figure 3-2 shows that Seoulites work 2,300 hours with an eight-day vacation per year, whereas Tokyo citizens work about 400 hours less than Seoulites and have double the vacation days.

Table 3-3 Change in Koreans' Work Attitude (in percentage)

	1979	1991
Employees' Attitude and Behavior toward Seniors and Supervisors:		
Compliance with Seniors' Opinions	77.3	40.6
Obedience to Superiors' Directions	90.6	65.3
Constituents' Value and Beliefs about the Group and Organization:		
Viewing the Company as a Second Family	94.3	59.2

SOURCE: Adapted from Yoo-Keun Shin and Heung-Gook Kim, "Individualism and Collectivism in Korean Industry," in Gene Yoon and Sang-Chin Choi, eds., *Psychology of the Korean People: Collectivism and Individualism* (Seoul: Dong-A Publishing, 1994), 189–208.

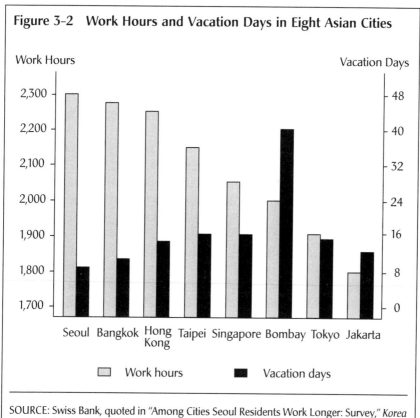

Figure 3-2 Work Hours and Vacation Days in Eight Asian Cities

SOURCE: Swiss Bank, quoted in "Among Cities Seoul Residents Work Longer: Survey," *Korea Economic Weekly*, November 7, 1994, 2.

SUMMARY

This chapter examined Korea's education and training systems to see how Koreans acquired knowledge. It also examined sociocultural factors to understand why Koreans work so hard. These two aspects underlie the process of technological capability building.

Deprived of natural resources, Korea invested heavily in human resource development as a way to survive in the changing international environment of the 1950s and 1960s. Other developing countries have also invested heavily in general education, but what was unique in Korea was the well-balanced expansion of all levels of education early enough to lay a foundation for subsequent industrialization. As a result, Korea was furthest in the direction of educational achievement, given per capita GNP, and achieved the highest educational attainment among NICs. The more rapid expansion of education than of economic development, however, created short-term unemployment problems, but subsequent industrialization soon absorbed the surplus. The formation of educated human resource stock enabled Korea to master mature production technology through the imitative reverse-engineering process. Yet the Korean government neglected to invest in research-oriented tertiary education to prepare for the future competition in knowledge-intensive industries.

Many Western scholars have attributed the rapid industrial progress of Korea and other East Asian tigers to Confucianism. This argument contradicts previous arguments that Confucian heritage retarded modernization in East Asia. It also fails to explain rapid industrialization in non-Confucian NICs. Confucian culture still permeates Korean society, but it has undergone significant modification by Christian values and Western civilization, leading to the formation of new Confucian ethics.

Neither traditional Confucianism nor new Confucianism alone explains the dynamic energy of Korean society. Many situational factors, particularly the impact of the Korean War, were also at work. First, the perseverance of Korean people in turmoil and hardship inflicted by foreign invasions, associated *han* psyche, disciplined work habits formed during exam hell school days, unfavorable physical conditions, and the memory of deprivation bred a hardworking trait into Korean workers. Second, compulsory military service molded young Korean men into disciplined organizational members, giving them invaluable opportunities to learn to manage not only small and large organizations but also complex logistical support systems. Third, the refugee exodus during the Korean War and urbanization afterward resulted in great geographical mobility in Korean society. Rapid expansion of industrial sectors caused much job mobility, making Korean society highly flexible. Furthermore, networking among clan members from school, family, and hometown made the society highly interactive, more effectively diffusing imported technology throughout the economy. Fourth, homogeneity and an independent spirit made Koreans highly nationalistic, a trait that grew stronger during Japanese colonial oppression. These factors combined in the Korean mind to instill a strong work ethic.

Political democratization in the late 1980s, however, triggered waves of militant labor strikes for three years, making significant changes in the power structure in the workplace and in attitudes among workers. The core of Korea's hardworking cultural traits has, however, endured the turmoil, and Koreans remain among the hardest working people in the world. Subsequent chapters provide more detailed examination of how government policies, foreign technology, and hardworking human resources worked together in selected industries to expedite technological learning through series of crises.

From Imitation to Innovation in Industries  PART II

4 Analytical Frameworks

The process of technological learning at firms is so dynamic and complex that it defies a simple analysis. As an attempt to shed light on the dynamic learning process from imitation to innovation in industries, this chapter introduces four analytical frameworks: global technology environment, institutional environment, dynamic learning process at the firm level, and technology transfer. Interrelations among the four frameworks are depicted in Figure 4-1. These frameworks are used as tools to analyze both incremental and discontinuous learning at Korean firms.

GLOBAL TECHNOLOGY ENVIRONMENT FRAMEWORK

This framework analyzes the global *technology environment*, presenting two technological trajectories: one in advanced countries and the other in catching-up countries. Technological trajectory refers to the evolutionary direction of technological advance observable across industries and sectors.

Technological change in catching-up countries stems largely from the acquisition, assimilation, and improvement of foreign technolog-

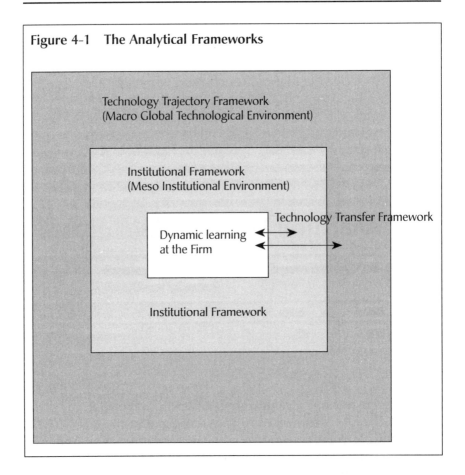

Figure 4-1 The Analytical Frameworks

ies. Foreign firms transfer these technologies as part of their own global business strategy to extend the life cycle of their products and technologies in the global market. For this reason, it is important for catching-up countries to understand the technology trajectory in advanced countries and global strategy of foreign technology suppliers. The catching-up countries should also understand the technological trajectory of industrializing economies. The interface between these two trajectories creates a dynamic technology environment, in which firms in catching-up countries have to operate. It is this environment that determines, to a significant degree, the strategy of these firms.

Technology Trajectory in Advanced Countries

William Abernathy and James Utterback postulate that industries and firms in advanced countries develop along a technological trajectory made up of three stages—*fluid, transition,* and *specific.*[1] Although the model is oversimplified to accommodate variations of technological change in different industrial sectors, it provides a useful framework to understand technological change in advanced countries.

According to this model, firms in a new technology exhibit a fluid pattern of innovation. The rate of radical, rather than incremental, product innovation is high. The new product technology is often crude, expensive, and unreliable, but it fills a function in a way that satisfies some market niche. At this stage, technical entrepreneurs form small new firms and new venture divisions within existing firms, competing on the basis of their capability in product innovation. The risk of total failure is highest at this stage. Product changes are frequent, as are changes in the market, so the production system remains fluid and the organization needs a flexible structure to respond quickly and effectively to changes in market and technology. These characteristics are typical of the early history of many existing industries, and new industries continue to show the same dynamics.[2]

As market needs become better understood and alternative product technologies converge or drop out, a transition begins toward a dominant product design and mass-production methods, adding competition in price as well as product performance. Cost competition leads to radical change in processes, driving costs rapidly down. Production capability and scale assume greater importance to reap scale economies. Strong, large firms take advantage of their capabilities in production, marketing, and management as well as R&D. In some cases, the original innovative firm can gradually build such resources. In other cases, larger firms with considerable capital and management resources absorb the small innovative firms.

As an industry and its market mature and price competition grows more intense, the production process becomes more automated, integrated, systematized, specific, and rigid to turn out a highly standardized product. The focus of innovation shifts to incremental process improvements in search of greater efficiency. When the industry reaches this stage, firms are less likely to undertake R&D aimed at radical innovations, becoming increasingly vulnerable in their competitive position. Industry dynamism may be regenerated through invasions by radical innovations introduced by new entrants.[3] Often these are innovations generated elsewhere that migrate into the industry. Some industries, however, are quite successful in extending the life of their products in this specific state with a series of incremental innovations to add new values.[4] At the later stage of this state, industries are typically relocated to catching-up countries where production costs are lower. Most traditional manufacturing sectors in advanced countries that lost their competitiveness to those of catching-up countries are at this stage.

The upper part of Figure 4-2 depicts the above model. The frequency of radical product innovations is high during the fluid stage but diminishes rapidly, while that of radical process innovations is high during the transition stage. In the specific stage, both radical product and radical process innovations are low. The figure also depicts the invasion of new radical ideas reversing the direction of the technological trajectory. However, this model might change significantly with a shift in the technoeconomic paradigm. For example, the spread of microelectronic technology across industries may enable mature industries to regenerate by becoming more flexible and information-intensive and by redesigning mature products to give new life.[5] The Abernathy-Utterback model is still useful in explaining the learning process of Korean firms in the past.

Technological Trajectory in Catching-up Countries

The course of technology development in catching-up countries has been somewhat different from that of advanced countries. On the basis of research in several different industries in Korea, I developed a three-stage model—acquisition, assimilation, and improvement—to extend Abernathy and Utterback.[6]

During the early stage of their industrialization, catching-up countries acquire mature (specific-state) foreign technologies from industrially advanced countries. Lacking local capability to establish production operations, local entrepreneurs develop production processes through the acquisition of packaged foreign technology, which includes assembly processes, product specifications, production know-how, technical personnel, and components and parts.

Production at this stage is merely an assembly operation of foreign inputs to manufacture fairly standard, undifferentiated goods. With low labor costs and little cost pressure in the protected market, the operation is relatively inefficient. The immediate technological task is the implementation of transferred foreign technology to manufacture products whose technology and market have been tested and proved elsewhere. For this purpose, only engineering (E) efforts are required. Foreign technical assistance is most significant in debugging problems in the initial implementation of production operations, but its utility

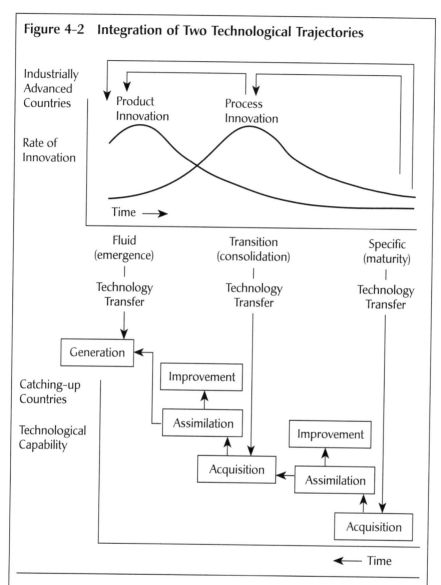

Figure 4-2 Integration of Two Technological Trajectories

SOURCE: This figure borrows ideas from James M. Utterback, *Mastering the Dynamics of Innovation* (Boston: Harvard Business School Press, 1994) and Jinjoo Lee, Zong-Tae Bae, and Dong-Kyu Choi, "Technology Development Processes: A Model for a Developing Country with a Global Perspective," *R&D Management* 18, no. 3 (1988): 235–250.

diminishes rapidly as local technicians acquire production and product design experience.

Once the implementation task is accomplished, production and product design technologies are quickly diffused within the country. Late entrant firms acquire technological capability by stealing experienced technical personnel from the early acquirers. Increased competition from new entrants spurs indigenous technical efforts in the assimilation of foreign technologies to produce differentiated items. Technical emphasis is placed on engineering and limited development (D&E) rather than research (R). By assimilating imported technology, local firms are able to develop related products through imitative reverse engineering without the direct transfer of foreign technologies.

The relatively successful assimilation of general production technology and increased emphasis on export promotion, together with the increased capability of local scientific and engineering personnel, lead to the gradual improvement of technology. Imported technologies are applied to different product lines through local efforts in research, development, and engineering (R,D&E). In proceeding along this trajectory at acquisition, assimilation, and improvement, firms in catching-up countries reverse the sequence of R,D&E in advanced countries.

Integration of the Two

Linking the technological trajectories of Abernathy and Utterback with mine, Jinjoo Lee and his associates postulate that the three-stage technological trajectory in catching-up countries takes place not only in mature technology in the specific stage but also in growing and emerging technologies in the transition and fluid stages.[7] As shown in Figure 4-2, firms in catching-up countries that have successfully acquired, assimilated, and sometimes improved mature foreign technologies may aim to repeat the process with higher-level technologies in the transition stage in advanced countries. Many industries in the first tier of catching-up countries (e.g., Taiwan and Korea) have arrived at this stage. If successful, they may eventually accumulate indigenous technological capability to generate emerging technologies in the fluid stage and challenge firms in the advanced countries.[8] When a substantial number of industries reach this stage, the country may be considered an advanced country.[9] So far, Japan may be the only catching-up country that reached this stage in the twentieth century. This framework provides an understanding of dynamically changing global technology environment, under which institutions and firms have to operate.

INSTITUTIONAL ENVIRONMENT FRAMEWORK

The acquisition of technological capability is a complex learning process at all levels of society. For firms in catching-up countries, there can be many sources of technological learning. These may be grossly categorized into three groups: the international community, the domestic community, and in-house efforts at the firm level. There are also five important factors that significantly influence the learning process: market and technology environment, public policy, formal education, socioculture, and organizational structure. Figure 4-3 depicts the major sources of technological learning, the firm's interactions with these sources, and the factors influencing the interactive process.

International Sources

The international community is perhaps the most important source of technological learning for firms in catching-up countries, as changes in the technological trajectory in advanced countries creates favorable windows of opportunity for those striving to catch up.[10] The arrow from the firm toward the international community, as depicted in Figure 4-3, shows how existing technological capability enables a catching-up firm to exploit unfamiliar technologies available in the international community. Technological capability includes not only substantive technical knowledge but also the capacity to identify sources of useful complementary expertise outside the country.[11] Technological capability also enables the firm to recognize the value of new external information, to strengthen its bargaining power in technology transfer negotiations, and to assimilate the transferred knowledge. It also makes the firm more proactive as it is highly sensitive to emerging technological opportunities. The firm aggressively seeks new opportunities to exploit and develop its technological capability. This capability also enables the firm to predict more accurately the nature and commercial potential of technological progress.[12] Thus, firms that develop a broad and active network with the international community strengthen their capacity to identify others' capabilities and to learn from them in order to build own technological capability.

The arrow from the international community to a firm indicates how foreign technology transferred to the firm strengthens its techno-

92 FROM IMITATION TO INNOVATION IN INDUSTRIES

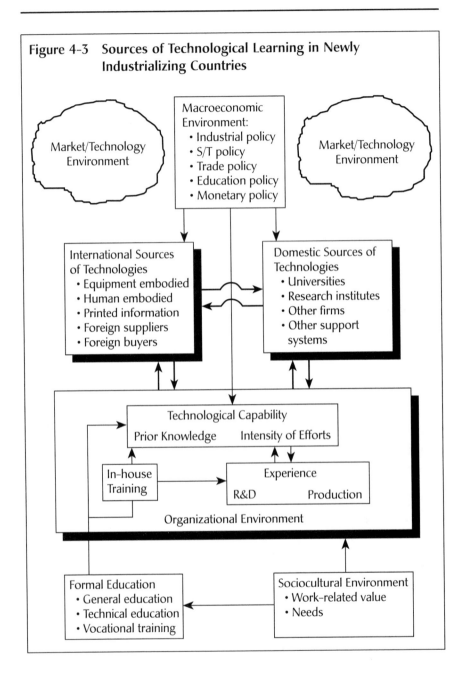

Figure 4-3 Sources of Technological Learning in Newly Industrializing Countries

logical capability by raising the level of the existing knowledge base, an essential component. This process is often called international technology transfer.

Domestic Sources

Technological capability may also be raised through interactions with the domestic community. The community's existing technological capability enables a firm to identify and explore complementary expertise available within the economy. Local universities, government R&D institutes and other public support agencies, buyers and suppliers, and other firms within the economy could be important sources of scientific and technical information new to the firm. Joint research projects with universities and research institutes could give it a significant rise in technological capability. The observation of advanced equipment in use by other firms or in exhibitions at trade fairs is a major source of imitative reverse engineering.[13] In short, technological capability enhances the competence to exploit external information, while its transfer strengthens firms' knowledge stock, raising technological capability.

In-house Efforts

Figure 4-3 also depicts the interactive mechanism between existing technological capability in a firm and its production experience and R&D activities. Existing technological capability enables the firm to operate and maintain production systems efficiently. Technological capability may be developed as a by-product of operations through learning by doing. This is particularly important for firms in catching-up countries. The more firms become practiced, the more they become capable at activities in which they are already engaged. In addition, production experience enables firms to recognize and exploit new information relevant to particular production methods to improve their own processes.

Technological capability is also generated as a by-product of a firm's R&D, particularly when knowledge is less explicit and codified and more difficult to assimilate in a technologically progressive environment.[14] The more difficult learning is, the more knowledge has to have been accumulated via R&D for effective learning to occur. The more difficult the learning environment, the higher marginal effect of R&D on technological capability.[15] R&D activities enable firms to be aware of the significance of new external signals and exploit available information more effectively. Technological capability also enables firms to identify the sorts of associations and linkages they may never before had considered, leading to creativity in research, development, and engineering activities.[16]

In short, technological capability at the firm level is acquired and accumulated mainly through three mechanisms: interactions with the international community, interactions with the domestic community, and in-house efforts. Further, these three activities intersect and reinforce one another. Effective interactions with both international and domestic communities facilitate in-house efforts, while effective in-house efforts promote interactions with external communities, both through the process of technological learning. The process involving interactions and consequent technological learning are significantly affected by five factors: the market/technology environment, formal education, socioculture, organizational structure, and public policy.

Five Influencing Factors

The first factor, the market and technological environment, affects to a significant extent not only the behavior of a firm, suppliers, customers, and policymakers but also the interactions among them. The process of technological changes and market forces operating thereon compel the firm to intensify its efforts to strengthen internal activities and in turn develop technological capability. It also compels the firm to intensify external activities to strengthen its learning from outside sources. In this vein, an export-oriented industrialization strategy, as discussed in Chapter 2, forces local firms to survive and grow in the more competitive international market than in the highly protected import-substituting local market.

The second factor, the government, can make a significant impact on the process of technological learning through both direct and indirect measures such as industrial, trade, and science/technology policies (see Chapter 2). Such policies affect a firm's interactions with the international community by regulating the inflow of foreign technology. They affect the firm's interactions with the domestic community by influencing the availability and efficacy of local supporting institutions and the quality of educational institutions. And they affect the firm's interaction with the market environment by shaping industrial organizations. That is, these policies set macroeconomic environments in which firms have to operate, thus affecting directly and indirectly the process of technological learning.

The third factor, the structure and quality of the formal education system, affects the accumulation of technological capability at the firm level. The importance of education in industrialization is well known from the economic history of Western countries. New recruits from the formal educational system provide firms with a continuous inflow of new knowledge and skills, which upgrade their technological capability for future learning.

The fourth factor influencing the process of technological capability acquisition is the sociocultural environment. This includes the beliefs, norms, and values in the society (see Chapter 3) that have significant effects on the formation of work ethics, which in turn influence the mind-set and behavior of people in the firm.

The fifth factor is organization and management. Even within the same socioculture, there are significant differences in the way an organization is structured and managed. These characteristics determine the incentive within the organization that elicits the energy and skills of the people. Many studies show that organizational properties are much more important than the characteristics of its participants in predicting the adoption of changes.[17] A conducive organizational environment fosters not only effective learning by its members but also its translation into organizational capability. In contrast, a rigid organization stifles the creativity of its participants, hindering both individual and organizational learning.

DYNAMIC LEARNING PROCESS AT THE FIRM LEVEL

The foregoing two frameworks provide an environment in which firms have to learn technologically. Understanding the dynamically changing global technology environment and a network of supporting institutions alone can explain neither the different growth rate between catching-up countries nor that between firms within Korea. Many catching-up countries have attempted at one point or another to pursue a similar strategy with few results. Even within the same country and a similar economic and technological environment, some firms are more effective than others in strengthening competitiveness through effective learning.

Understanding the dynamic process of a firm's technological learning is essential, because technological change is localized at the firm level.[18] Firms develop their technological capability through in-house efforts augmented by interactions with domestic and foreign institutions, constrained by regulations, and stimulated by government incentives in the dynamically changing global technology environment.

Thus, the learning effectiveness of individual firms that gives rise to their technological capability is a central issue in technological development. When an economy has many firms that grow dynamically by sustaining competitiveness through effective technological learning, the economy enjoys international competitiveness and healthy growth.[19]

Technological capability includes not only capacity to assimilate existing knowledge (for imitation) but also capacity to create new knowledge (for innovation). Technological learning, whether to imitate or innovate, takes place at two different levels: individual and organizational. The prime actors in the process of organizational learning are the individuals within a firm. Organizational learning is not, however, a simple sum of individual learning; rather, it is the process that creates knowledge, which is distributed across the organization, is communicable among members, has consensual validity, and is integrated into the strategy and management of the organization.[20] Individual learning is, therefore, a necessary condition for organizational learning, but it is not by itself a sufficient condition. Only effective organizations can translate individual learning into organizational learning.

Knowledge and Learning

Technological change, through either imitation or innovation, is a process in which a firm identifies real or potential problems, then actively develops new knowledge to solve them. At this point, it is important to introduce the two dimensions of knowledge: explicit and tacit. Explicit knowledge refers to knowledge that is codified and transmittable in formal, systematic language. Thus, explicit knowledge may be acquired from books, technical specifications, designs, and material embodied in machines. Joseph Badaracco calls it "migratory knowledge."[21] In contrast, tacit knowledge is so deeply rooted in the human mind and body that it is hard to codify and communicate and can be expressed only through action, commitment, and involvement in a specific context. Tacit knowledge can be acquired only through experience such as observation, imitation, and practice.

Ikujiro Nonaka postulates that the organization creates new knowledge through building both explicit and tacit knowledge and, more important, through the dynamic process of four different types of conversion between these two dimensions of knowledge: tacit to tacit, explicit to explicit, tacit to explicit, and explicit to tacit. Conversion from tacit to tacit, called socialization, takes place when tacit knowledge within one individual is shared by another through training, while conversion from explicit to explicit (combination) takes place when an individual combines discrete pieces of explicit knowledge into a new whole. Conversion from tacit to explicit (externalization) can be said to have taken place when an individual is able to articulate the foundations of his or her tacit knowledge, whereas conversion from explicit to tacit (internalization) takes place when new explicit knowledge is shared throughout a firm and other members begin to use it to broaden, extend, and reframe their own tacit knowledge. Such conversions tend to become faster in speed and larger in scale as more actors in and around the firm become involved in knowledge conversions. Using Japanese examples, Nonaka and Hirotaka Takeuchi provide excellent detailed discussions of a spiral model of organizational knowledge creation, showing how an upward spiral starts at the individual level and moves up to the organizational level.[22]

Technological capability at a firm is not a collection of explicit knowledge; rather, it is largely a collection of tacit knowledge. The firm may have some proprietary explicit knowledge such as firm-specific blueprints and standard operating procedures, but those are useful only when tacit knowledge enables its members to utilize them. Richard Nelson and Sidney Winter also note that much of the knowledge that underlies the effective performance of an organization is tacit knowledge embodied in its members.[23]

Absorptive Capacity

Effective knowledge conversions to lead to productive technological learning require two important elements: existing knowledge base, of course mostly tacit knowledge, and the intensity of effort. Wesley Cohen and Daniel Levinthal call it absorptive capacity.

First, existing tacit knowledge, as an essential element in technological learning, influences learning processes today and the nature of learning tomorrow. That is, today's tacit knowledge enables individuals and organizations to create tomorrow's increased tacit knowledge through various forms of knowledge conversion. The second important element is the intensity of effort or commitment. It is insufficient merely to expose individuals and firms to explicit knowledge. Without conscious efforts of individuals within a firm to internalize such knowledge, learning cannot take place.

These two variables, existing knowledge and the intensity of effort, in an organization constitute, as presented in Figure 4-4, a two-by-two matrix that indicates the dynamics of technological capability.

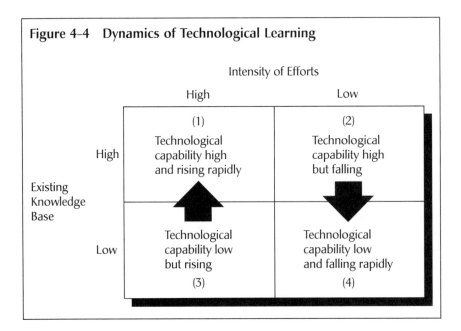

Figure 4-4 Dynamics of Technological Learning

When both existing tacit knowledge and the intensity of effort are high (quadrant 1), technological capability is high and rapidly rising. On the contrary, when both elements are low (quadrant 4), technological capability is low and falling. Organizations with high existing tacit knowledge and low intensity of effort (quadrant 2) might have high capability but will lose it gradually, since existing tacit knowledge becomes obsolete as technology moves along its trajectory. Such organizations gradually move down to quadrant 4. In contrast, organizations with low existing tacit knowledge but high intensity of effort (quadrant 3) might have low technological capability but will acquire it rapidly, as both continuous and discontinuous learning can take place through significant investment in learning, moving progressively to quadrant 1. In short, it can be said that the intensity of effort or commitment is a more crucial element than existing tacit knowledge for long-term learning and competitiveness of firms.

Crises and Discontinuous Learning

How then should a firm manage the intensity of effort? When does the firm and its members actively search for new knowledge? When do individuals within the firm vigorously commit their energy to knowledge conversion? When does a spiral pattern of knowledge conversion take place more rapidly and on a larger scale? To state it differently, when does discontinuous learning take place?

Cumulative technological learning can take place under normal circumstances. Discontinuous learning, however, takes place normally when a crisis is perceived in market competition and a strategy is implemented to turn the situation around. In such a case, the firm has to invest heavily, by hiring new personnel, in the acquisition of new tacit and explicit knowledge as well as in knowledge conversion activities to overcome the crisis in the shortest possible time. Just as the word *crisis* in Chinese character (*weiji*) is a combination of two characters (threat and opportunity), some firms manage to turn a crisis into an opportunity to transform their technological capabilities in a discontinuous manner and enhance their competitiveness. A crisis may be creative in this sense; otherwise, it can be destructive.

A crisis may be generated naturally when a firm loses its competitive standing in the market[24] or intentionally when an external principal or top management evokes a sense of crisis by proposing challenging goals.[25] Intentionally evoked crises may be imposed by the external coalition on a focal firm or industry in general. In catching-up countries, particularly where the state plays an orchestral role in industrialization, the government could impose a crisis by setting challenging goals for firms in a strategically designated industry. This is called an imposed crisis.[26]

Or the dominant coalition within a firm could intentionally construct a crisis, which is largely a negative word for mediocre managers. It may mean imminent, unfolding disaster, most possibly resulting in management failure and loss of face. Thus, crisis-oriented learning is discouraged. But for visionary entrepreneurs, crisis construction may be a strategic means of opportunistic learning, bringing about a valuable transformation in the firm. This is called constructed crisis.[27] An effective learning organization may frequently evoke constructed crises and institutionalize the process and structure to make discontinuous learning possible and to turn the crises into opportunities. It may be hypothesized that the owner/entrepreneur may be in a better position to introduce constructed crisis than the employed manager, as the former has stronger, centralized power without competing shareholders. In this vein, the tycoon of family-owned Korean *chaebols*, if he is entrepreneurial, might be in a more advantageous position to generate more constructed crises than managers.

Focal Levels in Firms

In the catching-up process, the shop floor is undoubtedly the focus for cumulative learning, as transferred technology is first implemented there and later incrementally improved to achieve optimal productivity.[28]

The strategic importance of top and middle management should not, however, be overlooked in late industrialization.[29] Their role is vital in discontinuous learning. It is entrepreneurial-minded top management that introduces constructed crises. This forces discontinuous learning that articulates metaphors and symbols to give organizational directions, creates task-force teams to manage organizationwide learning process, provides resources to support learning activities to make crises creative, and clears away any obstacles in the learning process.

It is the middle management that translates the ideas of the top into reality on the shop floor in managing constructed crises. Middle management is at the intersection of the vertical and horizontal flow of crucial information in the firm, managing task-force teams in which close interactions among members and crucial knowledge conversions take place. Nonaka's suggestion of middle-up-down management addresses the same issue.[30]

TECHNOLOGY TRANSFER FRAMEWORK

For firms to learn effectively, technology transfer from foreign companies in advanced countries can be an important source of both explicit and tacit knowledge. To analyze the behavior of firms in the acquisition of foreign technology, another framework is introduced that describes behavior operating in two dimensions. In the first, technology transfer may or may not be mediated through the market. In market-mediated technology transfer, the supplier and the buyer may negotiate payment for the transfer, either embodied in or disembodied from the physical equipment. Foreign technology may also be transferred to local users without the mediation of market; in this case the transfer usually takes place without formal agreements and payments. In the second dimension, the foreign supplier may take an active role, exercising significant control over the way in which technology is transferred to and used by the local recipient. Alternatively, the supplier may take a passive role, having almost nothing to do with the way the user takes advantage of available technical know-how either embodied in or disembodied from the physical items. These two dimensions—the mediation of market and the role of foreign suppliers—offer a useful two-by-two matrix, shown in Figure 4-5, to identify and evaluate different mechanisms of international technology transfer.[31]

In other words, firms in catching-up countries have many alternative mechanisms in acquiring foreign technology. Foreign direct investment, foreign licenses, and turnkey plants are major sources of formal technology transfer in quadrant 1. The purchase of capital goods transfers machine-embodied information (quadrant 2). Printed information such as sales catalogs, blueprints, technical specifications, trade journals, and other publications, together with observation of foreign

Figure 4-5 Evolution of Technology Transfer in Catching Up

	The Role of Foreign Suppliers	
	Active	Passive
Market Mediated	Formal mechanisms (Foreign direct investment, foreign licensing, turnkey plants, consultancies) (1)	Commodity trade (Standard machinery transfer) (2)
Nonmarket Mediated	Informal mechanisms (Technical assistance of foreign buyers and vendors) (3)	Informal mechanisms (Reverse engineering, observation, trade journals, advanced reverse engineering, etc.) (4)

SOURCE: Linsu Kim, "Korea: The Acquisition of Technology," in Hadi Soesastro and Mari Pangestu, eds., *Technological Challange in the Asia-Pacific Economy* (Sydney: Allen and Unwin, 1990): 145–157.

NOTES: 1. Merge/acquisition and strategic alliances, which are essential mechanisms in transferring technology or technology capability available in advanced countries, are not included in this classification, as they are strategies relevant only in the fluid stage, in which Korean firms have to generate new technology at the frontier.

2. The two dimensions—market mediation and supplier's role—were originally introduced by Martin Fransman, "Conceptualizing Technical Change in the Third World in the 1980s: An Interpretive Survey," *Journal of Development Studies,* July 1985.

plants, serve as important informal sources of new knowledge for firms in catching-up countries (quadrant 4).[32] Foreign suppliers and buyers from original equipment manufacturers often transfer critical knowledge to producers to ensure that products meet the buyers' technical specifications (quadrant 3).[33] In addition, reverse brain drain or return of foreign trained professionals and moonlighting foreign engineers give significant rise to technological learning of firms in catching-up countries.[34]

If firms in catching-up countries have absorptive capability, they can effectively acquire foreign technology without transactions costs (quadrants 3 and 4). When technology is simple and mature and patents have already expired, these firms, particularly small ones, with sufficient capability (high tacit knowledge and high intensity of efforts) do not have to purchase technology through formal mechanisms; rather, they can reverse-engineer foreign products, producing knock-offs and clones.

SUMMARY

This chapter introduced four analytical frameworks that I use as tools to analyze incremental and discontinuous learning at Korean firms. The first framework analyzes the technological environment, in which firms in catching-up countries have to formulate and implement technological strategy along dynamically changing technological trajectories. At the specific state of the trajectory, it may be relatively easy for catching-up firms to acquire mature foreign technologies, which might be generally available for them to imitate freely or to purchase at a bargain price from foreign suppliers. Rapid industrialization in catching-up countries has, however, pushed up wage rates faster than productivity, resulting in the rapid erosion of competitiveness in labor-intensive light industries. As a result, catching-up firms have to compete against more industrialized countries by creatively adding values on mature products or, in reverse, entering the transition state through enhanced technological efforts.

The second framework examines the institutional environment that provides sources of technological learning. The international community offers foreign direct investment, foreign licensing, turnkey plant transfer, the purchase of capital goods, and migration of technical personnel. It may be the major source of technology for catching-up countries, as market-proven technologies are readily available in advanced countries. In the local community, public research institutes, universities, and other firms may also provide valuable assistance.

The third framework theorizes the dynamic learning process at the firm level. Technological learning or the acquisition of technological capability is the acquisition and assimilation of existing knowledge and, more important, the creation of new knowledge. When successful it proceeds through a spiral process of conversions between explicit and tacit knowledge. To this end, the existing knowledge base and the intensity of efforts are important ingredients in learning. Cumulative learning takes place through learning by doing, but discontinuous learning takes place in crisis. Effective learning firms construct crises intentionally to develop organizational systems and manage their processes to make the crises truly creative.

The final framework categorizes four major modes of technology transfer across national boundaries. The mode of transfer is determined largely by a buyer's absorptive capability. If the buyer has sufficient capability, it can effectively acquire foreign technology without transaction costs and produce knockoffs and clones through reverse engineering.

These frameworks are used as tools to analyze the dynamic process of rapid technological learning at Korean firms and the role played by the supporting institutions and the government in the dynamically changing global technology environment.

5 The Automobile Industry: Crisis Construction and Technological Learning

"Only a handful of car manufacturers would survive the global shake-out of the 1990s and none of South Korea's five automakers was to be among them, having been driven out or relegated to niche markets dependent on alliances with Toyota, Honda, Nissan, Volkswagen, Ford, or General Motors," predicted one economic journal in 1992.[1] Nonetheless, five Korean automakers are determined to become leading automakers on their own in order to contend in the world market.

Korea's automobile industry has grown phenomenally since its birth in 1962, as shown in Table 5-1. Production increased tenfold in the first decade, tenfold again in the second decade, and twentyfold in the third. As a result, Korea has risen rapidly in the ranks of the world's auto producers. It was not even on the charts in 1980—Korean production was about one-tenth that of Brazil, which ranked tenth—yet rose to eleventh in the world in 1986, to ninth in 1991, and sixth by 1993. The Korean government initially envisioned its car industry's growing to fifth in the world by the twenty-first century. Korea's car makers, however, pushed even harder and reached fifth place in 1994 by producing 2.3 million cars, surpassed only by the United States,

Table 5-1 Growth of the Automobile Industry in Korea (in thousands)

	Year							
	1962	1965	1970	1975	1980	1985	1990	1994
Production								
Hyundai	–	–	4.3	7.1	61.8	240.7	676.0	1,134.6
Kia	0.07	0.03	5.7	20.0	34.1	87.2	377.3	619.9
Daewoo	1.7	0.1	16.6	9.3	25.7	45.0	201.2	340.7
Others	–	–	1.7	0.4	2.8	7.5	48.0	216.5
Total	1.77	0.14	28.4	36.8	124.4	380.4	1,302.5	2,311.7
Exports								
Hyundai	–	–	–	–	16.2	120.0	225.4	393.0
Kia	–	–	–	0.01	4.7	1.4	85.8	210.5
Daewoo	–	–	–	–	4.2	5.6	34.2	99.8
Others	–	–	–	–	0.1	0.9	1.7	34.7
Total	–	–	–	0.01	25.2	127.9	347.1	738.0

SOURCE: Based on data provided by the Korea Automotive Industry Cooperation.

Japan, Germany, and France.[2] (See Table 5-2.) In addition, Samsung, the largest *chaebol*, announced plans to join existing Korean firms in producing cars beginning in 1998.

Korea's auto exports also increased rapidly, from 1,341 in 1976 to 737,943 in 1994, making automobiles the nation's seventh largest export item behind electronics, textile products, machinery, steel products, and footwear in 1992.[3] Korea's successful entry to the U.S. market in the 1980s with a subcompact car made by Hyundai repeated West Germany's success in the 1950s with Volkswagen and Japan's success in 1970s with Toyota.[4] How have Korean automakers grown technologically fast enough to emerge as new contenders in the world market? How has the industry interacted with the government in this process?

IMITATION DRIVE IN THE AUTOMOBILE INDUSTRY

In the 1950s, more than a hundred primitive garages manually fabricated and assembled a few automobiles a year based on used military parts and components and experience maintaining military vehicles. The Korean Army and Air Force vehicle renovation depots overhauled imported Japanese and American military vehicles to stretch their life cycles. These military depots were the breeding grounds for the experienced technicians with necessary tacit knowledge who would later staff the primitive automobile fabricators.[5]

However, Korea's modern automobile industry can be said to have begun in 1962, when a local firm, Saenara, established the first well-structured assembly plant to produce Japanese subcompact cars in Korea at the instigation and promotion of the Korean government. As part of its First Five-Year Economic Development Plan, the Korean government enacted the Automotive Industry Promotion Law of 1962, which provided tariff exemptions for imports of parts and components, tax exemptions for assemblers, and local market protection from foreign cars. This led to the birth of the first modern assembly plant, a semi-knocked-down (SKD) type of operation, in Korea.[6] Technical assistance and SKD parts came from Japanese Nissan and most of the senior engineers from military vehicle renovation depots.[7] This company evolved into Daewoo Motor.[8]

Three locally owned assemblers emerged soon after: Hyundai began in 1967 to assemble Ford cars, Asia Motor in 1969 to assemble Fiats, and Kia Motor, a motorcycle producer, in 1974 to produce a Mazda model. What is noteworthy is that, unlike other developing countries but like Japan, Korea pursued a unique and independent strategy of developing its automobile industry independently of the multinational automakers in the international oligopolistic market, in which twenty producers from seven countries regularly accounted for more than 92 percent of world production.[9]

Hyundai, one of the two largest *chaebols* and by far the largest and most successful automaker, decided from the start that if it was to become a power in the international automobile industry, it would have to be its own master. (In 1979 Japan's Mitsubishi Motors assumed a 12 percent equity share in return for access to technology, but Hyundai has maintained full independence in global strategy.) Kia, the seventh largest *chaebol* with a background in bicycles, motorcycles, motortricycles, and small trucks, also entered the industry as an independent firm. Kia gave equity stakes totaling 20 percent to Ford, Mazda, and Itochu in attempts to acquire crucial technology, but it has maintained its management independence, pursuing its own technology and marketing strategy. As a result, it has surged to become Korea's second largest producer. In contrast, despite its head start as

Table 5-2 Top 10 Automobile Producing Countries in the World (in thousands)

1950		1960		1970		1980	
United States	8,005	United States	7,905	United States	8,283	Japan	11,042
United Kingdom	738	Germany	2,055	Japan	5,289	United States	8,009
Canada	387	United Kingdom	1,810	Germany	3,842	Germany	3,878
Soviet	362	France	1,369	France	2,537	France	3,378
France	357	Italy	644	United Kingdom	2,098	Soviet	2,199
Germany	306	Soviet	523	Italy	1,854	Italy	1,611
Italy	127	Japan	481	Canada	1,159	Canada	1,323
Australia	126	Canada	397	Soviet	916	United Kingdom	1,312
Japan	31	Australia	326	Spain	536	Spain	1,181
Czech	31	Brazil	133	Australia	473	Brazil	1,165
Korea	n[a]	Korea	n	Korea	28	Korea	123

THE AUTOMOBILE INDUSTRY 109

1990		1991		1994	
Japan	13,486	Japan	13,245	United States	12,316
United States	9,783	United States	8,810	Japan	10,554
Germany	5,163	Germany	5,015	Germany	4,351
France	3,769	France	3,610	France	4,017
Soviet	2,134	Spain	2,081	**Korea**	**2,311**
Italy	2,121	Soviet	2,012	Canada	2,303
Spain	2,053	Italy	1,878	Spain	2,142
Canada	1,926	Canada	1,872	United Kingdom	1,694
United Kingdom	1,567	**Korea**	**1,497**	Brazil	1,580
Korea	**1,321**	United Kingdom	1,454	Italy	1,534

SOURCE: This table is based on *Market Data Book* published by *Automotive News*, 1995.

NOTES: For years 1950 through 1980, Korea was not in the top 10.
[a] n denotes negligible.

Korea's first automobile company, Daewoo, in a joint venture with General Motors (GM), was so constrained by GM's global corporate strategy that it found itself trailing Hyundai and Kia. Finally, after years of discord, Daewoo bought out GM's equity share in 1992 to pursue an independent global strategy.

The Korean government played a significant role in developing the automobile industry, imposing crises while providing supports to make those crises creative rather than destructive. For example, the government established a domestic content schedule in 1966, which it implemented through various incentive policies. The preferential allocation of foreign exchange was tied to the degree of localization achieved, consequently pushing the domestic content ratio from 21 percent in 1966 to more than 60 percent in 1972 and to 92 percent by 1981, transforming the assembly operation from an SKD to a completely knocked-down (CKD) arrangement.[10]

The government designated the automobile industry as a strategic sector to promote and offered, among other things, various preferential financing and tax concessions, which made it easy for producers to expand production facilities. As mentioned in Chapter 2, these two measures were among the most crucial the government employed in directing the private sector. The rapid industrialization should, however, be attributed as much to miraculously dynamic industrial activities at the firm level as to effective policy intervention.

Initial Assembly Operation

Hyundai's entry into the automobile industry illustrates the way Korean automobile producers acquired their initial production capability. Lacking experience in automobile production at the outset, Hyundai formed a task force in 1967.[11] Team members with strong project management and engineering backgrounds came from Hyundai Construction, while others were poached from existing auto producers with auto production experience, providing requisite variety in experience and knowledge. The recruited engineers increased Hyundai's level of tacit knowledge related to automobile production.

In 1968 Hyundai entered an Overseas Assembler Agreement with Ford, whereby Hyundai was to assemble a Ford compact car on an SKD basis.[12] Ford transferred this technology in packaged form to Hyundai with explicit information, including blueprints, technical specifications, and production manuals. The agreement also provided for training Hyundai engineers at Ford sites and dispatching ten Ford personnel to Hyundai. This expedited the translation of Ford's explicit knowledge into tacit knowledge at Hyundai and to transfer Ford's tacit knowledge on procurement planning, procurement coordination, production engineering, process engineering, production management, welding, painting, marketing, and service to Hyundai. Other suppliers also sent engineers to set up equipment and train Hyundai technicians.[13] The most competent engineers trained by Ford were assigned to production and production engineering departments, because mastering production technology was most critical at the outset. In other words, the agreement with Ford enabled Hyundai to further upgrade both tacit and explicit knowledge related to auto assembly, moving up along the Y axis (toward higher prior knowledge level) in Figure 5-1.

At the same time, Hyundai constructed a crisis by setting an ambitious goal to accelerate plant construction in an attempt to minimize production lead time. Hardworking engineers, technicians, and construction workers lived together in makeshift quarters on the plant site, toiling sixteen hours a day, seven days a week. The crisis increased strong interactions among the members, intensifying various knowledge conversions spirally at the individual, group, and organization levels, moving Hyundai left along the X axis (toward higher intensity of efforts) in Figure 5-1, resulting in quadrant 1. Consequently, given

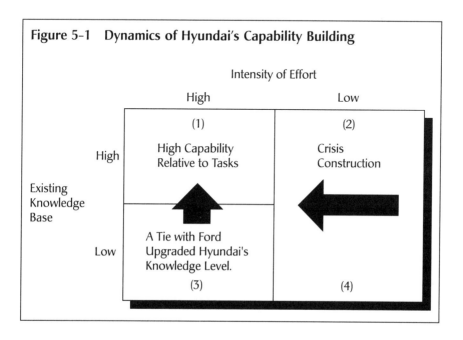

Figure 5-1 Dynamics of Hyundai's Capability Building

high prior knowledge and high intensity of efforts, Hyundai recorded the shortest time, six months, between groundbreaking and the first commercial production among the 118 Ford assembly plants around the world.

Hyundai also created a crisis for its production staff by setting an ambitious goal to acquire production capability in the shortest possible time. While plant construction was under way, teams rehearsed operations by disassembling and reassembling two passenger cars, a bus, and a truck over and over to routinize procedures, internalizing transferred explicit knowledge (production manuals) into tacit knowledge. At the plant's completion, workers had sufficient tacit knowledge to assemble cars with minimum trial and error. At the outset, technical emphasis was largely on mastering production capability to meet Ford's technical specifications. Rapid assimilation of production know-how enabled assembly process to evolve gradually from SKD to CKD operation.

Korean Car Development

In the aftermath of the first oil crisis and structural adjustments toward heavy and chemical industries, the government radically shifted its automobile industry policy from CKD assembly of foreign cars to the development of locally designed cars. Policy implementation to develop "Korean" cars was highly centralized by the government, personally directed by the nation's president at the top with the Ministry of Trade and Industry as a coordinating and implementing agency. In 1973 the government formulated the Automobile Industry Long-term Promotion Plan and ordered three passenger car makers—Hyundai, Kia, and Daewoo—to submit detailed plans to develop Korean cars. The president was briefed regularly on the progress.

The government plan was very specific. For instance, the indigenous model had to be new in the world, with a smaller than 1,500-cubic-centimeter engine and a local-content ratio of at least 95 percent, cost less than $2,000 to produce, and it had to be on the market by 1975. The government also specified a plant production capacity of more than 50,000 units per year when Korea produced merely 12,751 passenger cars annually. The government established seven principles to promote native model development and foster industry growth. These included, among other things, protection of the local market from new entrants and from new foreign knockdown imports, a significant tax reduction for locally designed cars, promotion of vertical integration leading to new business opportunities, preferential financing, tax concessions, and an administrative decree to guarantee a large market share for the Korean model.

This plan led to the appearance of two original new vehicles: Hyundai's Pony and Kia's Brisa. In response to the government's directive and incentives, in 1973 Hyundai submitted its master plan for a new plant with a capacity of 80,000 Korean cars, almost sixteen times the company's production of 5,426 cars that year, thereby constructing another major crisis. This was a major departure from the past strategy of merely assembling foreign cars. The plan required the development of a highly successful Korean subcompact car and a simultaneous drastic increase in both export volume and local market share in order to absorb the proposed production capacity. It was, indeed, a major crisis for Hyundai engineers. This event resulted in Hyundai's second major jump in technological learning.

Although lacking technological capability, Hyundai decided to obtain foreign technologies from many different sources in unpackaged form and integrate them on its own to maintain independence from foreign multinationals. Hyundai, however, had a clear goal of rapidly assimilating imported foreign technology in the shortest possible time. Prior knowledge accumulated from merely assembling largely foreign parts and components was inadequate for the new task. As the first step to overcoming the deficiency, Hyundai organized a project team whose members were to master literature related to various aspects of auto design and manufacture, accumulating tacit knowledge converted from explicit literature knowledge to enhance its prior knowledge level.

Hyundai approached twenty-six firms in five countries for various technologies: ten in Japan and Italy for style design, four in Japan and the United States for equipment in a stamping shop, five in the United Kingdom and Germany for casting and forging plants, two in Japan and the United Kingdom for engines, and five in the United Kingdom and United States for an integrated parts/components plant. These companies provided opportunities for Hyundai engineers to tour not only their sites but also those of the leading automobile manufacturing plants that had used suppliers' technology, enabling the highly motivated Hyundai engineers to relate the tacit knowledge derived from the printed word to physical operations. Through this process they gained significant insights into large-scale, modern automobile manufacturing systems. Hyundai then entered a licensing agreement with Italdesign for body styling and design and with Mitsubishi for gasoline engine, transmission, and rear axle designs and for casting technology. Engineers were sent to these suppliers for training.

How Hyundai assimilated style design technology is informative. It selected a team of five design engineers to study literature related to auto styling, then sent them to Italy to participate closely in the design process with Italdesign engineers. Hyundai set the team the ambitious goal of assimilating all of Italdesign's styling technology to enable them to undertake subsequent designs on their own, which the engineers were desperate to achieve. For a year and half, the highly motivated team shared an apartment near Italdesign, kept a record of what they were learning during the day, and conducted group reviews every evening. Such intensive interaction among the team members resulted in a most rapid spiral process of knowledge conversions and increased Hyundai's tacit and explicit styling knowledge significantly. These engineers later became the core of the design department at Hyundai, and one became the vice president in charge of R&D.

Although many engineers acquired necessary tacit knowledge related to different technologies, Hyundai did not have experienced engineers who could put them together. To minimize trial and error, Hyundai hired a former managing director of British Leyland as its vice president and six other British technical experts for the successful development of its first original model for three years (1974–1977), increasing the firm's prior level of tacit knowledge. These technical experts, as the chief engineers of chassis design, body design, development and testing, die and tooling, body production, and commercial vehicle design departments, played a crucial role in helping Hyundai engineers convert explicit knowledge supplied by licenses into tacit knowledge and to integrate diverse tacit knowledge into a workable system. After the British engineers left, Hyundai employed moonlighting Japanese engineers to troubleshoot problems.

Comparative Analysis

Although foreign direct investment is regarded as an important channel for transferring foreign technology to developing countries, this is not necessarily the case.[14] A comparative analysis of technological learning process and market performance between independent Hyundai and Daewoo, a joint venture with GM—the largest company with the largest R&D expenditures in the world—is instructive. Hyundai's approach constitutes a sharp contrast with the Daewoo-GM partnership, in which technical assistance was always acquired from the parent company. Technology transfer in a package contract or a joint venture is apt to lead to a passive attitude on the part of the recipient in the learning process, as the performance of the transferred technology is guaranteed by the supplier. In contrast, when a local firm unpackages technology transfer and independently takes the responsibility to organize imported technologies and components from multiple sources and to integrate them into a workable mass-production system, it does entail a major risk. But this forces and motivates local participants to assimilate foreign technologies as rapidly as possible throughout the process, because recipients, not the foreign suppliers, must take the total blame if it fails.[15]

That is how Hyundai developed its first model Pony with 90 percent local content in 1975, and it quickly improved its quality in subsequent years, making Korea the second nation in Asia with its own automobile.[16] As a result, Hyundai's local market share in passenger cars increased from 19.2 percent in 1970 to 73.9 percent in 1979. Hyundai exported 62,592 cars to Europe, the Middle East, and Asia, accounting for 67 percent of Korea's total auto exports in 1976–1980 and 97 percent of total passenger car exports from Korea in 1983–1986. Pony comprised 98 percent of Hyundai's exports during these periods.

In contrast, constrained by GM's global objectives, Daewoo had relied solely on GM for technology sourcing, having done relatively little in the way of developing its own technological capability and even less in developing its own product designs. The investment in product and process improvements undertaken by Daewoo between 1976 and 1981 was only 19 percent as great as those undertaken by Hyundai, although its production capacity, on average, was approximately 70 percent as large. As a result, though their products were comparable in engine size and price, Hyundai was operating at 67.3 percent of capacity compared with 19.5 percent for Daewoo in 1982 (see Table 5-3). The differential in labor productivity was just as stark; 8.55 cars per head at Hyundai compared with only 2.61 at Daewoo. Consequently, Daewoo had only a 17 percent passenger car market share compared with 73 percent for Hyundai, reflecting consumer preference.

Not until 1983, a year after taking over managerial control from GM, did Daewoo begin to show marked improvement in product/process development and market performance. Daewoo management established a full-fledged R&D department, adopted the Japanese *kanban* (just-in-time) system, streamlined production, instituted a quality control program, and strengthened its marketing drive. Nevertheless, conflicts between the partners continued to plague the joint venture, giving the smaller Kia a chance to outpace Daewoo. The 1992 divorce

Table 5-3 Basic Parameters and Performance between Hyundai and Daewoo, 1982

	Hyundai Motor	Daewoo Motor
A. Capital (million won)	64.4	44.5
B. Number of workers	9,129	5,675
C. Sales (billion won)	116,000	76,000
D. Production (cars)	78,071	14,845
E. Exports (cars)	13,573	114
Capacity utilization (E/D)	67.3	19.5
Labor productivity (E/B)	8.55	2.61
Capital productivity (E/A)	1,212.0	33.6
Export coefficient (F/E)	17.4	0.8
Market share	73.0	13.0

SOURCE: Adapted from Alice H. Amsden and Linsu Kim, "A Comparative Analysis of Local and Transnational Corportations in the Korean Automobile Industry," in Dong-Ki Kim and Linsu Kim, eds., *Management behind Industrialization: Readings in Korean Business* (Seoul: Korea University Press, 1989), 579–596.

from GM finally freed Daewoo to set its own global strategic direction and navigate at its own ambitious pace.

Export-oriented Transformation

The second energy crisis prompted another change in government policy to bring about greater scale economies at the cost of market competition, reducing the number of passenger car producers from four to two. The government's original rationalization program was to have only one Korean passenger car producer by merging the two largest companies—Hyundai and the Daewoo-GM joint venture—and by suspending production by the other two—Kia and Asia. While the latter two ceased passenger car production, the merger between the first two did not occur. GM assumed that it would retain half the share of all Korean automobile production and use Korea as one of many sites for manufacturing "GM world cars" within its global strategy. Hyundai, however, insisted that GM be limited to a minority position in the merged company, that Hyundai be given independent management control, and that Hyundai be allowed to pursue its own global strategy in both domestic and export markets. Since those involved were unable to resolve their disagreement, the proposed merger was aborted. This failure signaled the waning influence of the state, marking the end of government-directed development and the beginning of industry-initiated growth.

The second oil crisis was also a disaster for the automobile industry. Gasoline prices soared, car sales nose-dived, and losses mounted. At this juncture Hyundai decided to make a major investment to develop the next generation front engine, front wheel drive (FF) car in order to push it in the North American market, attempting once again to turn the crisis into an opportunity.[17] Hyundai's proposed capacity was 300,000 units per year; at the time Hyundai was producing 57,054 passenger cars, using only 32 percent of its capacity (150,000 units), and Korea was producing a mere 85,693 units per year. Clearly, Hyundai was determined to turn the domestic market-oriented automobile business into a highly export-oriented one, a goal that industry analysts within Korea and abroad dismissed as total nonsense. But once again Hyundai constructed a major crisis and turned it into an opportunity, achieving its third huge leap in technological learning.

Hyundai approached several major automakers—Volkswagen, Ford, Renault, and Alfa Romeo—for FF technology as a way to diversify its technology sources. However, all these companies demanded equity and management participation and viewed Hyundai as a local assembly subsidiary for their FF cars. Hyundai eventually approached Mitsubishi again; in 1981 Mitsubishi had agreed to license engine, transaxle, chassis, and emission control technology to Hyundai. In return, Hyundai gave Mitsubishi a 10 percent equity share, but it did not include management participation.[18] Hyundai not only retained all managerial control but reserved the right to imports parts and technology from Mitsubishi's competitors and to compete directly in Mitsubishi's own markets. Hyundai, however, sourced body styling from Italdesign and constant velocity joint technology from British GKN and Japanese NTN.[19]

In addition, Hyundai acquired more foreign technologies from various automobile sources than its Korean competitors. Through 1985 Hyundai signed 54 licenses compared with 22 for Daewoo, 14 for Kia, and 9 for Ssangyong. Hyundai's sources included Japan (22), United Kingdom (14), United States (5), Italy (5), West Germany (3), and others (5), indicating significant diversity. Mitsubishi accounted for only half the licenses from Japan, reflecting Hyundai's independence in acquiring technological expertise.[20]

With the experience of developing and manufacturing Pony since 1976, Hyundai had a sufficient base of prior tacit and explicit knowledge to assimilate FF car design and manufacturing without assistance from the foreign engineers. There were, however, three important learning aspects at this stage. The first was manufacturing a car to meet the most stringent U.S. safety and environmental requirements. The second was adopting computer-aided design/computer-aided manufacturing (CAD/CAM) and assembly line control systems and developing a transfer machine. This led to full computerization from design to manufacturing and to parts/components handling at Hyundai, laying a critically important foundation for the firm to develop cars on its own. The third was the construction of a proving ground, completing the necessary infrastructure for its next strategy.

For the first aspect, Hyundai, in March 1979, organized a project team to develop a long-term plan to computerize design and manufacturing. The team collected literature and catalogs on CAD/CAM and spent the next fourteen months internalizing explicit literature into tacit knowledge. Based on that knowledge, the team purchased an IBM computer system and Toyodenki's plotter and undertook an in-depth study of Mitsubishi's CAD/CAM system in operation. The team was then expanded to include two or three representatives from each department that would be affected by the CAD/CAM system, "socializing" the tacit knowledge of the original members to the new members. During the next nineteen months the expanded team determined the scope of CAD/CAM application and undertook a comprehensive study of available alternative software packages. Hyundai selected the Catia program developed by French Dasso Aerospace in May 1982, then did preparatory work for almost thirty-six months before implementing the system.

Hyundai completed the FF plant in February 1985, tripling its capacity from 150,000 to 450,000 units per year. Its FF Excel passed both emission and safety tests in 1986 and began exporting to the U.S. market in February 1986. In that year Hyundai sold 168,882 Excels in ten months, exceeding its ambitious plan by more than 60 percent and turning its loss into profit. In 1987 Hyundai sold 263,610 more Excels in the United States; Excel became the best-selling import car of the year, overtaking Nissan's Centra, Honda's Civic, Subaru's DL/GL, and Toyota's Corolla. Hyundai's success in developing and exporting a subcompact appears to have prompted GM to source its Pontiac LeMans from Daewoo.

INNOVATION DRIVE IN THE AUTOMOBILE INDUSTRY

Although Hyundai was quite successful in pushing the Excel in the North American market in the mid-1980s, it soon faced a technological dilemma. Mitsubishi, its major source of important FF technology, and other foreign suppliers were unwilling to share their latest technology with Hyundai.[21] But Hyundai lacked the technological proficiency to keep up with its competitors in the North American market in improving car quality. Consequently, like the Japanese car exporters in the 1970s, Hyundai found its Excel listed at the bottom of *Consumer Reports'* automobile ratings, which fatally tarnished its image in the U.S. market. This experience prompted Hyundai to develop an extensive R&D network within Korea and abroad to acquire its own technological capability. "We didn't know the export market before, but now our eyes have been opened," said the president of Hyundai.

Originally Designed Models

"Korea's automakers take on the world again. The West once scoffed at Japan's plans to exports its cars. Now Detroit and other automakers may be underestimating this new global challenge too," warned *Fortune* magazine in 1995.[22] In 1994, for example, the fiercely independent Hyundai unveiled the Accent, the first subcompact it designed—its predecessors were based on Mitsubishi designs—which was benchmarked on the Toyota Tercel for performance and the Chrysler Neon for cost.[23] The new subcompact has energy-absorbing front and rear crumple zones, dual airbags with a state-of-the-art self-diagnostic sensing system, and a four-channel antilock brake system. A big success in both the domestic and export markets, it became the best-selling car in the domestic market and the unexpected rush of orders from abroad resulted in a three-month backlog. How has Hyundai Motor Company been transformed from imitative learning by doing to innovative learning by research?

Hyundai's R&D efforts date back to 1978, when the company established a primitive R&D laboratory to design face-lifts of existing compacts and subcompacts. Efforts to develop its own capability, however, began to take shape in 1984, when it opened its Advanced Engineering and Research Institute to develop its own engines and transmissions. The laboratory also spawned the Passenger Vehicle R&D Center for the design of new passenger cars and the Commercial Vehicle R&D Center for the development of new buses, trucks, and special vehicles. In addition, it set up the Manufacturing Technology Center to design its production system. To augment its in-house R&D, Hyundai established joint laboratories with research-oriented local universities, one with the Korea Advanced Institute of Science and Technology and the other with Pohang University of Science and Technology.

In 1986 Hyundai opened the Hyundai American Technical Center, Inc. in Ann Arbor, Michigan, to monitor technological change related to the automobile industry and to perform emission testing and the Hyundai Styling Studio in Los Angeles to sense the needs of American consumers. Furthermore, Hyundai set up a technical center in Frankfurt to attempt to monitor technological change in Europe and design and engineer new cars for the European market. Hyundai established an R&D center in Japan in 1995 as a step toward entering that country's market in 1997.

Hyundai's investment in R&D personnel and projects is impressive. First, as shown in Table 5-4, the number of research engineers at Hyundai has increased, from 197 in 1975 to 3,890 in 1994, accounting for nearly 10 percent of total employment. Almost half of them have a postgraduate engineering degree. Second, Hyundai recruited many Korean engineers from American universities, some with experience at General Motors and Chrysler. For instance, all but a few of the thirty-five senior research engineers with Ph.D.'s at its Advanced Engineering and Research Institute were trained in the United States. Third, Hyundai also invested heavily in further training for its engineers. The number of R&D scientists and engineers sent abroad for purposes of short-term training and observation to long-term graduate degree programs increased from 74 in 1982 to 351 in 1986. Fourth, its R&D investment also increased sharply from W 1.1 billion ($2.2 million) in 1975 to W 400 billion ($501.3 million) in 1994. R&D investment grew from 1.8 percent of sales in 1982 to 4.4 percent in 1994, almost 60 percent higher than that of such domestic competitors as Daewoo and Kia.

The development of its alpha engine illustrates how Hyundai struggled to become independent of Mitsubishi, which licensed Hyundai to produce its old engines but refused to share its state-of-the-art models. Lacking experience in designing even a carburetor engine, let alone an electronically controlled one, Hyundai determined to develop a state-of-the-art engine, creating another major crisis in technological learning. Despite skepticism that it would end up developing an engine comparable only to Mitsubishi's engine of thirty years earlier, in 1984

Table 5-4 R&D Investment at Hyundai Motor Company (in 100 million won)

	1975	1978	1982	1984	1986	1988	1990	1992	1994
Hyundai									
Sales	30	216	430	669	1,906	3,411	4,656	6,079	9,052
R&D	1.1	5.4	7.9	22.7	79.5	116.0	190.4	248.8	400.0
R&D as a percent of sales	3.5	2.5	1.8	3.4	4.2	3.4	4.1	4.1	4.4
Number of researchers	197	381	725	1,298	2,247	2,459	3,418	3,192	3,890

SOURCE: Adapted from data provided by Hyundai Motor Company.

Hyundai organized a task force directed by its executive vice president with a vision of developing the most modern engine. But no one on the team had any experience in engine design, and no car with an electronically controlled engine from which Hyundai engineers could learn was available locally.

The task force was divided into several groups: (1) research on hydrodynamics, thermodynamics, fuel engineering, emission control, and lubrication; (2) research on kinetics and dynamics related to engine and car design and CAD; (3) research on vibration and noise; (4) research on new ceramics; (5) research on electronics and control systems; and (6) research on manufacturing control and CAM. More than 300 R&D personnel received training overseas before the engine project was officially launched in 1984. The team members collected all available English and Japanese literature about engines and transmissions and mastered the contents to raise their tacit knowledge. Hyundai then entered into an agreement with British Ricardo Engineering, which provided initial assistance in technical training for engine design. Next, Hyundai hired two Korean experts who had gained engine development experience with Chrysler and General Motors after earning Ph.D.'s at American universities. In 1985 Hyundai hired an experienced engineer from Ricardo for three years.[24]

Despite the training and consulting services of Ricardo and the three experts, Hyundai engineers repeated trials and errors for fourteen months before creating the first prototype. But the engine block broke into pieces at its first test. New prototype engines appeared almost every week, only to break in testing. No one on the team could figure out why the prototypes kept breaking down, casting serious doubts, even among Hyundai management, on its capability to develop a competitive engine. The team had to scrap eleven more broken prototypes before one survived the test. There were 288 engine design changes, 156 in 1986 alone.[25] Ninety-seven test engines were made before Hyundai refined its natural aspiration and turbocharger engines; 53 more engines were produced for durability improvement, 88 more for developing a car, 26 more for developing its transmission, and 60 more for other tests, totaling 324 test engines. In addition, more than 200 transmissions and 150 test vehicles were created before Hyundai perfected them in 1992.

Despite the doubters, Hyundai's alpha engine outperformed comparable Japanese models. Hyundai's natural aspiration engine took 11.1 seconds to reach 100 kilometers per hour compared with 11.3 seconds by the Honda CRX 3V. Hyundai also outperformed Honda in fuel efficiency. Success in developing the alpha engines (1.3 and 1.5 liters) led to the development of beta engines (1.6, 1.8, and 2 liters), making Hyundai completely independent of foreign licensing in engines for midsize, compact, and subcompact cars. Hyundai's new 1.8 liter, 16-valve double overhead camshaft engine, for example, takes only 9 seconds to reach 100 kilometers per hour, outperforming a similar model of Japan's Toyota.[26]

Hyundai invested $437.5 million and spent fifty-two months perfecting the Accent, its subcompact with the alpha engine. The company freed teams of its engineers to come up with the car they would buy and gave them a Cray supercomputer to help incorporate such safety features as antilock brakes and dual airbags in the snazzy design. "We have created an eye-catching design that will appeal to the young," said a young engineer at Hyundai's engineering center.[27] In 1995 Hyundai unveiled the Avante, a new compact with the beta engine. These two models obviated further royalty payments to foreign automakers.

Hyundai is still behind the high-class Japanese and U.S. manufacturers, but the quality gap has definitely narrowed. Its aim is to meet Japanese quality but at a more competitive price.[28] Nevertheless, Hyundai became an important technology exporter, earning royalties for its exports to Thailand, Egypt, Zimbabwe, the Philippines, Malaysia, and elsewhere. For instance, Hyundai received about $900,000 as a down payment and a running royalty of $90 per car from a Malaysian automaker.

Innovating and improving car quality by enhanced R&D operations, Hyundai won several quality accolades overseas. Canada selected Elantra as the car of the year in 1992. It also won first place at international auto rallies in Australia, Greece, and Malaysia. The National Road and Motorists Association of Australia selected the Elantra as the best car in 1992 and 1993.

As a result of continual R&D efforts, Hyundai sustained the largest domestic market share during the first quarter of 1995, when its Accent was the best-selling subcompact, the Avante the best-selling compact, the Sonata II the best-selling midsize car, and the Grandeur the best-selling full-size car in Korea. Hyundai also bounced back in exports, particularly in new markets, from 225,393 in 1990 to 392,239 in 1994. In Australia, for one, Hyundai is the best-selling import car, representing 13.8 percent of total imports, beating Mazda's 13.6 percent, Honda's 10.4 percent, and Toyota's 9.7 percent. Hyundai also took first place among foreign auto sales in Brazil and Puerto Rico.

Beginning with exports of 1,042 Ponys in 1976, Hyundai exported one million cars by 1988, another million by 1991, and its third million by 1994, accounting for 42 percent of its total production and 68 percent of Korea's total auto exports.[29]

Hyundai increased its output approximately tenfold every decade. It had taken Toyota twenty-nine years and Mazda forty-three years to produce one million cars;[30] it took Hyundai only eighteen.[31] Hyundai Motor was the thirteenth largest automobile producer in the world and the largest in the Third World in 1994, having steadily ascended from sixteenth in 1991. Aspiring to place among the global top ten by the year 2000, Hyundai is expanding its manufacturing capacity, adding another 400,000 cars per year in 1996 to its previous volume of 1.26 million.

Hyundai is spending more than $5 billion on R&D from 1995 to 2000 in a bid for a breakthrough in environmentally friendly cars, lifting its R&D outlay from 4.4 percent of sales in 1994 to 7 percent by 2000. The proportion of R&D funds devoted to environmentally friendly vehicles will rise from 40 percent to more than 60 percent. Hyundai is working on two alternatives—electric-and solar-powered vehicles. It began to concentrate on electric cars in 1991 and more recently entered into a cooperative agreement with the U.S. Ovonic Battery, which produces a nickel-metal hydrogen battery. The research with Ovonic was expected to provide a key to commercial production of electric cars by the end 1996, within twelve months of new U.S. vehicle emission restrictions. In other words, Hyundai is still determined to become a player in the United States, the world's largest car market.[32]

Sequence of Product Development

Figure 5-2 and Table 5-5 summarize the foregoing discussions, illustrating how Hyundai sequenced product development and accumulated technological capability. Figure 5-2 shows that Hyundai first acquired production experience in the assembly of foreign compact and large models for the eight years from 1968 to 1976 before it attempted to develop its own model. Inexperienced Hyundai had to enter into technical assistance agreements with many foreign suppliers. As new vehicle development sequenced from subcompact to compact to medium-size and large cars, the number of years between them decreased steadily. It took seven years (1976–1983) between subcompact and compact, five years (1983–1988) between compact and medium-size, and four years (1988–1992) between medium and large cars. Hyundai's completely native model also sequenced from subcompact

THE AUTOMOBILE INDUSTRY   125

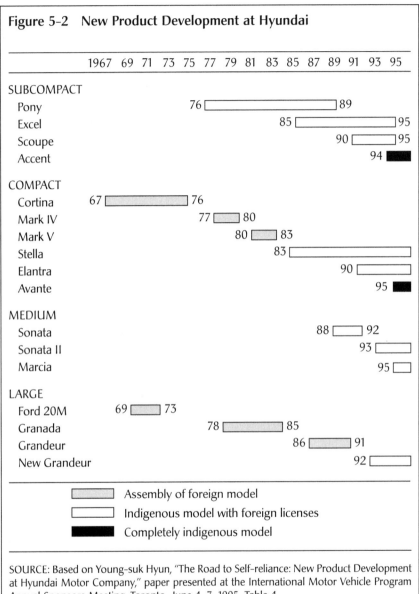

Figure 5-2   New Product Development at Hyundai

SOURCE: Based on Young-suk Hyun, "The Road to Self-reliance: New Product Development at Hyundai Motor Company," paper presented at the International Motor Vehicle Program Annual Sponsors Meeting, Toronto, June 4–7, 1995, Table 4.

Table 5-5 Increasing Localization of Technology for Indigenous Models

	Year Developed	Styling	Body Design	Power Train	Chassis Layout	Total
Subcompact						
Pony	75	1	1	1	1	4
Excel	85	1	3	1	2	7
Scoupe	90	3	3	3	2	11
Accent	94	3	3	3	3	12
Compact						
Stella	83	1	3	1	2	7
Elantra	90	3	3	1	2	9
Avante	95	3	3	3	3	12
Medium-size						
Sonata	88	3	3	1	2	9
Sonata II	93	3	3	1	2	9
Marcia	95	3	3	2	3	11

SOURCE: Based on Gyun Kim, "A Study of the Development of Technological Capability of Korea in the 1980s," Ph.D. diss., Department of Economics, Seoul National University, 1994, and Young-Suk Hyun, "The Road to Self-reliance: New Product Development at Hyundai Motor Company," paper presented at the International Motor Vehicle Program Annual Sponsors Meeting, Toronto, June 4–7, 1995.

NOTES: 1 = Under licensing.
2 = Improved based on licensed technology.
3 = Completely indigenous.

(1994) to compact (1995), requiring a single year. It is logical for an inexperienced company in a catching-up country to begin with a subcompact model, as its competitive edge rests more on price than quality in comparison with larger models.

Table 5-5 provides a more detailed picture of technological learning at Hyundai over the years. Hyundai developed the Pony in 1975 under foreign technical assistance with the localization score (degree of indigenous inputs in car design) of four. It then designed the body for Excel and improved its chassis layout on the basis of imported technology with a localization score of seven, showing a significant stride in technological learning. The score increased to eleven for Scoupe and twelve for Accent. A similar trend is also apparent in compact and medium-size models. It is interesting to note that the starting score was seven for compact and nine for medium-size models, proving that experience accumulated in one model provided a platform for a subsequent model and so on up the line.

SUMMARY

Despite skepticism that Korean automakers would survive the global shakeout of the 1990s, Korean chaebols have enjoyed phenomenal growth in the past three decades to comprise the fifth largest producer in the world. Unlike that of other developing countries, their increase was initiated and driven largely by local firms. Hyundai illustrates how Korean firms expedited technological learning in a short time.

Hyundai has been the most vibrant in technological learning among automobile companies in catching-up countries, having transformed itself from a mere assembler of Ford cars to a designer of its own cars and engines. Assembly technology from Ford in 1967 and various other technologies imported from sundry sources to produce Pony in the mid-1970s were mature and at the specific stage in advanced countries. Assimilating and improving these technologies through learning by doing enabled Hyundai to challenge more advanced technologies related to front engine, front wheel drive cars. Core technologies were again imported from advanced countries. Mastering the FF technologies provided a platform for Hyundai to develop state-of-the-art engines. In other words, Hyundai reversed the sequence of technological trajectory in advanced countries.

Many institutions played an important role in Hyundai's rapid progress. Hyundai Construction, existing auto producers, and military vehicle renovation depots provided crucial tacit knowledge at the outset. British Leyland engineers played a significant role in integrating technologies imported from various sources and expediting technological learning. Foreign suppliers such as Ford, Italdesign, Mitsubushi, and Ricardo Engineering provided important technologies at critical points. Crisis construction and hardworking Korean engineers and production workers enabled Hyundai to acquire, assimilate, and improve imported technologies.

Unlike firms in other developing countries, Hyundai pursued an independent strategy in fostering technological capability. Its process of advancing from one stage to the next through the preparation for, and the acquisition, assimilation, and improvement of foreign technology appears to be spiral. Both the acquisition of prior knowledge and intensity of effort played a major role in expediting technological learning.

First, in catching-up firms, relevant knowledge is available elsewhere in various forms. The acquisition of prior knowledge through literature review and poaching of experienced personnel may be effective ways of identifying and acquiring technology and facilitating learning in the subsequent phases. The mobility of trained personnel has been a major source of new tacit knowledge at Korean firms and of technology diffusion in many Korean industries. Like the Japanese, Korean firms implicitly guarantee lifetime employment. But unlike the Japanese, Korean workers enjoy great freedom to hop from one firm to another as opportunities open in industrial expansion. As a result, the average monthly turnover rate of Korean manufacturing firms is more than 5 percent, even higher than the 4 percent of the United States and more than double that of Japan.[33] Such high mobility resulted in the rapid diffusion of technology within and across the industry in Korea.

Second, crisis construction was a major means of opportunistic learning and a valuable facilitator of technological transformation at Hyundai and other Korean firms. Crises preempted opposition to change and served as an antidote to inertia, enabling the company to marshal consensus on goals. Crises also boosted the intensity of efforts, rendering them creative rather than destructive. The construction and resolution of crises are characteristically grounded in a prophetic, single-minded vision of a proactive manager's creative thinking. That is, crisis construction is an evocative and galvanizing device in the personal repertoires of visionary top managers.[34] An entrepreneurial tycoon of family-owned Korean *chaebols* might enjoy a more advantageous position than employed managers in constructing and resolving crises.

As a result, Hyundai was able to maintain its position in quadrants 1 and 3 in Figure 5-1, rapidly learning to catch up with leading automakers in advanced countries. After four major jumps in technological learning, Hyundai is in a position to generate new knowledge in order to survive not only in the international market but also in the domestic market, which will open to Japanese producers in the near future. Hyundai is doubling its production capacity to ascend to tenth largest automaker in the world by the year 2000, and it planned to increase its R&D investment from 4.4 percent of sales in 1994 to 7 percent in 1995 and beyond. As long as Hyundai manages to construct and resolve crises (intensifying efforts) and increase its R&D investment (raising knowledge level) in the future, it will remain a contending Korean automobile producer.

6 The Electronics Industry: From Reverse Engineering to Strategic Alliance

Its electronics industry surged so rapidly in one generation that Korea became the fourth largest producer in the world in 1994, after the United States, Japan, and Germany[1] and the second largest producer of consumer electronic products since 1990, after Japan.[2] Unlike that of other developing countries, such growth has been largely driven by Korean *chaebols* and other local firms rather than by multinational subsidiaries or joint ventures.[3]

Although small-scale assembly of vacuum tube AM radios for the domestic market started in 1958, the Korean electronics industry really got its start in the mid-1960s with the production of black and white TV sets and audio equipment through the international transfer of production technology. Since then, Korea's production, excluding parts and components, has grown remarkably, from $47 million in 1970 to $22.5 billion in 1994, as shown in Table 6-1. The consumer electronics industry has been heavily export oriented, foreign shipments accounting for 73 percent of production in 1975, 75 percent in 1981, and 53 percent in 1991.

The industry is highly concentrated. Although small and medium-size firms have mushroomed, four *chaebols*—LG,[4] Samsung, Daewoo,

Table 6-1 Growth of the Electronics Industry
(in millions of dollars)

	1968	1970	1975	1980	1985	1990	1994
Production							
Consumer products	12.9	30.4	270.0	1,148	2,669	10.141	12,621
Industrial products	6.7	17.4	93.6	364	1,518	6,345	9,892
Total	19.6	47.8	363.6	1,512	4,187	16,486	22,513
Exports							
Consumer products	0.1	9.0	198.3	1,020	1,752	5,727	7,319
Industrial products	3.6	0.4	35.8	169	783	3,481	5,807
Total	3.7	9.4	234.1	1,189	2,535	9,208	13,126

SOURCE: Korea Development Bank, *Korean Industry in the World, 1994* (Seoul: Korea Development Bank, 1994).

and Hyundai—have dominated production and exports. The oligopolistic market structure led to significant competition among them. LG Electronics (brand name GoldStar) is the pioneer of Korea's electronics industry and a pillar of the LG chaebol. It produces more than 150 items, ranging from home appliances to minicomputers, with nine overseas manufacturing bases, 62 marketing subsidiaries, 5 R&D outposts around the world, and is still expanding its overseas operation rapidly. It sold $6.4 billion and exported $3.6 billion (50 percent) in 1994.

Samsung joined the industry in 1969, eleven years after LG. Investing heavily in technology and human resource development, it became a multibillion-dollar, Korea-based multinational electronics firm with 8 production bases, 43 marketing subsidiaries, 9 R&D outposts, and 2 service firms around the world. Sales totaled $14.6 billion and exports $10 billion (68 percent) in 1994. Among all firms in developing countries, Samsung is considered the most technologically aggressive with the largest pool of engineers. If its semiconductor and telecommunication businesses are excluded, it competes neck and neck with LG.

Daewoo entered the industry in 1983 by acquiring the dwindling Electronics Division of Taehan Electric Wire Company.[5] After the take-over, Daewoo Electronics, with an aggressive globalization strategy, grew rapidly from $1 billion in 1986 to $3.2 billion in 1994. With 23 production bases, 26 marketing subsidiaries, and 3 research outposts overseas, Daewoo is the most enterprising of the *chaebols* in exploring emerging markets.

Hyundai Electronics, the youngest and smallest of the four electronics industry *chaebols* does not produce consumer electronics. Including its semiconductor and telecommunication businesses, it had sales of $2.59 billion and exported $1.89 billion (72.9 percent) in 1994. Hyundai, the most active in acquiring high-tech companies in advanced countries in an attempt to gain access to cutting-edge technology, has 8 overseas subsidiaries and 5 joint ventures around the world. How has the industry thrived so rapidly in one generation?

IMITATION DRIVE IN THE ELECTRONICS INDUSTRY

The state played a crucial role in the rapid growth of this industry, particularly during the early years. The government's import-substitution policy and tight control of foreign investment and contraband goods in the black market created attractive business opportunities for local entrepreneurs to enter the protected market in the early 1960s. However, growth was slow until late 1969, when the government designated electronics a strategic export industry.

The government promulgated the Electronics Industry Promotion Act in 1969 and released an ambitious Long-term Electronics Industry Promotion Plan;[6] it created the Electronic Industry Promotion Fund, offering preferential financing to foster scale economies in production as well as grants to develop and upgrade public support systems for standardization and R&D. The government also targeted ninety-five products for promotion, offering preferential financing and other incentives to their manufacturers. Yearly production targets were established. Progressive local content requirements were set to promote the parts and components industry. End products for the local market were completely protected from foreign competitors. Foreign investment was allowed largely in the production of parts and components and for re-export, and the government created an industrial estate for electronics to give rise to interfirm efficiency.

The plan included the government's determination to promote the electronics industry as a leading exporter. In 1969, when the industry was still exporting a mere $42 million, the government set the goal at $400 million for 1976, the last year of the plan. Preferential financing, tax concessions, foreign loan guarantees, and the control of entry by new firms formed the crux of the export drive. That is, the government not only set specific export goals and directives, forcing local firms to be competitive in both price and quality in the international market, it also provided incentives. This scheme induced a crisis, compelling local firms to acquire technological capability quickly while providing supports to make the crisis creative rather than destructive. Since marketing was largely in the hands of buyers from foreign original equipment manufacturers, local firms concentrated mainly on the acquisition of product design and production capabilities. In 1976, exports exceeded $1 billion, almost 259 percent of the established target, illustrating the extent of rapid learning in production and product design accomplished by the industry.

The government also took the initiative in organizing a yearly electronics show in an attempt to promote the diffusion of technical ideas in the economy and international marketing for Korean firms. In short, while the government played an important role in all strategic industries, its role in the electronics industry was extraordinary in the early years. Under this public policy environment, electronics firms have grown rapidly as a highly export-oriented industry.

Korea's first consumer electronics producer, LG Electronics, was begun in 1958 by the owner of a small, rudimentary face cream and plastic housewares company, which sensed an attractive business opportunity in the import-substitution policy. Lacking technological capability, the company hired an experienced German engineer to upgrade its tacit knowledge base. At about the same time, the company president embarked on an observation tour of several leading electronics firms in Japan, Europe, and the United States. The vision he formed from it and the German engineer led to LG's first business. In a small-scale garage operation, foreign components and parts were assembled into the first vacuum tube AM radio in the country through imitative reverse-engineering of a Japanese model.[7] The German played a key role in ordering the necessary equipment to set up the production system and training Korean technicians and assembly line workers. The tacit knowledge transferred from the German engineer to his Korean counterparts began to build technological capability at the organizational level. Assimilating the product design and assembly operation was so simple that relatively well-educated Korean engineers acquired enough tacit knowledge to replace the German within a year.[8] LG Electronics soon developed expertise in imitation and began producing such other home appliances as electric fans and refrigerators without foreign assistance.

Television Sets

LG Electronics imported several black and white television receivers to decide whether TVs could also be imitatively reverse engineered. Although LG had accumulated radio design and production experience for several years, it was beyond the firm's capability to reverse engineer TVs mainly because of the significantly large number of parts/components required and TV's greater technological complexity. Thus, in 1965 LG found it necessary to enter into a licensing agreement with Hitachi of Japan to import packaged technology for black and white TV production. The agreement included not only assembly processes but also product specifications, production know-how, parts/components, training, and technical experts, transferring a significant volume of explicit and tacit knowledge to LG Electronics, which sent seven experienced engineers and technicians to Hitachi for intensive training. This group was given the important task of assimilating and mastering TV production technology. Renting an apartment together, the engineers held group sessions every evening, reviewing and sharing the literature they had collected, their observations, and their training, facilitating rapid learning by the team; they played a pivotal role on their return home.

Even though it invested enough for licensing and overseas training, LG decided to have Japanese engineers supervise the installation and start-up of TV production systems to minimize trial-and-error time. These people played the most vital role in the initial implementation of transferred Japanese technologies by transferring their tacit knowledge to LG engineers and helping them internalize explicit knowledge such as production/quality control manuals and technical specifications. But the utility of the Japanese diminished within a year as the local Hitachi-trained technical personnel acquired enough tacit knowledge through production and design experience.

LG Electronics was able to apply the manufacturing competence accumulated over the years to subsequent assembly of other consumer electronics, such as cassette recorders and simple audio systems, without foreign assistance. The rapid assimilation of imported technologies and their application to other products may be attributed largely to the founder's entrepreneurial strategy of acquiring technological independence and fostering high intensity in learning efforts by relatively well-educated native technical personnel.

Three other TV set producers that started at about the same time acquired and assimilated production ability the same way. Subsequent entrants—ten by 1975—however, lured experienced engineers and technicians from existing firms, resulting in effective diffusion of tacit knowledge from established firms to new ones. LG Electronics, as the first and largest producer, was a major source of such personnel for new entrants. A similar pattern is evident in other electronic products of the same period.[9]

When black and white television sets eventually encountered a rapid decline in the export market, the color TV set became the next target appliance to sustain increasing exports. For black and white TVs, the Korean companies had moved up the production learning curve on the strength of the protected local market prior to competing in export markets. Color TV producers would, however, have to export from the start, because Korean channels did not broadcast in color.

No foreign color TV maker was willing to license technology to Korean makers to help them invade the U.S. market anew. LG Electronics and two other major firms jointly entered into a research contract with the Korea Institute of Science and Technology (KIST), a government R&D institute (GRI), to gain enough knowledge and experience in color TV technology. Experience gained from black and white receivers and learning from the joint research enabled local firms to strengthen their bargaining power in licensing core patents held by RCA in 1974. The R&D team worked around the clock for two years, searching and mastering foreign literature, reverse engineering foreign color TVs. After a series of trials and errors, LG developed a working model of its own color television set. It took another year to set up a mass-production system.

Microwave Ovens

The videocassette recorder and the microwave oven were next targeted for development. Both products went through a similar process. Samsung's approach to developing and commercializing microwave ovens illustrates how Korea acquired the necessary technological proficiency initially through reverse engineering and subsequently dominated the world market.

Intrigued by a new oven heated by microwaves, Samsung approached several Japanese and U.S. producers to license the technology. Turned down by them, Samsung, on the basis of its consumer electronics experience, formed a team in 1976 to design its own microwave oven by reverse engineering a foreign model for export markets, as few Koreans could afford it. Ira Magaziner and Mark Patinkin recount how Samsung reverse-engineered the oven and became one of the world's leading producers.[10]

Samsung had purchased a number of the world's top microwave ovens to choose the best parts of each for its prototype, which provided invaluable explicit knowledge to the firm. The team took the ovens apart, but its tacit knowledge was inadequate to figure out how they worked. Wiring and assembly of the case appeared simple, but many complex parts, including the magnetron tubes that generated the microwaves, were beyond Samsung's tacit knowledge. With only three magnetron producers, two in Japan and one in the United States, Samsung decided to source magnetron tubes from Japan.

It took the team a year of eighty-hour weeks to complete the first prototype, but the plastic in the cavity melted in a test. After more eighty-hour weeks of redesigning and readjusting, the second could not survive a test; this time the stir shaft melted. Finally, in June 1978, after two years, the team developed a model that survived the test; but it was too crude to compete in the world market. Samsung incrementally improved the product and developed a makeshift production line, producing one oven a day, then two, which it placed in local bakeries for feedback from users. The successful development of microwave ovens strengthened the bargaining power of Samsung to negotiate technology licensing with patent holders enabling it to acquire the necessary licenses to clear its way to the export market.

This was a common experience in Korea. When foreign firms were reluctant to transfer technology to emerging Korean competitors, Korean firms reverse engineered the technology. It was only after these firms successfully commercialized the product that foreign firms reluctantly licensed technology to them. It is useful at this point to differentiate the reverse engineering of mature, simple products in the early years from the advanced reverse engineering of sophisticated products to obtain licenses for valid patents. In this case, the purpose of licensing was not to learn technology but to pave the way into the export market.

Samsung decided to try its sales push in 1979, when it obtained Underwriter's Laboratory approval and produced more than 1,000 microwave ovens; in excess of 5 million were then being sold worldwide. In April 1980, the first order, for 240 ovens, came from Panama.

Samsung also sent 1,655 units to the United States and 3,230 to the United Kingdom to test their markets, taking the opportunity to learn the needs of overseas consumers.[11]

Samsung's lucky break came in late 1980, when J. C. Penney inquired whether Samsung could manufacture a low-priced microwave oven to sell for $299 in the U.S. market; the ovens were then selling for $350 to $400. Although the order entailed a completely new design and heavy losses, Samsung accepted it to gain a foothold in the most sophisticated market in the world and to turn a primitive assembly line into an efficient large-scale system. Penney extended technical assistance to the Samsung team to ensure that its ovens would meet Penney's technical specifications.

Turning a primitive assembly line for five or six ovens a day into an efficient production system to meet the first Penney delivery date, only months away, was a major crisis for Samsung. Engineers and technicians labored around the clock; they began at dawn, worked until 10:30 P.M., took a brief nap, then went back to work for the rest of the night. The line took shape and production began, but debugging was inevitably necessary. Because the company couldn't afford to lose production, the personnel manufactured by day and fine-tuned the line at night. Production improved to ten ovens a day, then fifteen. Soon they were making 1,500 a month, enough to meet Penney's first order. Penney liked the ovens and a month later asked for another 5,000 and another 7,000 the following month. Again Samsung worked around the clock to meet the deadlines. Rapid growth in production accelerated learning by doing at Samsung.

Samsung's cost advantage, however, had been eroded by large producers, whose process innovations brought their prices down. To bring its cost down, Samsung had to develop its own magnetron tube, which it still sourced from Japan. Samsung approached two Japanese producers for technical licensing but was turned down. Then, in 1982, Samsung bought and transplanted to Korea the only U.S. factory that produced magnetron tubes, which was going out of business because it could not compete against Japan. Samsung invested heavily in improving productivity by automating its production processes, enabling it to sustain its price competitiveness.

Samsung's rapid assimilation of design and production technology of microwave ovens stemmed largely from the way its engineers and technicians worked. When General Electric (GE) decided to outsource its microwave ovens, the head marketing manager for Appliances asked Samsung managers for a proposal on cost breakdowns, production plans, and a delivery schedule. The next morning, "a group of engineers came in and they gave us their proposal. Their hair was messed up, their eyes bloodshot. Those guys had worked all night." Samsung engineers completed overnight a proposal that would have taken U.S. companies four to six weeks to develop.[12] GE sent its engineers to Korea to outline its technical specifications. Well-trained Korean engineers with enough tacit knowledge and high intensity of effort took advantage of the opportunity to absorb world-class skills from them.

"It was my first glimpse of Samsung since 1977 . . . I went to the R&D lab. It had gone from an old high-school science room to a large, modern operation. Instead of a handful of engineers, there were 500. Everything Samsung had said in 1977 that it would do, it had done," reported Magaziner and Patinkin.[13] Since then, Samsung's R&D projects have led to seventy-four local patents and six overseas patents related to microwave oven technology, enabling Samsung to become one of the most dynamic microwave oven makers in the world. Samsung's production rose more than a hundredfold in two years, from 1,283 in 1979 to 137,931 in 1981, almost tripled the following year, then doubled again in 1983. In 1984, only five years after its first crude, imitative prototype, Samsung's microwave production topped 1.3 million units. By 1994 Samsung was producing 4 million ovens in Korea and 0.8 million more abroad per year, controlling 17 percent of the global market. The world's second largest producer, Samsung trails only Sharp of Japan by a small margin. More than 95 percent of Samsung's production is exported.

Samsung's success in developing the microwave oven prompted LG and Daewoo Electronics to follow. LG first approached Sharp for technology transfer only to be turned down. In 1980, four years after Samsung's entry, LG Electronics organized a task force to develop a microwave oven. The late entrants stole experienced engineers and technicians from Samsung, bringing about effective diffusion of oven technology to the rest of the Korean electronics industry. It took two years for pioneering Samsung to develop its successful prototype, but it took LG only eight months to come up with a successful model, as the Samsung engineers provided a platform. LG Electronics then acquired the necessary licenses to export the product. Samsung magnetron technology even helped LG to license the magnetron tube technology from Hitachi, which had previously refused to license it to Samsung. Now LG produces as many microwave ovens as Samsung. Expansion under way in overseas production increased the three *chae-*

bols' capacity to 5 million units each and Korean firms surpassed Japan to become the largest microwave oven producer in the world in 1996.

INNOVATION DRIVE IN THE ELECTRONICS INDUSTRY

The government played a useful role in creating a demand for technological innovation in recent decades. For instance, the import-substitution policy created a growing market for the computer industry in the early 1980s.[14] The government imposed import restrictions on personal computers (PCs) and peripherals, creating a protected market for small local firms to enter and survive long enough to gain first-stage learning experience in PC manufacturing. The market was later liberalized in 1987 under pressure from the United States.

In addition, the government issued its own procurement orders to create an early domestic market, announcing in 1982 that it intended to purchase 5,000 PCs for public schools in 1983 and increasing the numbers thereafter. The government then created the National Administration Information System (NAIS), investing $170 million by 1988 and $555 million by 1995 and creating demand for more than 80 main computers and about 5,000 workstations. In addition, the government launched computerization of the postal system, the tax system, the national defense system, and the education-research network system, each of which required as much investment in both hardware and software as the NAIS. In procuring merchandise, the government first set technical specifications and targets for the local content ratio, then awarded contracts to the firms that met the requisites. These announcements attracted many newcomers to the industry and induced aggressive investment for in-house R&D to meet the government requirements.

The government also played a significant role in the supply side of technology, establishing several GRIs. The Korea Institute of Electronic Technology (KIET) was set up several years prior to the private sector's entry into computers and semiconductors in an attempt to gain first-stage experience in R&D on new technologies and to produce experienced researchers. KIET, which invested more than $300 million between 1980 and 1984, was sold to a private firm when the private sector had matured sufficiently to undertake the type of design work for which that institution was previously responsible. KIST played a pioneering role by developing prototypes of computers, robotics, and computer-aided design/computer-aided manufacturing. The Electronics and Telecommunications Research Institute played a coordinating role in a consortium with many local firms in developing computers, electronic switching systems, and semiconductor memory chips.

Intensifying R&D Efforts

Given the policy environment and increasingly dynamic market, Korean electronics firms have drastically expanded in-house R&D ventures, establishing several laboratories. LG Electronics, for example, developed an extensive R&D network, shown in Figure 6-1. It also established ten independent R&D centers, six product-specific R&D centers, and five overseas R&D centers. Samsung, Daewoo, and Hyundai Electronics also instituted extensive R&D networks at each strategic business unit in Korea. In addition, Samsung and Daewoo developed an Institute of Advanced Engineering to focus on long-term R&D projects, which set new directions for these companies. LG's Central Laboratory performs a similar function.

Chaebol electronics firms also initiated R&D networks with leading universities by placing their R&D laboratories on campuses in an attempt to augment their in-house R&D projects. With full funding from *chaebols,* Seoul National, Korea, Yonsei, and Hanyang Universities, and Korea Advanced Institute of Science and Technology (KAIST), have constructed large-scale laboratories to be occupied jointly by university and corporate personnel, marking a turning point in university-industry collaboration. LG Electronics, for example, developed a joint R&D laboratory at KAIST, a research-oriented graduate school of applied science, to develop digital measurement, factory automation, a manufacturing information system, and precision fabrication.

The dynamic growth of R&D at Samsung may be seen in Table 6-2. At Samsung Electronics, R&D spending increased drastically from W 5.6 billion ($8.5 million) in 1980 to W 713.3 billion ($905 million) in 1994. Investment has grown much faster than sales, raising its ratio to total sales from 2.1 percent to 6.2 percent during the same period. Consequently, Samsung Electronics has led Korean industries in R&D spending and patent registration. Its patent registrations rose from 17 in 1985 to 1,413 by 1994. Its foreign patent registrations also rose from 2 to 752 in the same period. The number of researchers grew from 690 in 1980 to 8,919 by 1994. The growth rates at other electronics firms are similar. Most leading research scientists and engineers were trained in the United States, Germany, and Japan, some bringing with them extensive experience in leading foreign electronics R&D laboratories.

Globalization of R&D rapidly expanded the boundaries of R&D

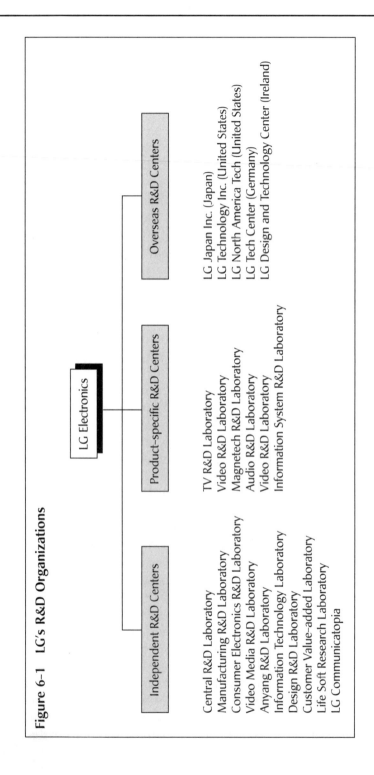

Figure 6-1 LG's R&D Organizations

Table 6-2 R&D Activities at Samsung Electronics

	1975	1980	1985	1990	1994
Total sales (W 100 million)	244	2,513	12,985	44,523	115,181
R&D investment (W 100 million)	NA	56	388	1,862	7,133
R&D/total sales (percentage)	NA	2.1	3.0	4.2	6.2
R&D personnel	NA	690	1,821	6,686	8,919
Local patent applications	NA	18	309	1,732	2,802
Local patents granted	0	4	17	640	1,413
Foreign patent applications	0	0	32	1,145	1,478
Foreign patents granted	0	0	2	128	752

SOURCE: Samsung Electronics Company.

endeavors in the Korean firms. LG Electronics, for one, has developed a network of R&D laboratories in Tokyo, Sunnyvale, California, Chicago, Germany, and Ireland. These facilities monitor technological change at the frontier, seek opportunities to develop strategic alliances with local firms, and develop state-of-the-art products through advanced R&D. LG Technology in Sunnyvale, for example, plays a pivotal role in designing the latest personal computers, display terminals, and high-resolution monitors, while the LG North American Laboratory in Chicago concentrates on high-definition TV, digital VCR, and telecommunication equipment. Samsung, Daewoo, and Hyundai Electronics have developed similarly extensive R&D branches. Samsung has R&D operations in San Jose, Maryland, Boston, Tokyo, Osaka, Sendai, Japan, London, Frankfurt, and Moscow; Daewoo has two in France and one in Russia; Hyundai has laboratories in San Jose, Frankfurt, Singapore, and Taipei.

Korean firms also globalize R&D through mergers and acquisitions. Hyundai has been the most aggressive at acquiring equity stakes in foreign firms as a way to gain access to cutting-edge technologies. In California, it acquired, among others, full ownership of Axil Computer, Santa Clara, for computer development; significant stakes in Laserbyte Corp., Sunnyvale, to gain access to magneto-optical disk drive technology; in Metaflow, La Jolla, to develop the SPARC compatible microprocessor; in Image Quest, San Jose, to develop thin film transistor–liquid crystal displays or flat panel displays; and in Maxtor, San Jose, to develop hard disk drive.

In 1995 Samsung Electronics acquired the controlling share (40.25 percent) of AST Research, one of the largest U.S. PC makers, for $378 million, placing Samsung among the five largest PC makers in the world. The acquisition gives Samsung access to more than 190 AST patents and its strategic alliance with IBM, Apple, and Compaq. Samsung also obtained a majority interest in Union Optical (Japan) and Rollei (Germany) to enhance its competitiveness in camera and optical equipment making.

In addition, Korean firms consider Russia an attractive alternative source for new technology, for Russian researchers have some world-class technologies. Samsung unveiled a prototype digital video disk recorder. The high-powered microchip laser technology required to make it was transferred from a leading Russian laboratory, the A. F. Ioffe Physico-Technical Institute in St. Petersburg. Other Samsung subsidiaries have signed contracts to import Russian technologies.[15]

Moonlighting Japanese engineers have been another valuable source of new knowledge. The *chaebols* invite Japanese retirees to visit their R&D and production facilities to solve specific engineering problems. This is a common practice in smaller companies in many industries as well.[16]

Flat Panel Display Development

The development of flat panel display (FPD) illustrates how Korean firms strive to emerge as innovators in the world market. Their move into this industry in the 1990s resembles the development of the semiconductor memory chip industry in the 1980s. When Korean firms made the strategic choice to invest in memory chips, Japanese firms dominated the burgeoning semiconductor market. In ten years, Korean firms, led by Samsung, were able to capitalize on soaring global demand (see Chapter 7). Korea is determined to repeat that success in FPDs, in which Japan again dominates the world market, and Koreans again see an industry ready to take off. They refer to it as the second meal, after semiconductor chips, to feed Korea's electronics industry.[17]

Flat panel display (active matrix)[18] is based on a combination of passive matrix liquid crystal display (LCD) technology and semiconductor technology. Thus, in technology, fabrication, and assembly it mirrors the semiconductor industry. Firms with a strong background in passive matrix LCD and semiconductor technologies are in a good position to build flat panel display technology.

The involvement of Hyundai Electronics in passive matrix LCD dates back to 1988, when it organized an LCD business unit. Lacking capability, Hyundai first imported the stick form of twisted nematic LCD from Oprex of Japan in 1990 and fabricated it into cell form. At the same time, Hyundai sent its engineers to Oprex for training in production and LCD design and imported a complete production system from Japan. This enabled the firm to gain a significant volume of both tacit and explicit knowledge. Training and in-house R&D led to the development of Hyundai's own twisted nematic LCD within months and super–twisted nematic LCD by 1993. Hyundai could then increase its output more than a hundredfold in three years, from 116,000 units in 1990 to 15.22 million in 1993.[19]

Based on its experience in passive matrix LCDs and semiconductors,[20] Hyundai organized a task force to develop flat panel display. It also approached Japanese and American LCD firms, including Oprex, for technical assistance to expedite learning, but none was willing to share the emerging technology with the Korean firm. Alternatively, in 1992 Hyundai established a joint venture, Image Quest Technology, in San Jose with a group of leading American LCD engineers spun off from Colory Inc. Hyundai invested more than $16 million in developing a 10.4-inch thin film transistor video graphic array (VGA) module prototype and setting up a pilot plant at Image Quest. The joint research brought Hyundai engineers, with their strong background in passive matrix LCDs and semiconductors, up to a par with Japanese competitors.

Two other semiconductor firms, Samsung and LG, are as, if not more, advanced as Hyundai in FPD technology. Samsung developed 14.2-inch FPD with a thickness of less than 3 centimeters in 1994 and 3.1-inch polysilicon FPD in 1995. The polysilicon method, which embeds drive integrated circuits (ICs) on panels to increase the light transmission efficiency up to 80 percent, enables the producers to extend the display size up to 100 inches and diminish defect rates by eliminating the combining process. In 1995 Samsung developed 22-inch FPD screen, one inch larger than the world's previous biggest LCD device produced by Sharp of Japan. This signals Korean companies as innovators in FPD technology. As a result, Korean firms are attractive candidates for strategic alliances with Japanese firms. LG Electronics established a fifty-fifty joint venture R&D with Alps Electric (Japan) to expedite the development of the next generation FPD, like plasma processing and LCD panel processing.

The rush is on among Korean firms to establish production facilities. Samsung Electronics, invested $375 million to complete an FPD plant and began producing 10,000 units a month in February 1995.

The capacity was expanded step by step to 80,000 units a month by the end of 1995. A second plant is under way as part of Samsung's vision to become one of the world's three largest FPD manufacturers. LG Electronics completed its production plant in the second half of 1995 and Hyundai completed its plant in 1996.

SUMMARY

The Korean electronics industry has, within a generation, developed from scratch into the fourth largest producer in the world. In some products, Korean firms have become new contenders in the international market, a transformation driven largely by local *chaebols* rather than multinational companies. When technology was mature and simple, as in the production of AM radios at the specific stage, local firms reverse-engineered foreign products. When technology was beyond the capacity of local firms, pioneering firms relied on foreign licensing and technical personnel, as they did with TV sets. Local firms did, however, pursue efforts to assimilate the imported technology in the shortest possible time. The assimilation of licensed technology enabled these firms to produce newer generations and a broader range of products without foreign assistance. Later Korean entrants acquired necessary capability largely by luring experienced technical and managerial personnel from pioneering firms, bringing about effective diffusion of imported technologies throughout the industry.

When technology was at the transition stage and foreign firms were reluctant to transfer their patented technology to Korea, local firms reverse-engineered it by intensifying in-house R&D, giving them stronger bargaining power in licensing technology from the patent holders. Such advanced reverse-engineering is distinguished from the simple reverse-engineering of mature products in earlier years. In this case, foreign licensing clears a path to the export market rather than to technology, as exemplified by the success in videocassette recorders and microwave ovens.

Facing rising resistance from foreign competitors, the *chaebols* continually intensified their R&D operations, establishing extensive networks of in-house laboratories in order to learn by research. At the same time, they established a number of R&D facilities in the United States, Japan, and Europe to monitor technological change and to tap high caliber Korean and foreign scientists. Korean firms also used mergers and acquisitions to gain access to frontier technologies. In some technological areas, Korean *chaebols* have grown sophisticated enough to enter strategic alliances with leading foreign competitors.

The government played important roles in the process of technological transformation in the electronics industry. The nation's import-substitution policy provided an attractive business opportunity for local entrepreneurs to enter the protected electronics industry. The ambitious goals of the government's export drive pushed the industry to transform itself technologically and become competitive in price and quality in the international market.

The government role has changed over time from acting as a developmental state to playing an indirect promotional role as Korea entered the technologically dynamic environment. The government was effective in the demand side of technology by creating a market through procurement. In this case, the release of technical specifications stimulated the industry to expedite learning to meet specifications in time for procurement. In addition, the government played an important role in the supply side of technology by strengthening public R&D capability and promoting joint research between industry and R&D institutes and between industry and academia.

7 The Semiconductor Industry: Leapfrogging into the World Frontier

Despite skepticism regarding its technological capability to enter and remain competitive in the semiconductor industry, Korea leapfrogged from a mere assembler of discrete devices to a major player in dynamic random-access memory (DRAM) chips in only a decade. It emerged as the second largest memory chip producer after Japan and the third largest semiconductor producer in the world after Japan and the United States. In memory chips, a report concludes, "already dominant in 4-megabyte DRAM semiconductors, Korea is expected to stay ahead of Japan in 16-megabyte and 64-megabyte generations, while also attempting to crack more profitable application-specific integrated circuits."[1]

As shown in Table 7-1, the industry's total output grew, on average, tenfold every decade, from $32 million in 1970 to $5.1 billion by 1990 and in four years almost tripled again to $14.8 billion in 1994. Exports similarly grew from $32 million to $11.72 billion during the same period, accounting for 100 percent of production in 1980 and 88 percent in 1994. The semiconductor industry has been one of Korea's most vibrant businesses, and its products became the single largest export item from Korea in 1994, accounting for 13.3 percent of total exports.

Table 7-1 Semiconductor Industry Production and Exports (in millions of dollars)

	1966	1970	1975	1980	1985	1990	1994
Production	0.002	32	231	424	1,155	5,104	14,800
Exports	0.002	32	178	415	1,062	4,541	11,720
Events	Multinationals entered assembly operations in Korea (1965).		First Korean firm began to fabricate wafers and produce LSIs (1975).	Chaebols entered VLSI production under foreign license (1984).		Korea became independent in DRAM design and production (1988).	

SOURCE: Korea Development Bank, *Industry in Korea*, various years.

The industry is highly concentrated; the three largest *chaebols*—Samsung, Hyundai, and LG—dominate the field. Samsung is the largest memory chip producer and the seventh largest semiconductor producer in the world. LG and Hyundai rank sixth and seventh among the world's memory chip producers and twentieth and twenty-first among all semiconductor producers in 1994 (see Table 7-2). In addition, several firms assemble semiconductor devices on consignment. Korean firms grew from nothing to contending players within a decade. How did they manage to learn so expeditiously? What role did the Korean government play?

IMITATION DRIVE IN THE SEMICONDUCTOR INDUSTRY

Korea's semiconductor industry began in the mid-1960s, when several multinational firms—Signetics, Fairchild, Motorola, Control Data, AMI, and Toshiba—began assembling discrete devices in Korea to take advantage of local cheap labor.[2] Operations consisted merely of simple

Table 7-2 World's Largest Semiconductor Manufacturers

Semiconductor Producers and World Rank	1994 Sales	1994 Growth Rate	Dynamic Memory Chip Makers and World Rank	1994 Market Share
Intel (1)	10,121	27	Samsung (1)	15.1
NEC (2)	7,944	29	Hitachi (2)	10.6
Toshiba (3)	7,527	31	NEC (3)	10.4
Motorola (4)	7,237	21	Toshiba (4)	9.7
Hitachi (5)	6,485	29	Texas Instruments (5)	7.1
Texas Instruments (6)	5,280	29	LG (6)	6.4
Samsung (7)	4,893	61	Hyundai (7)	6.2
Fujitsu (8)	3,858	32	Mitsubishi (8)	5.8
Mitsubishi (9)	3,735	26	Micron Tech (9)	5.8
LG (20)	1,797	90	IBM (10)	5.8
Hyundai (21)	1,621	90		

SOURCE: Quoted in the economic daily newspaper API, from *Korea Money*, "Making Fortunes in Silicon Chips," March 1995, 36–40.

packaging processes—bonded assembly operations by the wholly owned foreign subsidiaries with all parts and components imported from the parent companies and re-exported to the consignors. The assembly operations, requiring only about six months' training of unskilled workers, involved little transfer of design and engineering capability to Korea.

In 1975 the government, as part of its heavy and chemical industries (HCI) drive, formulated a six-year plan to promote the semiconductor industry. Many *chaebols* (e.g., Lotte, Ssangyong, Kukje, Dong-Ah) showed great enthusiasm in entering it. However, unlike other HCIs, difficulty in obtaining foreign technology and high market risk associated with increasingly short product life cycles chilled their zeal. Consequently, different from other strategic HCIs, investment in the electronics industry was only $421 million by 1979, well below the planned $1.19 billion; most of the firms chose to pursue consumer electronics promotion.[3]

In 1975, however, the government made some efforts to develop advanced technical manpower, establishing the Korea Advanced Institute of Science and Technology (KAIST), a graduate school of applied science, which became a major source of high-caliber scientists and engineers. The government designated a national university to specialize in electronics engineering. In 1976 it established a government R&D institute, the Korea Institute of Electronics Technology (KIET) with R&D and very-large-scale integrated circuit (VLSI) production processes. But the government R&D was not flexible and dynamic enough to adapt to rapidly changing technology in semiconductors. So by 1984, when the government decided to sell the facility to LG, it was virtually obsolete. Nevertheless, KIET made significant contributions to the industry by producing a large number of R&D engineers experienced in semiconductors who moved to the private sector and played important roles.

Large-Scale and Very-Large-Scale Integrated Circuits

In 1974 Dr. Ki-Dong Kang, a Korean-American scientist with a Ph.D. from Ohio State University and semiconductor design experience at Motorola, established the first local firm, Korea Semiconductor Co. Samsung bought it out during a financial crisis in its first year. With a large stake in consumer electronics, Samsung acquired the company as a stepping-stone to securing necessary tacit knowledge related to semiconductors. Dr. Kang provided a significantly higher tacit knowledge base for Samsung and transferred it to Samsung engineers, who gained initial experience in semiconductor design and production, enabling the firm progressively to produce various transistors and integrated circuits on a small scale for consumer electronics.[4] Samsung also established the Semiconductor R&D Laboratory in 1982, which focused mainly on bipolar and metal oxide semiconductors (MOS).

The stakes grew substantially in 1983 when the four largest *chaebols*—Samsung, Hyundai, LG, and Daewoo—marshaled investment to start VLSI production, and odds seemed stacked in their favor: they had ready access to funds siphoned from their cash-cow industries, within *chaebols*, a motivated and highly skilled workforce recruited from abroad, and a low-labor-cost advantage. Although leading foreign producers refused to license VLSI technology to them, the Korean *chaebols* were able to locate a number of distressed small semiconductor companies in the United States that were ready to sell the Koreans what they needed most, chip designs and processes, to fuel cash for survival.

64K DRAM

Samsung, was turned down by Texas Instruments and Motorola in the United States and NEC, Toshiba, and Hitachi in Japan in its attempt to license 64K-DRAM technology.[5] Then, based on its eight years' experience in transistor and integrated circuit production, in 1982 Samsung organized a task force to formulate an entry strategy for VLSI. This required a major technological leap from previous operations: from 5-micron to 2.5-micron circuit width, from 3-inch wafer to 5-inch wafer, and from 1K/16K LSI (large-scale integrated circuits) to 64K VLSI. The team members spent six months collecting information, analyzing the technology and market, and formulating plausible strategies, significantly building Samsung's preparatory VLSI tacit knowledge. They then spent one month in the United States, meeting experts in the industry, particularly Korean-American scientists and engineers working in American semiconductor firms and teaching at American universities. They studied the market and industry structure and identified potential technology suppliers. The knowledge gained thereby enabled the members to make sense of their discussions and observations.

Next, Samsung identified troubled small firms from which to buy VLSI technologies. It licensed 64K-DRAM design from Micron Technology in Boise, Idaho, in a successful attempt to shorten learning and production time, adding explicit and tacit knowledge related to the VLSI. Design for a high-speed MOS process was picked up for $2.1

million from Zytrex of California, transferring explicit knowledge to Korea. Samsung sent its engineers to these suppliers for training as part of technological transfer, giving rise to Samsung's capability to assimilate the licensed technologies.

Samsung sequenced the absorption of technology from easiest to progressively more sophisticated: from assembly processes to process development, then to wafer fabrication and inspection. Samsung first imported 3,000 64K-DRAM chips from Micron Technology to assemble in Korea. With eight years' experience in LSI chips, Samsung assimilated VLSI assembly technology without much trouble. Samsung's assembly operation easily reached a 92 percent yield ratio, on par with Japan's. Having mastered those details, Samsung proceeded to assimilate design and process technologies.

However, substantial technological capability and research efforts were required to translate tacit and explicit knowledge related to those technologies acquired from two American companies into a production operation with a high yield ratio. For this purpose, Samsung organized two R&D teams to work collaboratively to assimilate and commercialize 64K DRAM.

The firm set up one R&D outpost in Silicon Valley in 1983 and hired five Korean-American Ph.D.'s in electronics engineering from Stanford, Michigan, Minnesota, and Notre Dame universities who had semiconductor design experience at IBM, Honeywell, Zilog, Intel, and National Semiconductors. These five plus about 300 American engineers, including several designers who had left Mostek, brought Samsung crucially important tacit knowledge to crack VLSI technology. Silicon Valley was a strategic location for collecting cutting-edge information and undertaking research to develop 64K DRAM. The high density of scientists and engineers in the vicinity offered a rich source of the critical information and expertise Samsung needed. The facility also provided opportunities for engineers in Korea to participate in training and research in the United States, enabling them to learn a significant amount of VLSI technology.

In Korea, Samsung organized another task force with two Korean-American scientists and Samsung engineers trained at technology suppliers' locations. The scientists had gained 64K-DRAM development experience in American companies, providing a significantly higher tacit knowledge level. Interaction between those in Silicon Valley and the team in Korea through training, joint research, and consultation gave a meaningful boost to both tacit and explicit knowledge in the Korean team in a very short time, better equipping Samsung engineers to digest VLSI technologies from Micron Technology and Zytrex.

As occurred at Hyundai Motor (see Chapter 5), Samsung presented the team with an ambitious goal to develop a working production system for 64K DRAM within six months. The team members lived together in makeshift quarters on the plant site and worked around the clock to assimilate imported technologies and develop processes. "I was so immersed in working on 64K DRAM that I stopped smoking and drinking. I hardly slept any more than three or four hours a day for six months," said Dr. Sang-Joon Lee, a Korean-American team leader.[6] In such a crisis, the goal was clear to the entire team. Personal dedication for long hours expedited knowledge conversion among them individually, which led to their rapid knowledge conversion and high rate of technological learning organizationally. Once again, a Korean crisis was managed creatively rather than destructively.

Given previous experience in semiconductor production, Samsung engineers managed to develop all but eight core technologies needed for 309 processes in 64K-DRAM production. After six months of hard work, the team in Korea succeeded in creating a working good die, allowing Samsung to hit the market with 64K DRAM in early 1984, some forty months after the American pioneer and about eighteen months after the first Japanese version became commercially available.[7] Korea, the third country in the world to introduce DRAM chips, greatly narrowed a technological gap with Japan and the United States. In short, the successful development of 64K DRAM resulted from the combination of licenses from small American firms, R&D in Silicon Valley, R&D in Korea, and collaboration between the two R&D teams.

Samsung's mass-production plant was designed and its construction supervised by a Japanese firm that had previously built a Sharp semiconductor plant in Japan. Engineers from Samsung's semiconductor business and from its construction subsidiary took an active part in the project, accumulating both tacit and explicit knowledge related to that type of construction.

Unlike Samsung, Hyundai invaded the semiconductor industry in 1983 with no experience in electronics, let alone semiconductors. Aware of the increasing importance of electronics in its automobile, shipbuilding, and heavy machinery businesses, Hyundai considered it essential to develop an electronics capability to strengthen its competitiveness in these industries. Hyundai first contracted with Dr. Kang, who had by then returned to Silicon Valley, to formulate a strategic plan for its entry into the electronics industry. Based on the plan, Hyundai recruited four Korean-American Ph.D.'s from leading American universities who had invaluable experience in semiconductors and computers at Xerox, System Control, Fairchild, and Ford. Hyundai planned to recruit seventy-five Korean-American scientists from the United States and another thirty-five talented scientists and engineers within Korea, many from Samsung, to form the core of its new business and the Semiconductor R&D Laboratory in Korea.

Hyundai first attempted to develop DRAMs on its own with minimum input from foreign firms. For this purpose, it, like Samsung, established a foreign R&D center, in Santa Clara, staffed by Korean-American scientists and local American engineers to undertake R&D work on semiconductors and to train Korean scientists and engineers. This center, on its own, successfully developed a circuit design for 16K static RAM (SRAM), which was transferred to Korea for mass production. Process technology was acquired from Vitelic of San Jose. Based on the technology, the Hyundai team in Korea developed a production method and obtained good die in December 1984 in a pilot run. However, lacking previous experience in electronics and semiconductors, Hyundai had serious trouble raising its yield ratio in mass production, leading to no shipments in 1985.

At this juncture, Hyundai shifted its strategic approaches. Deciding to source technologies from foreign suppliers, it pursued two alternative strategies. First, it became an original equipment manufacturer (OEM) for a major foreign producer to accumulate assembly experience. Hyundai began assembling 64K DRAMs for Texas Instruments with the latter's technical assistance, acquiring assembly and inspection skills. Second, it purchased designs for 16K SRAM and 64K DRAM from Vitelic. Together, these efforts improved the firm's yield ratio significantly. In 1986, some two years after Samsung started, Hyundai became the second Korean *chaebol* to produce 64K DRAM.

LG, experienced in consumer electronics and modest-scale semiconductor production, took a rather cautious approach, focusing mainly on producing nonmemory semiconductors for in-house consumer electronics businesses. In 1984, attempting to initiate VLSI production, LG acquired the R&D and production facilities operated by KIET, which by then were completely obsolete. It then licensed chip designs from Advanced Micron Devices and Zilog in the United States and entered into a joint venture with AT&T's Western Electric, but it was far behind Samsung and Hyundai in launching 64K DRAMs.

Daewoo, the fourth *chaebol*, with a background in consumer electronics and modest-scale semiconductor production, tried to start VLSI production through acquisition. In 1985 it invested some $13.4 million in the ailing Zymos Corp., acquiring 51 percent equity. Daewoo transplanted Zymos's wafer fabrication equipment to Korea, but drastically scaled down its semiconductor project and later gave up the idea of producing memory chips. Daewoo subsequently focused, on a small scale, solely on nonmemory semiconductors necessary for the telecommunications business.

In short, three Korean semiconductor firms expended significant efforts on entering into licensing agreements with foreign firms. Of forty-nine licenses related to wafer fabrication, Korea received thirty-seven from the United States but only three from Japan, reflecting Japanese reluctance to transfer the latest semiconductor technology to Korean *chaebols*.[8] In addition, these firms invested about $1 billion in facilities and $180 million in R&D in 1983–1986, equivalent, respectively, to 24.2 and 44.6 times the total investment made through 1982.[9] Korean firms attempted to learn as much as possible from advanced countries while striving strenuously to assimilate imported technologies in the shortest possible time.

256K DRAM

Having succeeded in mass producing 64K DRAMs in early 1984, Samsung again launched two task forces, one in Korea and the other in Silicon Valley, for 256K-DRAM development. To shorten the time gap with Japan and United States in commercializing 256K DRAM, the Samsung team in Korea once more decided to source circuit design from Micron Technology, but this time it did not have to get process technology. Experience with 64K DRAMs provided invaluable tacit knowledge for developing the process for 256K DRAM. Nevertheless, several challenging technologies for 256K DRAMs—the developing process for 2-micron circuits, 200-angstrom thin oxide fabrication, 1.1-micrometer metal pitch and chemical etching, test program and ceramic package assembly—imposed another crisis on Samsung. The team went through all available literature for 256K DRAM process and had intensive training at its supplier's site, again significantly raising its tacit knowledge base. Then, as they did for 64K DRAM, the team members entered crisis management mode, working around the clock for eight months. They succeeded in developing working good die in October 1984, reducing Samsung's four-year pursuit of the world pioneer in 64K DRAM to two years for 256K DRAM (see Table 7-3). Mass production began in early 1986, about eighteen months after the first introduction of 256K DRAM by advanced countries.

The Silicon Valley team, however, was given a different assignment: to develop the whole range of 256K DRAM, including circuit design as well as process design, on its own, to become independent

Table 7-3 Gap between Advanced Countries and Korea in the Semiconductor Industry

	64K DRAM	256K DRAM	1M DRAM	4M DRAM	16M DRAM	64M DRAM	256M DRAM
Development Time							
Pioneer in the United States & Japan	1979	1982	1985	Late 1987	Early 1990	Late 1992	Mid-1995
Pioneer in Korea	1983	1984	1986	Early 1988	Mid-1990	Late 1992	Early 1995
Gap	4 years	2 years	1 year	6 months	3 months	Same	Ahead of Japan and the United States
Sample Shipment Time							
Pioneer in United States & Japan	First half of 1980	Second half of 1984	Second half of 1986	Second half of 1989	Second half of 1991		
Pioneer in Korea	First half of 1984	First half of 1986	Second half of 1987	Second half of 1989	Second half of 1991	Second half of 1994	
Gap	3½ years	1½ years	1 year	none	none	First in the world	

SOURCE: Adapted from Korea Development Bank, *Korean Industry in the World, 1994* (Seoul: KDB, 1994), Table 5.

of foreign design suppliers. The team, in competition with its counterpart in Korea, spent seven months, twenty-four hours a day, reverse engineering 256K-DRAM chips developed by Japanese and American firms and studying production literature. The team completed circuit design in April 1985 and working good die in July 1985, about ten months behind its counterpart in Korea.

The Silicon Valley success had two important results. First, by developing the capability to design the 256K-DRAM circuit on its own, Samsung laid an invaluable foundation for the subsequent development of 1M DRAM. Through training and relocating personnel, expertise was effectively transferred to the Semiconductor R&D Center in Korea. Second, the quality of its working good die outperformed the Micron Technology model in several important areas such as soft error rate, electric static discharge, and information processing speed. Therefore, Samsung adopted it as the dominant 256K-DRAM design for mass production in Korea.

Two other semiconductor producers were not as successful as Samsung. Attempting to speed development of 256K DRAM, Hyundai, for example, tried to set up its production process and acquire design technology concurrently. It had few problems in purchasing the state-of-the-art manufacturing equipment, mostly from Japan, but Japanese firms refused to give Hyundai their design technology, making it difficult for the firm to find a design model compatible with the equipment purchased from Japan. Alternatively, Hyundai entered into a licensing agreement with Inmos of the United States, whose 256K-DRAM technology was the fastest available but had not been production tested.[10] When Inmos failed to supply the technology on time, Hyundai canceled the contract and once again, in June 1985, purchased a design from Vitelic. But throughout 1986 a critical yield ratio never reached beyond 30 percent. To learn more about production-tested 256K DRAM, Hyundai entered into an agreement with Texas Instruments to assemble the latter's tested 256K DRAM, letting Hyundai improve its own 256K-DRAM production to a profitable yield ratio. Its subcontract to Hyundai enabled Texas Instruments to move to the more profitable 1M DRAM.

Facing the entry of Korean *chaebols* into 64K and 256K DRAM, Japanese semiconductor producers hastened to dump their models at a fraction of the Korean producers' cost. This strategy had worked earlier, placing enormous financial strains on their American competitors. However, unlike single-business semiconductor producers in the United States, cushions provided by other subsidiaries within the diversified *chaebols* kept their semiconductor operation afloat during the financial crisis. Then the *chaebols* had a stroke of luck: When Japan acceded to export restraints on semiconductor trade with the United States, this and the Japanese firms' subsequent move to 1M DRAM afforded new opportunities for Korean firms to penetrate the U.S. market, allowing them to emerge as the dominant suppliers of 64K and 256K DRAM. Increasing demand and short supply also pushed up prices for 256K DRAM, which rose, for instance, from $2 in 1986 to $5 in 1988. The market remained firm for many more years, leading Korean semiconductor producers into the black and firmly establishing them in the semiconductor industry.

1M DRAM

With development of the mass-production system for 256K DRAM in its final stage, Samsung's R&D team shifted its research focus to 1M DRAM in September 1985. Despite the fact that Samsung could purchase designs from an American firm, it decided to go it alone. Once again the project was assigned to a team in Korea and one in Silicon Valley. In a sense it was competitive, because both were to pursue the same goal; in another sense it was collaborative, because they were to exchange information, personnel, and results.

Experience gained in 256K-DRAM development provided a prior tacit knowledge base, but unlike that for 256K, Samsung had trouble securing explicit knowledge in technical specifications, literature on production processes, and sample chips from pioneering Japanese and U.S. firms, which preempted imitative reverse-engineering. Design and process development for 1M DRAM required several significant technological changes from 256K DRAM. They include, among others, design shifting from N-MOS to energy-efficient C-MOS, requiring notable complications, circuit width from 2 to 1.2 microns, from double-ploy process to triple-ploy process, and increasing speed to 100–120 nanoseconds.

The team in Korea, headed by a Korean-American scientist, included five groups: circuit design, unit process, devices, process structure, and test programs. Once again, the research teams adopted the Korean style of crisis management, living in makeshift quarters and working day and night. They consulted extensively with scientists and engineers at universities and public research institutes in Korea and abroad, including their Silicon Valley colleagues. It was March 1986 when Samsung completed circuit design and July 1986 when it produced working good die, narrowing the gap with the Japanese pioneer from two years for 256K DRAM to one year for 1M DRAM. The Silicon Valley team succeeded in 1M DRAM development about three months later, indicating that the locus of R&D capability had shifted from California to Korea.

Striving to narrow the gap in marketing 1M DRAMs, and having gained substantial tacit and explicit knowledge in producing both 64K and 256K DRAM, Samsung risked building a mass-production system in parallel with the R&D efforts. This time it designed and constructed the systems, needing only some technical consultation from Japanese and American firms. Samsung began mass-producing 1M DRAM in late 1987, a year later than Japanese firms but in time to catch the rapid rise in demand.

In 1986 Hyundai, a late entrant in 1M DRAM, again acquired design and process technology from Vitelic. Assimilating it, Hyundai developed a 1.5-micron 1M DRAM process in May 1986 and 1.0-micron Hiper 1M DRAM in 1988, rapidly catching up with Samsung. In contrast, LG turned to Hitachi for 1M-DRAM technology. Hitachi decided to provide LG with technical assistance for its production in a move to secure a reliable OEM source, allowing Hitachi to devote its resources to the next generation of DRAM.

The chip-making firms invested enormous sums in both production facilities and R&D. By the end of 1988, three semiconductor producers had allocated more than $1.3 billion to building new facilities. Total R&D expenditures increased dramatically, from $13 million in 1983 to $95 million in 1987, which led to cutting Japan's lead.

At about this time, several foreign firms set up design houses in Korea to tap into the rising demand. LSI Logic, for instance, established a design house there to help Korean firms design application-specific integrated circuits (ASICs). Texas Instruments built a facility to produce bipolar MOS and ASICs.[11] These foreign subsidiaries provide Korean *chaebols* with additional sources of critical expertise.

INNOVATION DRIVE IN THE SEMICONDUCTOR INDUSTRY

But the road ahead was getting bumpier.[12] In 1986 Texas Instruments filed a suit against Samsung and eight Japanese chip makers charging infringement of patents for DRAM designs, while Intel filed a similar suit against Hyundai and its American design suppliers. Both Samsung and Hyundai ended up paying royalties on past and future sales of their memory products. Work on the next generation of chips, the

4M DRAM, meant competing neck and neck with Japanese and U.S. companies in exploring the frontiers of semiconductor technology. As the stakes in the chip game rose, the field of players grew smaller worldwide, meaning that few, if any, of those left in the game could be counted on to sell state-of-the-art chip technology to Korean *chaebols*. So the Koreans had to tackle 4M DRAM alone.[13]

4M DRAM

The cost of semiconductor R&D grew exponentially with each succeeding generation. Anticipating difficulty in acquiring foreign technology and seeking to avoid costly duplication in research and investment, in October 1986 the Korean government stepped in and designated R&D on 4M DRAM a national project. Electronics and Telecommunications Research Institute (ETRI), a government R&D institute (GRI), served as a coordinator in the consortium of three *chaebol* semiconductor makers—Samsung, LG, and Hyundai—and six universities. The objective was to develop and mass-produce 4M DRAM by 1989 and completely close the technological gap with Japanese firms. The consortium spent $110 million for R&D over three years (1986–1989); the government contributed 57 percent of the total expenditure, a disproportionately large share in comparison with other national projects.[14]

ETRI invited researchers from the *chaebols* to participate in developing core technologies jointly at ETRI facilities, but they were unwilling to work together. Each formed its own group, trying to succeed independently, so the ETRI program had to be dissolved.[15] The *chaebols* took different approaches; Samsung worked on a stack structure, Hyundai on a trench structure, and LG on a hybrid structure.[16] In 1988 Samsung was the first among them to announce the completion of its 4M-DRAM design, only six months after Japan's. LG was second, and Hyundai had to switch its research from trench to stack structure.

The *chaebols*' independent approaches are reflected in the patents generated by their 4M-DRAM R&D; Samsung registered 56, LG 40, Hyundai 38, the universities 3, and ETRI 11.[17] Samsung could mass-produce 4M DRAM at the about the same time as Japanese firms. Korean firms had finally caught up with the Japanese in memory chips.

The three *chaebols* invested heavily in developing improved versions. Hyundai developed 5S (a higher speed model) 4M-DRAM, stacked capacitor cell (SCC) 4M-DRAM shrink version, and Hyfac 4M DRAM, which was faster and smaller, improving the quality as well as productivity. In technical collaboration with Mosaid in Canada, Hyundai also developed worldwide/bytewide 4M DRAM. Hyundai developed 4M flash electronically erasable programmable read only memory (EEPROM) in collaboration with Bright Microelectronics, which Hyundai later acquired for $2 million, allowing Hyundai access to many of Bright's patents for flash memory technologies. Aggressive investment in production capacity and R&D eventually enabled the Korean *chaebols* to dominate the world market for 4M and 16M DRAM.

Beyond 16M DRAM

The government also designated the development of 64M DRAM and 256M DRAM as national R&D projects. Accordingly, it organized a similar consortium, involving ETRI as a coordinating GRI with three semiconductor producers. But since the three *chaebols,* having already built enough technological capability to work on their own, refused to share their knowledge with competitors, the consortium was virtually a mechanism to distribute the government's R&D subsidy. Actual R&D was undertaken competitively among the three firms. Samsung developed 64M DRAM ahead of the other competitors in August 1992, Hyundai followed, and LG, which had a technical collaboration with Hitachi, was last. All three firms continued to invest in R&D to improve 64M DRAM. Samsung developed the second-generation 64M DRAM with a circuit width of 0.32 micron, 40 percent smaller than the first generation, enabling the company to increase the productivity of an 8-inch-diameter silicon wafer. The second-generation model can be operative at a 3.3-volt power source with a process speed of 50 nanoseconds. In the second half of 1994 Samsung became the world's first supplier of commercial samples of 64M DRAM to such giant users as Hewlett Packard, IBM, and Sun of the United States.[18]

After investing $150 million in R&D over thirty months, in August 1994 Samsung succeeded in developing the world's first fully working sample of 256M DRAM, made with 0.25-micron C-MOS process technology, ahead of the government schedule and of Japan. Samsung also used its own patented technology to design a new architecture that facilitates input/output expansion and overcomes current operating speed limitations, making major improvements in the capacity to process vast amounts of data.[19]

As Korean firms reach the world frontier in dynamic memory chip technology, they have something to offer rival firms in Japan and the United States, opening new opportunities for strategic alliances. Samsung has teamed up with such rivals as Toshiba, General Instrument, ISD, Mitsubishi, NEC, Fujitsu, and so on (see Table 7-4). For example, in September 1994 it formed an association with ISD in which Samsung helps the U.S. company to develop next-generation chips. At the same time, Samsung has the right to use ISD's technologies on storage and reproduction of sound signals in semiconductors, permitting Samsung to combine this knowledge with its own to develop chips with a storage capacity of up to fifteen times the existing models.[20]

Korea's innovativeness in semiconductor technology is also reflected in patent applications. The number of semiconductor-related patent applications by Koreans, as shown in Table 7-5, increased sharply from 708 in 1989 to 3,336 in 1994, outpacing those by foreigners. Koreans accounted for 63 percent of the total. During those six years, LG topped the list of Korean firms with 3,182 applications,

Table 7-4 Samsung's Semiconductor Strategic Alliances

Date	Partner	Subject
Dec. 1992	Toshiba (Japan)	Development of flash memory chips
Jan. 1993	General Instrument (U.S.)	Broad-band agreement of HDTV chips
Apr. 1993	Array (U.S.)	Development of digital signal programming chips
July 1993	Mitsubishi (Japan)	Standard setting for cashed DRAM
Nov. 1993	Micron Technology (U.S.)	Development of synchronous DRAM, Windows RAM, triple-port RAM
Dec. 1993	Toshiba (Japan)	Development of LCD-motivation integrated circuit
May 1994	ARM (U.S.)	Development of microprocessing unit
Sept. 1994	ISD (U.S.)	Development of voice signal process chips
Jan. 1995	Toshiba (Japan)	Technical exchange for memory and nonmemory chips
Feb. 1995	NEC (Japan)	Production of memory chips in Europe
Apr. 1995	Fujitsu (Japan)	Technical exchange for TFT-LCD
Apr. 1995	Toshiba (Japan)	Development of 64M flash memory

SOURCE: *Korea Economic Weekly*, May 1, 1995, 6.

Table 7-5 Patent Applications re Semiconductor Chips

Classification	1989	1990	1991	1992	1993	1994	Total
Design							
Korea	130	95	220	196	166	171	978
Foreign	214	198	284	247	191	236	1,370
Subtotal	344	293	504	443	357	407	2,348
Manufacturing Process							
Korea	578	1,269	1,938	1,850	2,535	3,165	11,335
Foreign	751	889	952	913	1,019	1,317	5,841
Subtotal	1,329	2,158	2,890	2,763	3,554	4,482	17,176
Total							
Korea	708	1,364	2,158	2,046	2,701	3,336	12,313
Foreign	965	1,087	1,236	1,160	1,210	1,553	7,211
Total	1,673	2,451	3,394	3,206	3,911	4,889	19,524

SOURCE: Korean Patent Office.

followed by Samsung with 2,445 and Hyundai with 2,059. Meanwhile, applications by Japanese rivals are also increasing. Toshiba led with 1,127, followed by Hitachi with 546, Fujitsu with 343, Mitsubishi with 325, and Philips with 272, indicating that the Japanese apply for Korean patents in attempts to protect their technology in Korea and preempt reverse-engineering by Korean firms.[21]

Although LG depended on Hitachi for semiconductor technology, it attempted to strengthen its own technological capability. This is reflected not only in its top position in patent applications related to semiconductors but also in its software innovations. LG developed chip design software called Rendezvous and licensed it to Meta Software of the United States. Meta markets the software to American chip designers and pays an 8 percent royalty to LG, which expects to earn about $10 million within two years. Rendezvous helps semiconductor manufacturers to reduce the time required for chip design by more than 20 percent. LG not only integrated the technology for itself but marketed software to instruct other chip makers in it. "In the past, they came to us and said, 'Here is the chip design and how to make it.' But now we say, 'We need a chip. Here is our design. Do it our way,' " said Chang Soo Kim, executive vice president of LG Electronics R&D Center.[22]

Nonmemory Semiconductors

Korea emerged as a global contender in the memory chip business, but lags behind foreign competitors in nonmemory devices, which constitute more than three-fourths of the world's semiconductor chip market (about $101.3 billion in 1993). Korean semiconductor firms turned their attention to the nonmemory area with an ambitious vision of ranking among the world top ten in the new business by the year 2000. Their strategic plans range from intensive R&D and facility investments to tie-ups with foreign firms to vault into the new field. Accumulated technological capability in sub-half-micron process technology, advanced wafer fabrication, and test facilities, which stemmed from their DRAM experience, appears to provide a platform for these *chaebols* to venture into nonmemory technology.

Hyundai quickly moved into the nonmemory business through a worldwide R&D network. It established ASIC design centers in Taiwan and the United States and invested in Metaflow in La Jolla, California, to design a SPARC-compatible microprocessor in 1991. With that technical support, Hyundai developed engineering samples of reduced instruction set computer (RISC) chips for the first time in Korea in 1995. It also established a strategic alliance with Fujitsu.

In addition, Hyundai acquired a controlling interest in the nonmemory division of AT&T-GIS (now called Symbios Logic Inc.) for $340 million in November 1994. Thus Hyundai acquired access to 220 U.S. patents, 160 patents in other countries, and technical expertise available in the new firm, hoping to shorten its pursuit of the world leaders.[23] Hyundai has a strong base for advancing into the nonmemory market without having to pay heavy royalties, gaining an edge over other rivals. Symbios Logic, to intensify its R&D activities in nonmemory chips, also took over a research center in Colorado.

Hyundai established laboratories in Silicon Valley and Tokyo and intensified its domestic R&D, in 1994 alone investing almost $2 billion, about 11 percent of its sales, for R&D and plant expansions. Its Semiconductor R&D Laboratory II is involved in developing RISC computer chips, complex instruction set computer chips, and small computer system interface controllers.

Samsung, LG, and Daewoo are also moving swiftly into the nonmemory chip business. Samsung has been aggressive in developing strategic ties with foreign firms, including Toshiba, ARM of Great Britain, and ISD of the United States. Samsung has also taken over the U.S. HMS and IgT and signed a technical partnership with American Array Microsystem, in which Samsung holds a 20 percent equity stake. In 1995 LG earmarked more than $3 billion, the largest amount among domestic producers, in a bid to catch up with Samsung. For its nonmemory sector, LG hired 500 research engineers in 1995 and was aggressively seeking partnerships with foreign makers and overseas training for its engineers. Daewoo, which abandoned the risky dynamic memory business in the 1980s, decided to venture into the nonmemory sector by signing a wide-range contract with David Sarnoff Research, an affiliate of Stanford Research Institute and by establishing an R&D center in New Jersey. Daewoo spends more than $100 million to produce nonmemory chips with applications for the display function of multimedia devices.[24]

Rapid growth in the semiconductor market and Korea's dominance in memory chips resulted in enormous cash flow into the three Korean major semiconductor makers, enabling them to invest boldly in the nonmemory business. During the first six months of 1995 the three *chaebols* recorded $1.02 billion in nonmemory sales, representing 16 percent of their total chip sales and up from 9 percent in the same period of the preceding year. At Samsung, the proportion of nonmemory chips increased from 4 percent in 1994 to 18 percent in 1995.[25]

While the Korean firms emerged as new contenders in the global semiconductor market, they relied on foreign suppliers for almost 90 percent of production equipment, roughly 50 percent from Japan, 30 percent from the United States, and 10 percent from the European Union. The government recently launched a project to promote the semiconductor equipment industry in Korea by constructing a site for it in Chonan, some 100 kilometers south of Seoul. Six companies, most of them joint venture firms, have located there. The government hopes to raise the proportion of domestically produced equipment to 50 percent by 2001.[26]

SUMMARY

Korean *chaebols* sprang out of nowhere to become leading memory chip producers in a decade. In the 1960s several multinational companies invested in Korea to assemble discrete devices on a consignment basis, transferring little design and engineering technology to Korea. In the 1970s a few Korean firms began modest-scale production of three-inch wafers with a low yield ratio to meet in-house demands in consumer electronics. In the mid-1980s Samsung, Hyundai, and LG embarked on very-large-scale integrated circuit production based on design and process technologies acquired from financially troubled small U.S. semiconductor makers. Since then the three *chaebols* have caught up to and surpassed their Japanese and American rivals in DRAM.

How does technological learning in the semiconductor industry differ from that in the automobile and electronics industries discussed earlier? And why? There seem to be both commonalities and differences.

Technological learning in the semiconductor industry appears to share several features with the previous two industries. First, *chaebols* are major players in these industries, which have faced ups and downs in their evolution, but unlike the specialized U.S. manufacturers, the *chaebols* had cash-cow subsidiaries to keep their semiconductor operations afloat. Like Japanese conglomerates, the *chaebols* had advantages in pushing potentially lucrative but questionable businesses and later making stars of them.[27]

Second, the *chaebols* in these industries pursued an independent strategy in determining to become leading producers in the world market. Korean producers learn significantly from foreign multinationals but maintain their independence in management control and investment for learning and marketing strategy, sharing a national idiosyncracy. Multinationals from advanced countries dominate the markets in other newly industrializing countries (NICs) but not in Korea. In autos, leading Japanese, European, and U.S. producers dominate the markets in both Latin American and Asian NICs. In electronics, the Japanese giants dominate the markets in catching-up countries. In semiconductors, Taiwan recently entered the memory chip business, but Texas Instruments and Phillip control production.

Third, the learning process is similar in all three industries. Initial tacit knowledge was acquired through recruiting experienced engineers. Extensive search of explicit knowledge from literature and the observation of production sites enabled the *chaebols* to upgrade their prior tacit knowledge base significantly, gaining bargaining power in technology transfer negotiations. Then the *chaebols* used crisis construction to strengthen their intensity of effort to facilitate rapid conversions between tacit and explicit knowledge, expediting technological learning. Capability acquired at one stage provided a platform for subsequent stages.

Fourth, technology diffusion between producers took place most effectively through the mobility of experienced personnel. Engineers and technicians from the pioneering *chaebol* played a major role in diffusing manufacturing and design technologies to late entrants, enabling the latter to reduce their learning time notably. Hyundai Motor benefited significantly in building its initial tacit knowledge through experienced engineers from existing producers. LG Electronics was a major source of expert engineers and technicians for subsequent entrants to electronics. LG and Daewoo could shorten the development process for microwave ovens by pirating veteran engineers from pioneering Samsung. The latter also supplied experienced semiconductor engineers to following firms.

Fifth, Korean *chaebols* in these industries have developed sufficient capability to offer something to their rivals in advanced countries, opening new opportunities for strategic alliances. They have amassed the technological expertise to crack more complex products. The acquisition of equity shares in U.S. design houses and the opening of overseas outposts are expected to expedite technological learning of these *chaebols*, which aspire to be in the top ranks by the beginning of the next century.

There appear to be a few differences in the three industries. First, while the automobile and electronics industries progressed incrementally over three decades, the semiconductor industry made a quantum jump in a decade. The difference stemmed from the fact that Korea's technology base was very low when *chaebols* entered the automobile and electronics industries in the 1960s and there were few highly trained Korean-American scientists and engineers available to lure. In contrast, when Korea entered the semiconductor industry, the country had acquired a significant technology base and built a useful platform in electronics. There were also a substantial number of highly sophisticated Korean scientists and engineers who had been trained in leading American universities and gained experience with semiconductor designers and manufacturers.

Second, there were differences in use of R&D laboratories in California. In automobile and electronics, *chaebols* employed them as antennas to monitor and collect frontier technical information and conduct R&D with a view to transferring their results to Korea for production. But Samsung built internal competition between its California R&D facility and its counterpart in Korea in design and process development. That contest accelerated technological learning at each center. Furthermore, the carefully planned shuttling of scientists and engineers across the Pacific resulted in collaborations between the two R&D centers and created significant synergy in further accelerating technological learning in Samsung as a whole.

Third, the government formulated a series of promotional programs for the semiconductor industry. But unlike that of the other two industries, in which the state played a major role in directing the *chaebols*, Korea's success in the semiconductor industry should be attributed to business initiative rather than state initiative.[28] The state appears to be in an inappropriate position to play a decisive role in highly dynamic sectors like semiconductors. Korean *chaebols* were in a strong position to generate necessary financial resources through internal earnings as well as foreign credit and syndicated loans. Samsung used these mechanisms in entering highly capital-intensive VLSI production. GRIs played a useful role in helping *chaebols* crack 4M DRAM. But *chaebols* are now far more versatile and their R&D capability is more advanced than that of GRIs in this sector. Indeed, the other two industries are similar in terms of their latest products.

In short, technological complexity, the level of its base in the country, and firm strategy account for the differences in technological learning between the three industries.

8 Imitation and Innovation in Small Firms: Two Contrasting Patterns

Many studies conducted in the United States and elsewhere have demonstrated that small and medium-size enterprises (SMEs), particularly small young firms, were the most prolific creators of innovations and jobs. This is also true in Korea, though such firms are few in number. Despite their low expenditures on R&D, SMEs account for a disproportionately large number of innovations.[1]

In the early years of Korea's drive toward industrialization, however, most SMEs barely survived as petty traditional firms.[2] In contrast to the government's heavy involvement in promoting and supporting large firms (see Chapters 2, 5, and 6), SMEs were largely neglected, especially in the 1960s and 1970s. Korean government policy was heavily biased in favor of the *chaebols*. As a result, Korean SMEs accounted for less than half the shares of manufacturing employment and value-added for Japanese and Taiwanese SMEs.

Only in the early 1980s did the government belatedly realize the importance of SMEs and begin to support their growth. As mentioned in Chapter 2, the government introduced the compulsory lending ratio to earmark a certain percentage of bank loans for SMEs. The government also took initiatives in promoting the venture-capital industry and established several SME-related infrastructure such as technical extension agencies and training institutions.

Various SME support schemes made a notable change in the industrial structure. For instance, the SME share in manufacturing employment rose from 37.6 percent in 1976 to 51.2 percent in 1988, and the SME share of manufacturing value-added rose from 23.7 percent to 34.9 percent in the same period.[3] Nevertheless, imbalance between the large and SME sectors has mostly continued. SMEs suffered from a disproportionate allocation of financial, technical, and human resources and from a lack of supporting institutions. Dominance in the markets by large firms has impaired the healthy growth of SMEs, which, for instance, are at a serious disadvantage in recruiting competent technical personnel. Lack of collateral made it difficult for SMEs to take advantage of the loans earmarked for them. In addition, opportunistic behavior by large firms toward small subcontractors and increasing imports from low-wage China and other Asian countries have made it even more difficult for SMEs to survive in the markets. As a result, the number of SMEs to that went bankrupt steadily increased, from 6,156 in 1991 to 10,488 in 1994. A poor SME base is a major weakness in Korea's industrial structure.

Despite the predicaments, some traditional but dynamic small firms were able to surmount these obstacles, transform themselves over time, and become pioneers in their industries. This chapter focuses on five such SMEs. Four traditional dynamic small firms—Shinpoong Paper, Korea Shipbuilding and Engineering, Korea Steel Pipe, and Wonil Machinery—illustrate the pattern of imitative growth among SMEs. One technology-based small firm—Medison—presents a case of innovative growth.[4]

As described in the preceding chapters, large firms typically relied initially on foreign firms for the acquisition of manufacturing and design capabilities. The traditional dynamic small firms examined here relied mainly on reverse engineering existing foreign technology to commercialize new products. The technology-based small firm, however, relied heavily on in-house R&D and relations with local universities.

SHINPOONG PAPER COMPANY

Shingpoong, Korea's most profitable paper manufacturer, holds the largest market share in paperboard. As a result, it enjoys the highest stock price among paper manufacturers. When founded in 1960 by Chung Il-Hong, a former navy engineer, Shinpoong was a small, single-business firm. Over the past decades, however, it has proved itself technically adept and grown dynamically. Shinpoong's system of technological learning offers an interesting illustration of how a small firm can develop independently technological capability.

The first phase of Shinpoong's learning is associated with its initial production system in 1962. Unlike other papermakers, which relied on the transfer of turnkey plants from abroad, Mr. Chung was determined to install a significantly larger capacity than he could purchase on a turnkey basis with a U.S. AID loan. On the basis of import records, he estimated that the Korean market for paperboard was about six tons per day. He carefully studied paperboard production processes from industry literature, gaining tacit and explicit knowledge about them. He then visited Japanese papermakers to observe working systems. During his visit he identified secondhand machinery for a system scrapped by a Japanese paper producer, from which many parts were missing.

Despite doubtful critics, he decided to purchase it. Chung acquired an engineering background in the navy, but had no experience in papermaking or papermaking machines; thus, his plan to make the obsolete model workable was significantly riskier than turnkey transfer of a new foreign plant. He constructed his own crisis. Reviewing technical information from literature and from his observation of Japanese papermaking plants, he was able to develop a basic layout for his plant and to identify missing parts. Designing them, using a small Japanese machine shop to produce them, fitting them to the main system, and debugging it became a painful trial-and-error process. But such an iterative operation provided the president-engineer with invaluable opportunities to learn, step by step, the mechanisms of the system. He worked day and night with his assistants to finish the project in the shortest possible time.

In turnkey plant transfer, foreign suppliers take full responsibility for project engineering, project execution, and start-up of the transplant. By contrast, Chung had to assume total responsibility for his undertaking and learn all he could to make his secondhand system work. Through it, Chung personally gained a great deal of experience in papermaking machinery and engineering, providing invaluable opportunities for him to build his tacit knowledge in an upward spiral process of two-way conversions between explicit and tacit knowledge. The investment capability he gained and his production experience enabled Shinpoong to increase the six-ton-a-day system to one of twelve tons a day a year later and eighteen tons a day three years later.

The second phase of Shinpoong's learning took place in 1970, when Chung decided to install a new production system at his second plant in Sungnam, on the southern outskirts of Seoul. For this purpose, he received a license from the government to seek a foreign loan from Japan. This required that he purchase the capital goods from Japan, for the source of finance dictated the source of capital goods. The $700,000 loan would have been just enough to buy twenty-five tons a day of capacity, had he purchased the system from an established papermaking machinery firm. Instead, he decided to design his own forty-ton-a-day system and have a smaller Japanese firm manufacture it.

His experience in operating, expanding, and improving the initial system over eight years gave him the self-confidence to tackle the challenge. Chung had become a member of the American Pulp and Paper Technical Institute, perhaps its only Korean member. He wanted a broader contact base from which to monitor up-to-date technological development in advanced countries and to acquire relevant technical information. He also subscribed widely to foreign trade magazines and technical journals, which had been a major source of indispensable explicit knowledge and his technical ideas. He then made trips overseas to relate printed information to actual physical implementation, empowering him to do both basic and detailed engineering for the second system. With its large drawing board and stack of technical journals, his office resembled that of a design engineer more than that of a CEO.

The president also had a local capital-goods producer manufacture stock preparation equipment and dryers he designed, providing an opportunity for that producer to learn about papermaking machinery. With its help, the capacity of the second system was continually improved and expanded (the expansion of dryers usually leads to increased production capacity) to seventy tons a day by 1973 and eighty tons a day by 1975.

The third learning phase began in 1978, when Shinpoong decided to develop its third plant in Pyongtaek, forty miles south of Seoul, with a 140-ton-a-day system. Using his experience in the design, engineering, operation, and maintenance of his previous two models as a platform and with new technical information from recent literature, he developed both basic and detailed designs for Korea's first international-scale papermaking plant, which incorporated the latest papermaking technology.

This time, Chung decided to have a local capital goods producer manufacture his system and had four engineers from the supplier work closely with him. Under his supervision, this company developed 80 percent of the third system, made possible by the effective transfer of technology from a user to a producer. The remaining 20 percent was purchased from abroad. Chung was also motivated to use a local producer by the government's program to provide purchasers of locally produced capital goods with preferential financing for 70 percent of their necessary investment.[5] Chung estimated that it would have cost him three to four times the $10 million he invested had the new system been built abroad. Gaining experience from this order, the capital-goods maker later produced similar and modified versions of papermaking systems for other paper mills.

According to Chung, the new system represents a synthesis of all the equipment he had studied in the literature, seen operating in Japan and other countries, and worked with during his twenty years in the industry. But he designed it so as not to infringe on patents, both locally and abroad. His six formers, for instance, roughly resembled the Japanese Kobayashi conventional ultraformer but incorporated features of the American multiformer method. After the last former, the multi-ply sheet had the top ply applied from a short fourdrinier, which is the most significant technological innovation in the third phase. Chung was also proud of technical advances in his personally designed system; his presses dehydrated down to 56 percent, compared with 60 percent in conventional presses, resulting in energy savings. Two American engineers who visited Shinpoong to install a computer-assisted scanning system for on-line control of product quality noted that Shinpoong's new system was one of the most up-to-date paperboard making systems they had seen.[6] Shinpoong's success story was even reported in *Pulp and Paper International.*

In its technological development, Shinpoong had not licensed any agreements from foreign firms nor had it received any assistance from local universities, R&D institutes, or engineering firms. It relied completely on the ingenuity, highly effective learning proficiency, and hardworking characteristics of its president, who developed and used an effective network of local and Japanese capital goods producers that carried out his creative designs. He also used the American Pulp and Paper Technical Institute as a major source of new technical ideas.

Never having diffused his ingenuity to others in the firm, Chung preserved his technological capability individually rather than organizationally. This may be the reason Shinpoong could not diversify into a capital goods producing business in spite of its high capability.

KOREA SHIPBUILDING AND ENGINEERING CORPORATION

Korea Shipbuilding and Engineering Corporation (KSEC), now Hanjin Heavy Industries, is no longer a small firm but a subsidiary of the Hanjin, the sixth largest *chaebol* in Korea with more than 3,000 employees. Among its holdings are Korean Airlines and Hanjin Shipping, the largest shipping and transportation company in Korea. But as the first and a small shipbuilder at the outset, its technological learning exhibits the characteristics of a traditional dynamic small firm, organically evolving in accumulating technological capability.

KSEC, established in 1937 by Mitsubishi and other Japanese entrepreneurs, was nationalized in 1945, when the Japanese withdrew from Korea at the end of World War II. Under Japanese management, Koreans, who had largely done menial work, lacked both the technical and the managerial capabilities to operate the firm. The Japanese abandoned four small steel ships under construction, but the Koreans, not knowing what to do with them, left them untouched. Only several years later did the Koreans discover the blueprint of the ships by chance. When they finally figured out what to do with them a decade later, the half-finished ships had rusted so that they had to be scrapped.

KSEC acquired basic shipbuilding capability mainly through learning by doing from repairing ships. The Korean War brought to Korean shores many foreign freighters of various classes in need of emergency repairs. The repair business gave inexperienced KSEC engineers opportunities to gain explicit knowledge by studying and examining ships' drawings and blueprints and tacit knowledge by receiving substantial technical help from the foreign engineers aboard those ships. In this way KSEC engineers learned how modern ships were built. In repairing ships, KSEC progressed through a spiral process of learning. That is, mastering simple tasks allowed its engineers to tackle progressively more difficult tasks. By 1953 KSEC had repaired 963 foreign ships, both welded Western and riveted Japanese types.

The government also played a useful role in helping KSEC learn technologically. As a state-owned enterprise, KSEC, together with two national universities, was awarded a project to develop a series of standard ship designs to be made available to smaller Korean private shipbuilders. This state-funded enterprise enabled the firm to purchase volumes of similar standard ship designs published in Japan in the 1950s. Based on these, plus those obtained from the repair business and those discovered at its site, KSEC engineers imitatively developed Korean standard ship designs for freighters and tankers, gaining essential experience.

However, translating repair experience and design blueprints into actual shipbuilding was not a simple task. KSEC had to undergo a series of trials and errors in building the first few ships smaller than 25 gross tons (GTs). For example, the hull of its first welded ship was found to be bent on the day of its launch owing to differences in tension of various steel materials used. It took many months of trying one thing and another for the engineers to make the ship seaworthy.

The introduction of the government's first and subsequent Five Year Economic Development Plans in the 1960s significantly altered the growth of the industry, particularly for KSEC. The total tonnage built by the firm increased from 4,636 GTs in 1962 to 43,310 in 1971. The largest ship it built increased from 200 GTs in 1962 to 4,000 in 1968 and 12,000 in 1971. But acquisition of technological capability through learning by doing was relatively slow and inefficient.

Along the way, KSEC had to expand its dry-dock capacity. As shown in Table 8-1, such expansion with increasingly newer equipment relied heavily on foreign assistance not only for equipment but also for basic and detailed designs. KSEC, however, was achieving progressively greater localization of designs, equipment, and construction. By the 1960s KSEC could build facilities under the supervision of Japanese engineers. It had to rely completely on the Japanese supplier for basic and detailed designs, but KSEC engineers took an active part in developing the designs. They accumulated enough skill to undertake a significant proportion of detailed design for a 1970 expansion and generate imitatively both basic and detailed designs for the 1975 expansion. The local content ratio of equipment also increased significantly during the expansion process. These developments led to the birth of KSEC's construction division.

In 1971 KSEC received an order for a 12,000-GT ship, three times larger than the largest it had ever built. Despite more than two decades of accumulating experience, the company's capability was insufficient, so KSEC turned to foreign technical assistance. It purchased a complete design from Kawasaki in Japan and sent ten of its engineers to the Japanese firm for training. But Kawasaki was not cooperative in

Table 8-1 Import Substitution of Engineering at Korea Shipbuilding and Engineering Corporation

Year	Capacity Added	Design		Equipment	Construction
		Basic	Detailed		
1937	6,000 DWT[a]	Japan	Japan	Japan	Japan
1966	30,000 DWT	Japan	Japan	Largely Japan	Korea
1970	60,000 DWT	Japan	Japan	Largely Japan	Korea
1970	150,000 DWT	Japan	Japan/Korea	Largely Japan	Korea
1975[b]	150,000 DWT	Korea	Korea	Japan/Korea	Korea

SOURCE: Interviews with KSEC engineers.
NOTES: [a] Deadweight ton.
[b] Basically a copy of Japanese design adopted in 1970.

transferring know-how to the emerging Korean competitor. Thus, KSEC recruited as its chief engineer a Korean shipbuilding expert with more than twenty years' experience as a representative of the American Bureau of Ships (ABS) in Japan. This enabled KSEC to increase its tacit knowledge significantly. Under his engineering leadership, KSEC generated its own standard design for a 12,000-GT-class bulk carrier based on the firm's accumulated experience, Kawasaki's design, and supplementary informal technical assistance acquired through the new chief's personal contacts with other Japanese shipbuilders.

A year later, Gulf Oil ordered six oil tankers, ranging from 13,500 to 19,460 GTs, when the largest tanker KSEC had built was a substandard 356-GT-class vessel for a local shipping firm. The ABS, with authority to approve a design and supervise shipbuilding, approved KSEC's basic conception of the tankers, but Gulf insisted on purchasing proven designs from advanced countries. Given Japanese reluctance, KSEC turned to KDW, a German firm, for a complete design for a 13,500-GT oil tanker. KSEC went on to build four such tankers through 1975, and after that purchased only the basic conception from KDW for larger ones.

KSEC built twenty-one more oil tankers through 1983, including one as large as 32,000 GTs. It no longer relied on foreign sources for design, seeking only partial technical assistance from Norwegian SRS and DNV. Unlike the Japanese, the Europeans were willing to share technology with KSEC, as they were getting out of the shipbuilding business because the Japanese shipyards were eroding their competitiveness.

As the first modern shipyard owned by the state and privatized in 1968, KSEC produced a significant number of experienced design and yard engineers and technicians. They, in turn, later played crucial roles in emerging private shipyards such as Hyundai, Daewoo, and Samsung in the 1970s and 1980s.

KOREA STEEL PIPE COMPANY

Korea Steel Pipe Company (KSP), founded in 1967, is one of four steel pipe manufacturers in Korea; it produces carbon steel pipes, conduit tubes, structural pipes, other special pipes, and steel pipe machinery. It exports almost 70 percent of its output to twenty-four countries around the world.

There were no steel pipe producers immediately following the

1950–1953 Korean War. Many people recovered used pipes from ruined buildings. Sensing a business opportunity in steel pipe for postwar construction, the founder and his associate, an electrical engineer, gained a basic understanding of the process by observing and examining the operation of German equipment imported by a local bicycle company. Based on that experience, they developed a small steel pipemaking machine, using an automobile transmission for speed control and other war surplus materials. Since they lacked mechanical engineering capability, the initial process was so primitive that it was dangerous to operate and half the yield was defective.

The first major leap in technological development began with the arrival of Dong-Suk Ryu, a young engineer who had a mechanical engineering degree and four years' experience in machinery manufacturing with the state-owned Korea Machinery Corporation, the only modern machinery plant inherited from the Japanese.[7] Ryu's arrival at KSP in 1967 was a major infusion of tacit knowledge to the company.

During the first five years of Ryu's mechanical engineering leadership, KSP developed six pipemaking lines in its Seoul plant, manufacturing more than 70 percent of its equipment in its own engineering department; only critical parts were imported from Japan. During this period, Japanese suppliers of specialized electrical and machinery components informally provided KSP engineers with valuable technical information and ideas gained through their marketing activities to Japanese pipemakers. Subsequent lines were always significantly better than the previous ones, incorporating new ideas stemming from experience, new technical information from literature, and the observation of new equipment in Japan. Although these processes were primarily manual and slow, KSP's production capacity increased drastically, from 6,000 metric tons in 1967 to 54,500 by 1973.

The second major jump in learning took place in 1973, when a new plant was built in Inchon to meet increasing demands in both domestic and international markets. For the first time, KSP imported a foreign machine, a high-speed model from Japan with a production rate of 60 meters per minute, twice the speed of KSP's own models. The model not only let KSP improve its productivity but provided its engineers with new, sophisticated explicit knowledge about the machines. The supplier sent a number of its engineers to KSP to help the latter's engineers learn how to set up and operate the model, transferring crucial tacit knowledge to KSP. Within a year, the operating and maintenance experience of the high-speed Japanese model enabled KSP engineers to improve the firm's old models to match the Japanese one.

The third major jump took place in 1975, when KSP imported, again from Japan, the latest fully automated model. Japanese engineers accompanied the machine and transferred operating and maintenance technology to the buyer. At the same time, KSP sent its engineers to visit Japanese steel pipemakers. The KSP engineers, who had extensive experience in designing and operating the KSP lines, were most receptive of the new features embodied in the lines they had seen in Japanese firms.

While Shinpoong used external capital-goods producers to translate creative ideas into production processes, KSP produced its own capital goods, diffusing the chief engineer's ability to other engineers in the firm. By 1978 KSP's engineering capacity had become so competitive that it established a new subsidiary, Korea Steel Pipe Machinery Company (KSPM), under the leadership of Ryu, to capitalize on its engineering and machine-making expertise and market the capital goods to others. The design and engineering capability it accumulated over the years and its experience in operating the Japanese model enabled KSPM to develop an exact copy of the automatic model and to automate the first model it had imported. Only a year later, in 1979, KSPM developed its new automatic line, which was even better than the Japanese model. It had taken KSP only three years to assimilate the Japanese line and one year to develop an improved model of its own.

R&D in the real sense of the term was still at a formative stage. KSP, however, had an effective learning system within the firm, having established a flexible, collective decision-making process for producing a new line. Design engineers would formulate a basic idea and circulate it among all the firm's engineers and technical leaders to evaluate the idea and provide input for improvements. A final design was decided on only after several iterations of the same procedure, incorporating all ideas from those who had previously worked on a similar line and building a consensus among them. This procedure had proved to be most effective in translating many engineers' important tacit knowledge at the individual level into new tacit and explicit knowledge shared among the engineers at the organizational level, socializing such knowledge throughout the organization.

The fourth jump in technological learning took place in 1978, when KSPM entered into a number of technological collaboration agreements with Japanese and German firms. KSPM reached a point at which it realized the limit of imitative learning in increasingly complex knowledge. To expedite learning in internationally competitive technology, it was imperative to develop ties with well-known foreign firms, for such ties were also deemed important to KSPM's image with prospective foreign buyers.

KSP exported several models to developing countries, and KSPM retooled labor-intensive lines and exported them on a turnkey basis to Kenya and Bangladesh. It developed a highly sophisticated automatic model and sold it on a turnkey basis to Saudi Arabia. The Saudi buyer forced KSP to accept a 30 percent equity stake as a way to ensure efficient operation of the plant by KSP personnel. Such export projects had two advantages. One, they enabled KSP to fully exploit its technological assets, especially personnel, during a downturn in the domestic market—like other Korean firms, KSP does not lay off workers. Two, the adoption of a highly sophisticated export model led KSP personnel to apply it to subsequent designs for Korean clients.

WONIL MACHINERY WORK

Wonil Machinery Work, a small hot and cold rolling mill producer, began in 1948 as a machine repair shop spun off from a small machinery firm.[8] The founder, Jong-Sun Won, an experienced engineer, and his associates had ample opportunities to examine carefully many types of old machines they repaired. With this background, Won often designed and manufactured simple machines and tools to meet his clients' orders.

In the early 1950s, a small local steel fabricator asked Wonil if it could make a simple and inexpensive hot rolling mill. This order, the first large-scale machine Wonil was asked to design and manufacture, presented the company an opportunity to shift its business from repairing machines to specializing in rolling mills. As a first step, the founder and his assistants visited a local firm to observe an imported hot rolling line in operation, then began to search technical literature related to rolling mills. On the basis of observation, machine repair experience, and the technical literature, Wonil developed a simple rolling mill that was primitive but worked satisfactorily for the types of products the client needed. While steadily improving subsequent hot rolling models, Wonil developed auxiliary equipment such as coilers and plywood machines.

By the mid-1960s Wonil had accumulated enough technological capability to design and manufacture 3-high hot rolling mills and 2-high cold rolling mills. But it had to rely on Japanese sources for critical parts and components, the suppliers of which informally transferred important technical rolling mill design information. One Japanese electrical machine maker, which supplied critical electrical parts for hydraulic molding machines, gave Wonil monographs and Japanese technical journals on rolling mill design as part of its marketing efforts. At the same time, Japanese sales engineers, who had been exposed to Japanese rolling mill producers, provided Wonil with invaluable information and technical advice on mill design.

In 1966 Wonil's engineering team launched a project to create a blueprint for a more sophisticated 4-high nonreverse cold rolling mill, a technology widely used in advanced countries, in anticipation of increasing demand for high-quality cold rolling machines. During the first year the development process was very slow, as none of the local firms used such a complex model from which Wonil could learn. Company engineers had to rely largely on literature. But a year later a local firm imported that very model rolling mill and gave Wonil an opportunity to see the machine in operation and to obtain technical information, both written and verbal, from the user. Interaction with the user helped Wonil to speed up and significantly improve development of its own 4-high cold rolling mill design, the most important technical milestone in the company's history.

In the 1970s Wonil developed many important products, including 3-high 10-stand tandem structural rolling mills, a 2-high metal testing cold rolling mill, pipe hydraulic testing machines, laminating machines, and a continuous shearing line. The last was designated by the Korean government as innovative machinery, a classification that entitled the purchaser of the machine access to preferential financing. In 1976 the government designated Wonil a specialized firm to manufacture steel rolling mills, which made the firm eligible for preferential financing for capital investment and operation.

Throughout these years, Wonil frequently sent its engineers and technicians abroad to visit both rolling mills and rolling mill producers to identify new technological developments, to obtain sales catalogs and other technical information, and to observe the mills in operation. Such actions provided important foundations for Wonil either to improve its existing models or to imitate foreign models exactly or creatively.

Like KSP, Wonil realized the limit of imitative learning, particularly in technologically sophisticated areas. In 1981 it made a strategic shift and entered into licensing agreements with Josef Frohling and Moller and Neumann, both of Germany, for more refined models such as 20-high cold rolling mill. The strategy to depart from its self-reliant reverse-engineering approach was preparation for growing demands for more advanced models in both the local and international markets. Wonil thought it wiser to speed development of its capability by arranging agreements with leading German firms than by progressively upgrading over a long period of time through learning by observation and learning by doing.

MEDISON COMPANY

Medison, one of many technology-based small firms spun off from the Korea Advanced Institute of Science and Technology (KAIST), the research-oriented graduate school of applied science, is one of the most successful new venture companies in Korea.[9] The founder, Min-Hwa Lee, with a Ph.D. in electronics engineering, and his four cofounders were graduate students under Professor Song-Bae Park. Professor Park directed a 1984–1985 research project on ultrasonic scanner technology funded jointly by the government and a local medical equipment manufacturer. The project was one of the targeted national R&D projects in the mid-1980s.

When the medical equipment company decided to pull out of the project, the laboratory team searched for an alternative industry partner; national R&D projects required a partner willing to commercialize research results. In July 1985, failing to find another partner, the team led by Dr. Lee decided to spin off from KAIST to form a new venture as the requisite industrial partner. A person experienced in medical equipment marketing and a young man with experience in venture business management joined the five KAIST researchers. The team members had already published eight research articles by the time they founded Medison, and they published five more the following year in such international journals as *Ultrasonic Imaging* and *IEEE Transactions on Medical Imaging*. In addition, they had obtained four patents on ultrasonic imaging by the time Medison was founded, an indication of the team's impressively high level of both tacit and explicit knowledge.

The government played three important roles—R&D supporter, venture business financier, and market creator—in Medison's success. First, the government funded the initial R&D project for more than four years before and after the inception of Medison, leading to substantial progress in mission-oriented research on ultrasonic technology at a KAIST laboratory, which was effectively transferred to Medison. Second, the government assisted Medison indirectly through venture-capital financing. In its first year, Medison received a critical investment and a loan from the Korea Technology Development Corporation, the first venture-capital company established by the government in 1981 to promote new enterprises.[10] Third, the government created a market for Medison by restricting imports of foreign ultrasonic scanners. Owing to high tariff and nontariff barriers, small hospitals in rural areas could not afford to purchase foreign ultrasonic scanners, creating a rural market for Medison to penetrate. The government gradually liberalized the scanner market, but its initial protection enabled Medison to put down strong roots in the medical equipment industry.

Linear-only Scanners

The first-generation scanners were largely linear-only types to meet the growing needs of the domestic market. The team searched extensively in academic and trade journals, catalogs and technical reports from such leading medical equipment manufacturers as General Electric, Toshiba, and Aloka. This allowed Medison engineers to translate their academic knowledge into practical knowledge. Examining foreign models used by large general hospitals in Seoul also helped the team to emulate those scanners, not by reverse-engineering but by applying the research outcome of the national R&D project. The team established an ambitious goal of completing the development of a prototype within two months so they could exhibit it at the Korea International Medical Equipment Show (KIMES) in September 1985. KIMES offered the best opportunity for Medison to debut and get the widest exposure to local as well as foreign medical equipment dealers.

The research team rented a small room in a shanty inn near the KAIST campus. There they virtually lived together and worked around the clock for two months, translating their highly innovative patent for eight-point continuous dynamic focusing technology into a working model in time for the show. They were often spoon-fed so that they could continue their research without interruption. The team succeeded in meeting the deadline, and its working model was exhibited along with sophisticated designs from Toshiba, General Electric, and Aloka. The government bestowed an Industrial Achievement Award on the founder for one of the most innovative products introduced that year.

Medison placed working models in two university teaching hospitals in Seoul before it began marketing the product, SA-3000, in February 1986, selling some thirty units to rural hospitals in 1986. But the scanner was so unreliable that its image was blurry and often faded away. It broke down completely two or three times a month, forcing the team members to be on the road constantly to service their undependable products. It was a technical failure as well as a commercial disaster.

Facing problems with their continuous dynamic focusing technique, the team adopted a simpler existing technology, proven two-point focusing, to produce more reliable scanners. In desperate financial straits, they needed to develop a commercially successful model. Once again they worked day and night, this time for four months. Experience gained in developing the previous high-tech scanner and lessons learned from its users provided enough technological capability to develop a second, more reliable model, SA-3000A, which incorporated a unique digital scan converter (DSC) design developed by the team and was commercially successful. Medison sold more than 100 units during the first year, including exports to Turkey, Pakistan, Italy, Hong Kong, India, and Mexico, putting the business into the black.

Sensing a potentially large market not only in Korea but also abroad, Medison attempted to develop an inexpensive portable model and generated a compact, semiportable model, SA-100. Given the company's reputation from the SA-3000A and portability of the compact scanner, the model sold well among smaller rural Korean hospitals, but the scanner was noisy, poor in image, and low in heat resistance, leading to system breakdown. Although it was a disaster, it provided a platform for a more successful model. Based on this experience, in 1988 Medison came up with an inexpensive, reliable, fully-portable compact model, SA-88, for export to third world countries. After exhibiting the model at several European international medical equipment shows in 1989, Medison began exporting it to Europe, the Middle East, and Asia. By 1990 SA-88 had received U.S. Food and Drug Administration approval and became the best-selling portable model in developing countries for many years.

Linear/Sector/Convex Scanners

Medison progressively moved from linear-only models to linear/sector models and to linear/sector/convex models as a way to challenge the sophisticated market in advanced countries. This progress was based largely on its own R&D and joint research with KAIST. Medison developed its SA-4000 model in 1988, which incorporated patented uniform ladder algorithm (ULA) in sector display technology, significantly reducing location errors and in turn improving image quality. But its quality was noticeably inferior to that of comparable foreign models. In 1989 it developed a better scanner, a linear/sector/convex model, SA-4500, with a high-quality sector/convex image supported by ULA. This model dominated the domestic market even in the face of increasing foreign competition. During this time, the KAIST team completed Doppler technology and color-flow mapping technology. Medison incorporated the Doppler technology in its linear/sector/convex/Doppler scanner, SA-4800, which became a hot-selling model abroad. Doubling its sales almost every year, by 1990 Medison grew to 140 employees with sales of $10 million, half from exports.

Diversification

Medison, aggressive in diversifying into related businesses, established Meridian, a subsidiary to launch its bioenergy medical equipment business, integrating oriental medicine with modern bioenergy technology developed in Russia. A Medison research team spun off to form Meridian to concentrate on the exploration of new possibilities in modernizing oriental acupuncture and medicine. Medison also established Medidas to develop medical information systems such as its medical image display archiving system, teleradiology, and a picture archiving communication system. Medison also invested in Korea Multimedia Communication, Byte Computer, and Taeha Mechatronics for research in medical information systems and medical automation.

Globalization

Medison's globalization focused on three areas: marketing, production, and research. First, Medison established overseas marketing subsidiaries in the United States, Europe, Russia, China, Japan, and Singapore, indicating its determined marketing strategy in advanced as well as in developing countries. Second, Medison entered into a licensing agreement for an Indian firm to assemble its scanners on a completely knocked-down basis. Medison models are among the best-sellers in India. Shanghai Medison also began assembling scanners for the Chinese market. Third, Medison is developing a joint research program with Russian R&D institutes on an electrocardiograph, an endoscope, and Doppler technology. Fourth, Medison acquired 60 percent ownership of Kretz, an Austrian ultrasonic producer and one of the first firms to introduce ultrasonic devices. The Austrian firm is the most advanced in three-dimensional scanner technology.

With 250 workers Medison is still small, but it is a company of a new generation, quite different from the traditional dynamic small firms presented earlier. Unlike slow-moving firms, it is dynamic in technology development, moving rapidly along changes in frontier technology. In contrast to traditional dynamic firms, which focus predominantly on the domestic market with peripheral interest in developing countries, Medison is global, active in both developing and advanced nations.

SUMMARY

The 1960s and 1970s were a difficult time for Korean SMEs. Most struggled to survive in an environment severely lacking in resources and supporting institutions. Some traditional dynamic small firms were able to evolve organically over time, accumulating technological capability primarily through imitative reverse-engineering, which exhibited several common features.

First, these small firms commonly acquired their technological capability by reverse-engineering foreign products. Lacking financial and organizational resources to negotiate and finance foreign technology transfer, they had to use an imitative approach at the outset.

Second, successful imitative capability building often resulted from energetic technical entrepreneurs who, although their initial knowledge was not significant, played a central role in reverse-engineering. What was noteworthy was their learning capability. They were highly effective in translating the explicit knowledge of literature and that embodied in equipment into tacit knowledge, which enabled them to make sense of increasingly sophisticated explicit knowledge and translate it into higher tacit knowledge. That is, an experience in one stage was effectively used to tackle a more challenging task at the next stage, facilitating the spiral process of learning, which was largely cumulative.

Third, a quantum leap in technological capability is commonly associated with the arrival of technical personnel recruited from other firms. These people brought with them new tacit knowledge, enriching their firms' technological base and enabling the firms to tackle tasks that were previously beyond their competency. The mobility of experienced technical personnel is, indeed, the most effective means of diffusing technology within an industry and an economy.

Fourth, learning by observation appears to be an important means of imitative learning for traditional small firms. The opportunity to observe foreign products allowed technical entrepreneurs to substantiate improvised ideas conceived from the integration of their tacit and explicit knowledge acquired from literature. Thus, the availability of foreign products in local and foreign firms was instrumental in the firms' efforts to build their capability.

Fifth, the foreign suppliers of core equipment played an important role in informally transferring technologies related not only to the equipment they supplied but also to the main systems. These suppliers' engineers had significant knowledge related to the users of their core equipment and provided relevant literature and information to their Korean clients, helping them to expedite learning.

Sixth, it is extremely difficult to transform traditional dynamic small firms into technology-based small firms. The latter typically arise from the spin-off of highly educated scientists and engineers from research-oriented universities, R&D institutes, and high-technology corporate R&D centers. Medison is a good example of such a firm.

Seventh, the government had a relatively negligible role in the emergence and growth of traditionally small dynamic firms in the 1960s and 1970s. However, its role expanded in the late 1970s, when the state began promoting the local capital-goods industry. In the 1980s and 1990s, it played an increasingly important part in promoting the emergence and growth of technology-based small firms.

Finally, while *chaebols* have human, financial, and organizational resources to invest for expeditious technological learning, traditional dynamic small firms, lacking these resources, have to evolve over a long period of time. Technology-based small firms could produce a disproportionate share of innovations, but they are small in number, Medison being one of about ten that are internationally competitive. Innovation is encouraged by synergies being achieved between large firms, with all their resource advantages, and small firms, with all their entrepreneurial advantages.[11] For this reason, the scarcity of dynamic technology-based small firms is a major weakness in Korea's technological system. There are, however, many signs in the economy that a significant number of new technology-based small firms will emerge in the years to come. For example, the relatively new Venture Business Association has more than 100 members and its membership is increasing rapidly.

Conclusion and Implications

PART III

9 Korea's Technological Learning: Conclusion

Chapter 4 presented a global technology environment framework (see Figure 4-2) postulating that industries and firms in advanced countries evolve along a technology trajectory made up of three stages—fluid, transition, and specific. The fluid stage characterizes firms in a new technology, a new industry. The rate of radical product innovation is high, as competition depends mainly on performance. Then a transition begins toward a dominant design and mass-production methods, adding cost competition and giving greater importance to production capability and scale economies. As an industry matures and price competition grows more intense, the production process becomes more automated, integrated, systematic, and specific to turn out a highly standardized product. It is in this specific stage that industries typically relocate to catching-up countries.

The industries cited in the preceding four chapters indicate that Korea entered the specific stage of the technology trajectory model of advanced countries in the early 1960s. Furthermore, based on its cheap but well-educated and hardworking labor force, Korea imitatively reverse-engineered mature and labor-intensive foreign technologies. Most products of this period resulted from the imitation of foreign goods.

Then, facing protectionist policies in North America and Europe, eroding competitiveness caused by rapidly rising wages, increasing difficulty in acquiring foreign technology, and the consequent imperative to shift to higher-value, technology-intensive products, Korea, reversing direction, entered the transition stage in the 1980s. The country intensified its indigenous R&D in this stage to strengthen its competitiveness through creative imitation of sophisticated foreign technologies and its own innovation. Some selected industries entered the fluid stage in the 1990s to compete neck and neck with leading advanced countries. Innovation became their watchword.

Chapter 1 raised several questions regarding Korea's rapid industrial growth. For instance, how have Korea and Korean firms managed to achieve such phenomenal growth in technological learning? What major factors are behind their rapid technological growth? This chapter answers these questions. The conclusions are based as much on the industry cases presented earlier as on the more than 200 firms I studied in past decades, which attest to the judgments that have emerged.[1]

The diverse factors that interacted complexly to influence the direction and speed of technological learning in Korean industries are government, *chaebols,* education, export policy, technology transfer strategy, research, development policy, sociocultural systems, and private-sector strategy.

GOVERNMENT: AN EFFECTIVE ORCHESTRATOR?

The strong and highly centralized developmental Korean government, as discussed in Chapter 3, was relatively effective in orchestrating technological learning in the 1960s and 1970s. During these decades, industrial policy measures, which brought about the demand side of technology by creating the needs for it, were much more effective in expediting technological learning at the firm level than science and technology policy measures (except for education), which were designed to strengthen the supply side of technology by accumulating technological capabilities.

On the demand side, President Park Chung Hee and his technocrats learned effectively from Japanese industrial experience. The government designated several strategic industries for export promotion and deliberately created and fostered *chaebols* to marshal the scale economies inherent in mature technologies. It then pushed and pulled the *chaebols* to achieve the ambitious export goals, imposing a series of crises on the firms to accelerate technological learning in order to survive in a life-or-death struggle in the competitive export market. At the same time the government provided necessary supports for the *chaebols* to make the crises creative rather than destructive.

On the supply side, the government expanded educational institutions to provide workers with high tacit knowledge for the *chaebols*. However, government R&D institutes (GRIs) and other science and technology infrastructures were not effective, because mature technology was readily available and easy to master.

In short, the government had been relatively effective through the mid-1970s. In the mature and stable environment, it was in an advantageous position to sit in the driver's seat, using *chaebols* as the engine. Government technocrats were competent to identify winners and allocated necessary resources to achieve ambitious goals for growth.

However, the effectiveness of the government's developmental role waned significantly in the rapidly changing market and technology environments of the 1980s and 1990s. Unlike its role in the 1960s and 1970s, the state was in a less advantageous position than the private sector in understanding and responding timely to the dynamics of market and technological change because it deals directly with them.

On the demand side, the government introduced various measures—antitrust and fair trade legislation, trade liberalization, financial liberalization, and investment liberalization—to inject more market forces into economic activities. Promoting the liberalization on the surface, government technocrats behind the curtain tried to maintain their orchestrating role even in the 1980s and 1990s. Their self-interest in preserving bureaucratic power and inertia to continue existing practices inhibited the dynamic growth of private initiatives. As a result, many government developmental programs were inappropriately applied or many steps behind the private sector.

In addition, two factors made it difficult for the government to be effective in its developmental role. First, political corruption in the late 1970s and thereafter resulted in political collusion between the state and *chaebols*, leading to irrational allocation of resources. For instance, political leaders demanded a kickback from *chaebols* in exchange for a lucrative business license or rescue from financial problems. It appears that absolute power inevitably leads to absolute corruption. Second, the economic power of *chaebols* grew so strong and their impact on the economy so profound that even without kickbacks the government was often forced to rescue poorly managed firms, too numerous to name, from financial woes to protect other firms upstream and downstream. The state role as a crisis imposer had become that of a coddler.

On the supply side, the government drastically expanded educational institutions over the years to meet the increasing needs of industries. Progress was impressive in terms of quantity but dreadful in terms of quality owing to underinvestment.

By contrast, preferential financing and tax concessions were effective in promoting substantial R&D growth in Korean firms. In Korea, where the private sector takes major initiatives in R&D, accounting for more than 84 percent of the nation's total research investment in 1994, these incentives enabled the private sector to reduce the cost of R&D and human resource development.

The strong government was an asset in the early decades, enabling Korean industries to achieve phenomenal growth in large-scale, production-oriented, mature industries. It has, however, become a liability as its rigid bureaucracy inhibited the economy from responding creatively to the rapidly changing market and technology environment in recent decades.

CHAEBOLS: ASSET AND BURDEN

One of the most significant ways the Korean government influenced technological learning in the private sector was in fostering *chaebols*. The state deliberately created and nurtured them as engines for rapid economic development. These *chaebols*, the backbone of industrialization in labor-intensive industries in the early decades, have been the major source of Korean production and exports.

Chaebols played a major role in expediting technological learning in industry for several reasons. (1) The *chaebols*, which were in the most advantageous position to attract the best-qualified entrants to the workforce, accumulated technological capability rapidly. This resulted in their forming a high tacit knowledge base. (2) The *chaebols* developed organizational and technical resources to identify, negotiate, and finance foreign technology transfer, capitalizing on their ability to acquire higher-level explicit and tacit knowledge from the international community. (3) Their demonstrated economic viability and political collusion enabled them to obtain new business licenses and preferential financing from the government and reinvest the funds to accelerate learning in new projects through organized in-house training and development efforts. (4) The highly diversified but centrally controlled *chaebols* applied experiences gained in one field of business to another, resulting in rapid diffusion of technological capability across subsidiaries. (5) The government imposed crises by forcing technologically challenging new industrial projects on them. Meanwhile, the government provided these firms with supports to keep them afloat until they learned enough to compete in a new industry. (6) Cushioned by their size and diversified portfolios, they could engage in risky and expensive new businesses. They fostered repeated attempts to turn imposed or constructed crises into opportunities. (7) The *chaebols* spearheaded the drastic expansion and deepening industrial R&D operations in Korea. And (8) They have the technical and financial resources to globalize their R&D activities and to monitor and tap state-of-the-art technologies at the frontier. As a result, Korea has ascended to the status of a world-market contender in such capital-intensive, large-scale industries as shipbuilding, steel, semiconductors, automobiles, synthetic fibers, petrochemicals, and consumer electronics. In addition, *chaebols* were a leading force in the globalization of Korean businesses.

However, behind the success of the *chaebols'* rapid technological learning lie serious tolls on the market and on small and medium-size enterprises (SMEs). Collusion with political powers resulted in the misallocation of resources and economic inefficiency at the macro level. The concentration of economic power in the hands of a small number of *chaebols* also resulted in such monopolistic exploitation at the micro level as creating scarcities, price gouging, and predatory behavior in the protected domestic market. The most serious consequence of the asymmetric promotion of *chaebols* was the impediment to the healthy growth of SMEs. Consequently, the lack of a supportive SME network caused heavy dependence by automobile and electronics *chaebols* on Japanese component suppliers.

These problems, however, are likely to be mitigated. Ongoing political reform in Korea is expected to make a major impact on efforts to eliminate corruption caused by the collusion of political powers and *chaebols*. Continuing import liberalization should limit opportunities for the *chaebols'* monopolistic exploitation of the domestic market.

Chaebols, as noted earlier, created many problems by their predatory behavior, but they are still more assets than liabilities in Korea's technological learning. They play a major role in strengthening Korea's technological capability and spearheading the globalization of Korean businesses because they have the necessary organizational, technical, and financial resources. With Korean *chaebols* participating in the economy of almost every country on the globe, the government should promote the healthy growth of SMEs to develop effective subcontracting links between large and small firms.

EDUCATION: FROM DRIVING FORCE TO BOTTLENECK

Chaebols are populated with well-trained Koreans who have empowered the Korean engines. Deprived of natural resources, the government and parents invested heavily in education, drastically expanding educational institutions, when Korea was very poor. Other catching-up countries also invested heavily in education, but what was unique to Korea was the well-balanced expansion in all levels of education prior to the launching of the industrialization drive. However, more rapid expansion of education relative to economic development created a short-term unemployment problem: high numbers of unemployed among the educated represented a serious social issue in the 1960s. The formation of educated human resources, albeit of poor quality, laid an important foundation for the subsequent reverse-engineering of mature foreign technologies.

The rapid expansion of Korean formal education produced a vast body of human resources, people with enough initial tacit knowledge to make sense of explicit knowledge embodied in foreign technology and to absorb tacit knowledge transferred to them in the early decades. Formal education also imbued important social norms and beliefs, which were essential to organized technological learning. The lack of valuable natural resources in Korea played a positive role in its development of abundant human capital. Furthermore, such resources, together with entrepreneurship, competitive capability, hard work, and determination, enabled Korea to prosper in a hostile environment.

Underinvestment in education in later decades has, however, resulted in a major bottleneck in Korea's technological learning, a problem that is most acute at the university level. Given deterioration in the quality of education and research at universities over the past three decades, all but a few universities have remained primarily teaching-oriented rather than research-oriented undergraduate institutions. Such relatively low tacit knowledge compared with increasingly complex technological tasks facing Korean firms is suspected to drag down R&D productivity in Korean firms. The scarcity of research-intensive universities also preempted the emergence of technology-based small firms. The government has contemplated enacting major educational reform.

There is, however, an encouraging sign regarding the quality of university education. The number of scientific publications by Koreans cited by the *Science Citation Index* increased slowly from 27 in 1973 to 171 in 1980, but rapidly to 1,227 in 1988 and 3,910 in 1994,[2] climbing from thirty-seventh in the world in 1988 to twenty-fourth in 1994.[3] Although the ranking is still quite low compared with Korea's 1994 rank of eleventh in gross national product (GNP), Korea achieved the highest annual growth rate (28.97 percent) in 1973–1994. Other large-growth countries include Taiwan (17.16 percent) and Singapore (11.96 percent). In other words, although Korean university R&D had long been weak, emphasis on university research resulted in significant achievements in building basic research capabilities.[4]

EXPORT-ORIENTED STRATEGY: A MAJOR SOURCE OF STIMULUS

The government's import-substitution and export policies also had decisively important influence on technological learning in industry. Import-substitution policy created the domestic market for *chaebols* to enter new industries and enjoy infant industry protection. More important, export promotion policy significantly affected technological learning in industry by creating a highly competitive market environment in which *chaebols* had to survive. At least five major effects may be mentioned.

First, this policy created business opportunities, concurrently imposing crises causing firms to undergo life-or-death struggles in the competitive international market. To survive the crises, Korean firms had to accelerate learning by importing and rapidly assimilating production technology from abroad. As the export promotion policy continually placed pressure on firms to sustain competitiveness in the changing international technology and market environment, export-oriented firms acquired more foreign technologies than import-substituting firms. Therefore, export-oriented industries accounted for the majority of Korean licensing and capital-goods imports. Furthermore, restrictions on foreign direct investment (FDI) forced firms to take an independent approach to assimilating imported technology, which provoked them to accelerate learning.

Second, Korean exporters made lump-sum investments for capacity in excess of local market size to achieve economies of scale. This resulted in crises, forcing local firms to accelerate technological learning to improve productivity and in turn international competitiveness to maximize capacity utilization.

Third, surviving in the dynamic international market required continual local efforts to improve imported technology. Export-oriented firms were forced to invest heavily in technological learning to sustain their competitiveness in both quality and price in the international market.

Fourth, the government always stood behind relatively well-managed firms in crises, providing necessary supports to make them creative rather than destructive. Much like a swimming instructor, the government forced firms into scary waters, then helped them stay afloat until they learned to swim. The assured government support emboldened Korean firms to attack successively more difficult technological challenges. In this fashion, the firms made quantum jumps in technological capability through discontinuous learning.

Finally, Korean firms relied heavily on foreign buyers of original equipment for marketing their products internationally. These buyers provided priceless help to Korean firms in acquiring necessary capability through interactive tutorial processes, allowing them to focus their efforts primarily on acquiring production capability.

As a result, firms in export-oriented industries learned significantly more rapidly and grew faster than firms in import-substituting industries. Likewise, countries with export-oriented industrialization grew faster than those with import-substituting industrialization.

Export-oriented strategy can be an effective means of imposing a crisis on manufacturers. Such a strategy creates a highly competitive market in which firms in catching-up countries have to accelerate technological learning to survive.

TECHNOLOGY TRANSFER POLICY

In the industrialization of catching-up countries, foreign technology transfer plays a major role in accelerating technological learning, providing higher tacit and explicit knowledge and useful interaction with foreign suppliers for effective learning.

The Korean government restricted the inflow of FDI and foreign licenses (FLs) to protect the local market from multinational companies. Instead, it promoted technology transfer through imports of foreign capital goods to strengthen international competitiveness of capital-goods-consuming industries at the cost of retarding development of the local machinery industry. The restriction on FDI enabled Korean firms to maintain independence from management control of multinational corporations in Korea, which set an important ground rule for the direction of Korean firms' technological learning. The restriction on FLs enabled Korean firms to strengthen their bargaining power in negotiating transfer of mature, but complex technologies.

But the promotional policy for capital-goods imports forced Korean firms to rely heavily on reverse-engineering of the foreign goods. The restrictions could have negative results, for example, slow learning owing to restricted inflow of foreign technologies and dependency on foreign suppliers owing to unrestricted inflow of their goods. However, well-trained, hardworking Koreans were motivated to maximize technological learning from readily available foreign goods, and they had sufficient tacit knowledge to reverse-engineer them successfully.

The government gradually relaxed the restrictions on FDI and FLs in the 1970s, as Korean industries progressed in absorbing increasingly more complex technologies. Flexible adjustment of public policies in response to the changing economic environment is essential to those policies in meeting industrial needs constructively and in effectively facilitating technological learning.

RESEARCH AND DEVELOPMENT POLICY

Given the inadequacy of Korean university research, the government developed a network of R&D institutes (GRIs) to play a major role in advanced industrial R&D. The Korea Institute of Science and Technology (KIST) and its spin-off GRIs spent a large proportion of the nation's total R&D funds in the early decades, but they suffered from poor linkage with industries in the 1960s and 1970s. Most Korean government-recruited scientists and engineers came from either academic institutions or R&D organizations that undertook advanced research, but there was no demand from industries for the kind of expertise GRIs could offer. The discrepancy was that these researchers lacked manufacturing know-how related to developing prototypes, which were in great demand early on. Consequently, Korean researchers could not compete with foreign licenses in supplying detailed blueprints and other manufacturing specialization, nor were they able to assist industries in solving teething problems in the crucial initial stage.[5]

In attempting to establish an effective linkage between GRIs and the private sector, the government coerced large firms to undertake joint research with the GRIs. Some large firms initiated joint research efforts, which ended for the most part in disappointing results. Private firms were preoccupied with developing production capability, while GRIs offered expertise in helping firms enhance investment and innovation capabilities. In short, the supply of GRI technological capability cannot be effective in the absence of demand from the private sector.

Despite these problems, GRIs produced many significant research results. The private firms, however, shunned the commercialization of these results, as they were skeptical about the institutes' engineering and production competence. After several failed attempts to transfer the results to the private sector, KIST, for instance, established its own production subsidiaries to commercialize them and a holding company to finance and supervise the subsidiaries.

Nevertheless, GRIs played an important role in helping firms acquire foreign technology in the early years of industrialization. The R&D facilities helped firms strengthen their bargaining power in acquiring foreign technology. Joint research with GRIs provided opportunities for firms to acquire prior knowledge about technology, enabling them to identify prospective suppliers. Once the technology was imported, experience gained in joint research enabled firms to assimilate and adapt it rapidly.

GRIs also played a significant role in informally transferring and diffusing technology within the economy through reverse-engineering foreign technologies. For example, when a Japanese company refused to transfer polyester film production to Korea for fear of losing its market there, a Korean chemical firm, in collaboration with KIST, successfully reverse-engineered the technology. Korea has become one of the world's major suppliers of audio- and videocassette tapes.[6] In his study of Latin American countries, James Utterback concludes that the major role of GRIs in catching-up countries is to facilitate and lubricate transfer by assisting the private sector's acquisition of foreign technology either formally or informally.[7]

The most important, though unintended, GRI role during an early stage was to generate experienced researchers when the private sector failed to employ R&D investment. Then, in the 1980s, when *chaebols* began establishing corporate R&D centers to respond to market competition, these experienced researchers spun out of the GRIs to play a pivotal role in private R&D centers.

GRIs have also been a backbone of national R&D since 1982. Projects cover a wide range of mission-oriented applied research from aerospace to application-specific integrated circuits, paving the way for the private sector's subsequent entry. For industrial R&D, the mission-oriented approach is generally believed to be less effective than the diffusion-oriented, which rarely set specific technological objectives. Rather, the diffusion-oriented approach seeks to provide a broadly based ability to adjust to a technological change throughout the industrial structure.[8] An extensive network of effective institutions, from which the firms could get necessary support in developing new products and processes, is an important instrument in this approach.

Over the years, however, the role of GRIs vis-à-vis *chaebols'* corporate R&D centers has weakened for two reasons. First, the GRI centers have been far less dynamic than those of corporations. The former are controlled by the government bureaucracy, whose rigid regulations stifle the vibrant life of creative individuals. However, the latter, controlled by their markets, respond dynamically to market and technological changes for survival. Second, GRIs encounter difficulty in retaining competent researchers, who jump either to academic institutions, which offer prestige and freedom, or to corporate laboratories, which offer better economic incentives.

In addition, the government has been so preoccupied with mission-oriented projects that it failed to develop effective infrastructure for SME promotion. The technical extension networks developed in the 1980s did not prove adequate for encouraging such enterprises to grow technologically. In the 1990s, Korea belatedly established a few industry-specific R&D laboratories for SMEs, but their effectiveness is still in question.

Korean experience indicates that the role of government institutes should evolve. In the early years of industrialization, GRIs should provide the private sector with technical assistance to enable it to strengthen its bargaining power in technology transfer and assimilate and adapt imported technology rapidly. In other words, GRIs should not be evaluated by the number of patents or significant research they generate and transfer to the private sector but rather by the number of experienced researchers they train, individuals who can play a pivotal role in private-sector industrial R&D. They should also be evaluated through their role in helping the private sector transfer foreign technology economically and assimilate and improve it effectively.

When *chaebols* developed their own extensive R&D network, GRIs should have adjusted their roles to find their own niche. GRIs are still in a favorable position to develop technologies related to environment, agriculture, public health, nuclear energy, and other non-commerce-oriented projects. These require so much economic externality that private firms find it difficult to appropriate R&D outcomes. GRIs and other supporting institutions could also play crucial roles through extension services in helping SMEs acquire technological capability.

SOCIOCULTURAL FACTORS

Another important influence on rapid technological learning in industry in the early decades was sociocultural environment, which set a stage for Korean behavior and the people's social interactions. Cultural and situational factors worked together to shape the Korean mind-set.

Cultural Factors

Confucian culture still permeates Korean society. However, traditional Confucian values have been significantly altered by Christianity. The new Confucian ethics—an amalgam of the family and collectively oriented values of the East with the pragmatic, economic-goal-oriented values of the West—is most visible in Korea. It emphasizes education, clan, harmonious interpersonal relations, action, and discipline. These cultural characteristics must have played a critical role in inculcating a set of values in the Korean mind. For instance, Koreans, like other east Asians, value education. Historically, traditional as well as new Confucian ethics puts great emphasis on education. Koreans also believe more strongly in the great and direct return on education than most developing societies in which upward mobility depends largely on vested social interests; hence the greater private demand for education and learning in Korea. Education is a vitally important prerequisite to technological learning.

Situational Factors

Situational factors appear to have influenced the instillation of the Korean work ethic more strongly than cultural factors. The perseverance of Korean people in turmoil and hardship inflicted by foreign invasions, the associated *han* psyche that produces energy, disciplined work habits formed during "exam hell" school days, the dense population and severe cold that forced Koreans to work competitively, and the memory of deprivation bred the hardworking trait into the country's workers.

Of all situational factors, the 1950–1953 Korean War brought the most lasting, and paradoxically, positive impact on the subsequent industrialization of Korea. The war caused a major exodus from North Korea to the south and social turmoil, amalgamating people not only from different geographical areas but also from different families and classes. This made Korean society a lot more flexible, mobile, and free from social segregation than it was before the war. Furthermore, compulsory military service brought together young men from diverse geographical, social, and family backgrounds to undergo the same experiences for an extended period, breaking long-standing social barriers. These young men received military training, accepted the strictest discipline, experienced tightly intertwined organizational life; enlisted men and noncommissioned officers learned to manage small groups, while officers learned to command large organizations. They also learned to handle sophisticated military technology and manage complex logistical support systems using modern transport and communications. In other words, despite the fact that the war destroyed the majority of industrial and infrastructure facilities Korea had inherited from the Japanese and caused more than one million civilian casualties, it laid an important foundation for later industrial development by destroying the highly rigid class society and creating a new order of social flexibility in Korea. Were it not for the war, it would have taken far longer, with far more social barriers to be surmounted, for Korea to become industrialized.

Cultural and situational factors have had a decisive role in instilling a strong work ethic among Koreans. A strong desire for education formed a requisite knowledge base, and a hardworking population gave rise to an intensity of effort, which led to rapid technological learning in Korean firms. In this sense, cultural and situational factors are the most decisive prerequisite to technological learning.

LEARNING STRATEGY IN THE PRIVATE SECTOR

In the dynamic environment of the macroeconomic level, Korean firms deployed various strategies for expediting imitative technological learning. These strategies include the sequence of capability building, the differing learning approaches of apprentices and imitators, four learning phases, R&D investment, organization/management, crisis construction, and technology transfer.

Sequence of Capability Building

Korean firms had deliberate strategies for developing technological capabilities. Using different types of production technology—small-batch, mass-production, and continuous-process[9]—they sequenced differently three grossly categorized technological capabilities: production, investment, and innovation.[10] All firms, large and small, emphasized the acquisition of production capability at the outset in order to bring about immediate and effective implementation of production operations. But large firms soon diverted their efforts to acquire different types of capability to maximize the fruits of their efforts.

Large firms using small-batch systems, for example, shipbuilders and machinery makers, shifted their emphasis from the initial production capability to design capability, as they usually create highly differentiated commodities in a most flexible production system. Although effective production management is essential to maximizing productivity, the most important competitive advantage of these industries lies in their own capability or technical ties with foreign firms to design and produce vastly differentiated, custom-ordered products. Investment capability (capacity to design and erect new production systems) is less important for them, as expansions can be achieved by adding capital. Table 9-1 shows the sequence of capability building in different production systems.

Large firms using mass-production systems, for example, in the electronics and automobile industries, produced fewer differentiated products in a more systematized system, calling for capability both to design products and to optimize production systems. For this reason, large firms in these industries also depended on foreign licensing but to a lesser extent than those with small-batch operations, reflecting the degree and frequency of product differentiation. Emphasis then shifted to acquiring of investment and innovation capabilities. The ability to expand a production system, which is more complex than a small-batch system, and the ability to innovate products were equally important.

Industries using continuous-process systems, for example, chemicals, cement, paper, and steel, produced the least differentiated products in a highly systematized and capital-intensive process. This places primary emphasis on investment capability soon after acquisition of initial production capability. Since the proprietary know-how inherent in the details of a production process can make a significant difference in the productivity of these industries, the initial systems of large chemical, cement, and steel plants were established on a turnkey basis by Western firms.

Dynamic traditional small firms, however, regardless of type of production system, continued to focus mainly on production capability to create imitative goods by reverse engineering. Emerging technology-

Table 9-1 Sequence of Capability Building

Production Pattern	Firm Size	Sources of Initial Technology	Indigenous Efforts to Assimilate Foreign Technology	Emphasis on Acquisition of Technological Capability[a]
Small-batch and Unit Production	Large	Foreign licensing	High and rapid	Production→ Innovation
	Small[b]	Own imitative efforts	Low and slow	Production
	Tech-based Small	Own innovative efforts	High and rapid	Innovation→ Production→ Investment
Large-batch and Mass Production	Large	Foreign licensing	High and rapid	Production→ Investment ↘ Innovation
	Small[b]	NA[c]	NA[c]	
Continuous-Process Production	Large	Turnkey and consultancies	High and rapid	Production→ Investment→ Innovation
	Small[b]	Imitative	Low and slow	Production

SOURCE: Linsu Kim and Hosun Lee, "Patterns of Technological Change in a Rapidly Developing Country: A Synthesis," *Technovation* 6, no 4 (1987); 261–276.

NOTES: [a] Production refers to capability to operate and maintain systems, investment to capability to design and erect new systems and expansions, and innovation to capability to innovate and improve products and processes.
[b] Emerging technology-based small firms exhibit dynamic behavior in capability building and innovation.
[c] Small firms in the electronics and automobile industries deploy small-batch technology rather than a large-batch system.

based small firms, however, sequenced from innovation capability to production capability to investment capability.

Small-batch industries proceeded sequentially from production capability to innovation capability, whereas mass-production industries sequenced from production capability, then to investment and innovation capabilities simultaneously. In contrast, continuous-process industries began with production capability, then moved to investment and finally to innovation capabilities. These sequences in different industries appear to be logical and rational, offering implications for firms in catching-up countries to allocate resources properly.

Apprentices versus Imitators

There also appear to be several commonalities across the aforementioned industries. First, large firms were initially dependent on acquiring foreign production technology. Why? Given the scale of large investment required and the lack of technological capability and experience in the early years, local firms were highly motivated to look to experienced foreign firms. With their help, the locals were ensured of swift construction and smooth start-up of their production processes, and they acquired technological information and training to manufacture goods with stringent specifications. It may also be that large local firms possessed an adequate organizational capability to negotiate and finance foreign technology imports. Such firms are known as apprentices.

On the other hand, small firms across the industries took an imitative approach in developing the initial processes and products and evolved slowly in acquiring technological capability. The initial processes, developed in-house, were quite primitive ones based on related foreign products. One reason for this was that these firms had neither the financial resources nor organizational capability to identify and negotiate collaborative agreements with foreign suppliers. Also, it was relatively easier to adopt primitive production technology for a small operation than for a large one. Small firms catered to a market that did not demand sophisticated products. Such firms are known as imitators.

Imitators characteristically achieved a major leap in technological capability through technical personnel stolen from larger firms or by importing new equipment. Technical personnel brought in higher tacit knowledge, while new equipment provided higher explicit knowledge. Technological diffusion within these imitator industries spread rapidly through the mobility of experienced engineers from large to small firms.

Nevertheless, both apprentices and imitators deployed deliberate and aggressive strategies to acquire their own technological capabilities by striving to assimilate foreign technologies from the very outset.

Phases in Technological Learning

For apprentices, these efforts, as shown in Table 9-2, may include four phases: (1) preparation, (2) acquisition through technology transfer, (3) assimilation through enhanced in-house efforts in learning (leading to the rapid import substitution of personnel, engineering, and components), and (4) improvement, making incremental advancement on imported technology and applying it to related products.

When *chaebols* set up their initial production systems on a large scale, they resorted to foreign licensing. LG Electronics's licensing of black and white TV set production and Hyundai Motor's acquisition of production technology from Ford are examples.[11] In such cases, Korean firms appear to have progressed through all four phases. First, without adequate tacit knowledge to challenge new technology, *chaebols* took preparatory measures to gain necessary tacit knowledge, including luring experienced personnel from outside, extensive search and mastery of the literature, observation of technology in operation, and joint research with local public R&D institutes. The tacit knowledge gained from experienced personnel, albeit insufficient alone, made it possible for the team members to comprehend the advanced explicit knowledge in literature. The members were then sent to observe facilities in operation in advanced countries, where they had opportunities to relate their tacit knowledge from literature to actual physical settings.

In the second phase, the tacit knowledge base helped Korean firms identify the sources of technology and strengthen their bargaining power against foreign suppliers in technology transfer negotiations. Then, the acquisition of foreign licenses brought in higher explicit knowledge (designs, technical specifications, production manuals, etc.) from abroad. Training by foreign technology suppliers (transfer of tacit knowledge embodied in foreign personnel to Korean engineers and technicians), accompanied by explicit knowledge, enabled highly motivated Koreans to assimilate the technology rapidly.

In the third phase, Korean firms intensified their in-house efforts to expedite the assimilation of imported foreign technology. The comprehensive explicit knowledge and effective training provided by foreign suppliers were indispensable for effective technology transfer. More important, however, were the high tacit knowledge base and the

Table 9-2 Patterns of Capability Building

Phases	First Stage	Second Stage	Third Stage	Fourth Stage
Learning Phases				
Preparation	Poaching experienced personnel; literature review; observation tour	Literature review; observation tour; foreign personnel	Literature review; observation tour	Poaching scientists; literature review
Acquisition	Packaged technology transfer; foreign personnel	Unpackaged technology transfer	Unpackaged technology transfer	Acquisition by research; overseas R&D; foreign expatriates
Assimilation	Learning by doing	Learning by doing	Learning by doing	Learning by research
Improvement/ Application	Learning by doing	Learning by doing	Learning by doing	Learning by research

NOTE: This table is based on a specific Hyundai Motor Company experience.

intensity of effort of the Korean firms. This made foreign technology licensing effective, as tacit knowledge can be built largely through experience. Assimilation of "know-how" took place primarily through learning by doing in production during the initial stage. To expedite assimilation with minimum trial and error, Korean firms often hired foreign engineers as tutors for an extended period, as was the case at Hyundai Motor.

In the fourth phase, Korean firms improved imported technology in order to adapt it to local market needs. Given a high tacit knowledge base and intensity of effort, it was not at all difficult for Korean firms to bring about incremental improvements to satisfy changing needs of both domestic and overseas markets. Tacit knowledge gained in assimilating imported technology was applied to similar products. There were two motives behind efforts to assimilate and improve imported foreign technologies. First, dependence on foreign sources for new ventures and expansions is costly and limits the economic activities of recipient firms with restrictive clauses in technology transfer contracts. Second, the freedom and ability to institute even minor improvements in product design and production operations can lead to significant betterment of a firm's competitiveness.

After successfully completing these four phases, a Korean firm was usually ready to enter more sophisticated technological areas. If foreign firms were still willing to license technology to Korean firms—and they often were—the Koreans again cycled through the preparation, acquisition, assimilation, and improvement phases. Hyundai Motor, for instance, thoroughly studied literature related to design technology and scheduled observation tours of several firms in advanced countries. Then Hyundai licensed foreign technologies from many different sources. At the same time it recruited capable foreign engineers to increase its tacit knowledge base to assimilate the more sophisticated foreign technologies. This time it assumed full responsibility for integrating those technologies, which it licensed in an unpackaged form.

In some industries, the four phases were repeated more than once in the third cycle of Table 9-2 as they advanced from simple to more sophisticated technology and foreign suppliers were continually willing to transfer it. This occurred in Hyundai Motor's move from Pony in the mid-1970s to Excel in the mid-1980s and Samsung's move from 64K to 256K DRAM.

When a Korean firm faced even more sophisticated technology far beyond its accumulated capability and foreign firms were reluctant to transfer patented and copyrighted technology, the firm typically cracked the technology through advanced reverse engineering.[12] Microwave ovens, videocassette recorders, and some semiconductor memory chips are examples. At this stage, "know-why" is as, if not more, important as know-how. During Stage 4 the firm underwent a similar process from the preparation phase through improvement phase. The preparation phase involved literature study, recruiting high-caliber Korean-American scientists, and often developing R&D outposts. Advanced reverse engineering in Stage 4 required more learning by research than learning by doing. Only after Korean firms developed the technologies did foreign firms reluctantly license them for export.

A relatively well-educated workforce and the continued inflow of Korean-American scientists and engineers helped sustain the growth of tacit knowledge to match the rapidly advancing technological frontier. This equipped Korean firms to crack emerging technologies, narrowing the gap with advanced countries. The firms hastened the catch-up process largely by constructing crises to intensify efforts. The impact of knowledge and effort was present in every stage of the four phases.

Some Korean industries completed all four stages and stand near the technological frontier. They must generate new technology without recourse to reverse engineering, advanced reverse engineering, or licensing. From here on in-house R&D, R&D outposts, mergers and acquisitions, and strategic alliances may be the major mechanisms for generating new knowledge.

Heavy Investment in R&D

Facing the need to shift to higher-value technology-intensive products, Korean industries drastically raised their R&D investments in recent decades. Though the Korean economy recorded one of the world's fastest growth rates, R&D expenditures rose even faster than GNP. R&D increased its share of GNP from 0.32 to 2.61 percent in 1971–1994, surpassing that of the United Kingdom. This is an encouraging sign for Korea's innovation drive.

Korea's growth rate is the highest in the world. For instance, the average annual growth rate of nations' R&D investment per gross domestic product (GDP) in 1981–1991 is highest in Korea, 24.2 percent, compared with 22.3 percent in Singapore, 15.8 percent in Taiwan, 11.4 percent in Spain, and 7.4 percent in Japan. The average annual growth rate of business R&D per GDP is also highest in Korea, 31.6 percent, compared with 23.8 percent in Singapore, 16.5 percent in Taiwan, 14 percent in Spain, and 8.8 percent in Japan.[13]

Other important indicators of Korea's rapid growth in industrial R&D are patent registrations in Korea and abroad. Korean patents have risen significantly in the past two decades compared with the previous two, increasing a mere 48 percent in 1965–1978 but almost tripling in 1979–1989 and almost tripling again in 1989–1993. This reflects the expanding importance of intellectual property rights in the face of declining reverse-engineering. The gap is still great when it is compared with advanced countries, but Korea is catching up rapidly. Furthermore, the Korean share of local patent registration also swelled from 11.4 percent in 1980 to 39.7 percent in 1993, indicating rising R&D activities. Korea was fifth in the world in 1993 in the number of industrial property applications, following Japan, the United States, China, and Germany, which is impressive compared with its eleventh rank in GNP.[14] For industrial property applications by local residents per population, Korea ranks second, following Japan.[15]

U.S. patent registration is often used as a surrogate measure of international competitiveness. The number of U.S. patents held by Koreans is far below that of the Taiwanese, let alone those of advanced countries. The cumulative number of U.S. patents granted to Koreans between 1969 and 1992 is only 1,751 compared with 4,978 to Taiwanese. But Korea jumped from thirty-fifth in rank among the thirty-six countries listed in a National Technical Information Service report, with five patents in 1969, to eleventh, with 538 patents, in 1992 for an average annual growth rate of 43.32 percent, the highest among the countries in the report. This indicates once again that Korea has been gaining rapidly in international technological competitiveness.[16]

Finally, although Korea began investing in R&D relatively late, it has spent heavily in that area to strengthen its technological competitiveness in the past decade. This again demonstrates Korea's determination and can-do spirit in technology-intensive as well as in labor-intensive industries.

Organization and Management

The government functioned as manager of the program of forced-march industrialization that enabled Korea to achieve significant progress in a decade or so. In the beginning, the 1961 military coup enabled the government of Park Chung Hee to free itself from the rent-seeking tendencies of Korean politicians and bureaucrats that marked Syngman Rhee's government.[17] Business licenses and financial resources were allocated on the basis of economic efficiency. But corruption set in gradually and such tactics returned, making the state the most critical source of uncertainty for firms. In allotting the means and resources critical to success and exercising other administrative powers, the government could make a firm a winner or a loser.

In this environment, with the state the major source of constraints and contingencies, Korean firms developed "conservation-of-power rationality."[18] They sought collusion with powerful politicians and technocrats to gain access to lucrative businesses and to maximize the predictability of the environment. Few Korean businesses could have grown into *chaebols* without such political patronage.

Once it became a *chaebol,* the most critical capability for a business was the top manager's political skills at developing and sustaining such collaborative relationships with the government. It was also his entrepreneurship that selected lucrative businesses. With so much of the firm's success resting in the top manager's personal skills, Korean industry naturally adopted a top-down management style. This imperative combined with the rule of military government over three decades fostered management that resembled a military bureaucracy, hierarchical and centrally controlled but relatively less formal. The notion of Confucian traditions fit comfortably with this style.

Unlike formal bureaucratic organizations, Korean firms were adaptable to change once the "commanding general" made a decision. These organizations were quite compatible with and efficient in imitative reverse-engineering and production-oriented tasks in the 1960s and 1970s.

The developments in business environment pose new competitive challenges for Korean management. The slowdown of the world economy, protectionist policies in North America and Europe, the rapid growth of real wages, rising challenges from second-tier catching-up countries, and import liberalization in their protected home market all require major reorientation in the organization and management of Korean firms. Furthermore, economic democratization and the consequent disorderly labor movement increase workers' dissatisfaction with a military-type, centrally controlled hierarchy.

The efficiency-oriented militaristic organization can be a major hindrance, however, to raising the innovation capability of Korean firms through R&D. The bureaucratic system adopted to maintain order in a large firm in its early stage is too slow to respond to the dynamically changing technological environment a firm faces in its later stages. In addition, the development of human resource management techniques has been seriously retarded in Korean firms because they are organized around a task-oriented military bureaucracy.

Many *chaebols* are aware of the problems facing their organizational and managerial style, and they are making major changes. They find, however, that while organizational structure and management system can be changed overnight, changing the behavior of managers and organization members to make them compatible with a new system is more difficult and takes a long time. Most Korean managers and workers have never experienced any other type of organization.[19] *Fortune* magazine reports that it takes six to fifteen years to change organizational culture,[20] requiring perhaps 5 to 10 percent of a firm's annual budget to bring about cultural change.[21]

Korean *chaebols* have to transform themselves into innovation-oriented, initiation-viable organizations. This type of organization requires a decentralized, self-contained, strategic business unit structure; an organizational climate that nurtures creative individuals and efficient small groups; effective and flexible lateral coordination across R&D, marketing, and production responsibility; and bottom-up communication to identify and respond quickly to market opportunities and threats and technological possibilities, which is almost the opposite of the existing bureaucracy in Korean firms. This transformation is one of the most formidable tasks facing Korean *chaebols*.

Another major weakness in management is the high transaction costs involved in the typical interorganizational relations of Korean firms. The exploitation of small and medium-size enterprises by large firms in the form of deferred payments and the wide practice of offering financial kickbacks have raised firms' costs, particularly for SMEs. This, together with a public policy biased against Korean SMEs, has retarded their growth in efficacy. As a result, end-product producing *chaebols* have to rely heavily on Japan for high-technology parts and components, thus critically constraining innovation at firms of all sizes. Without fluid supports from capable small-parts and component suppliers, Korean firms will continue to lag behind in product and process innovation and remain vulnerable in price and quality in competition with Japanese rivals.[22]

Crisis Construction

The government has often imposed crises on *chaebols* to realize overly ambitious goals. The most dramatic case was the promotion of heavy and chemical industries (HCIs) at far greater intensity, much earlier, and in a far shorter time than originally envisioned as a way to create a defense industry in the wake of the Nixon doctrine. The hasty creation of HCIs on a gigantic scale without adequate preparation in technological capability resulted in misallocation of resources, rapid inflation, wage increases, and further concentration of economic powers in a few *chaebols*. The most significant effect of the HCI drive, however, was a major crisis in technological learning. Overcoming the crisis prompted Korean firms to make a great leap in technological capability.

In the militaristic Korean firms, top management used crises as a major means of opportunistic learning, as discussed in Chapters 5, 6, and 7. Hyundai Motor, for one, constructed a series of crises to expedite technological learning by setting overly challenging goals in acquiring and assimilating foreign technologies. A similar learning process is also evident, albeit to a different degree, in other Korean companies and industries. To mention a few, electronics, shipbuilding, steel, and machinery firms underwent a similar process of crisis construction and expeditious learning in catching up, which are widespread in Korean manufacturing, where the quality of final products can easily be tested by users.[23]

Technology Transfer Strategy

Discussions on technological learning in the electronics industry illustrate an interesting pattern in foreign technology transfer in Korean firms. When technology was simple and mature and patents had already expired, Korean firms with sufficient tacit knowledge and intensity of effort did not purchase it through formal mechanisms; rather, they reverse-engineered foreign products, producing knockoffs or clones (Figure 9-1, Stage 1). This was particularly true for small firms.

When the technology was complex yet sufficiently mature (specific stage in Figure 4-2, Chapter 4) for foreign firms to transfer it willingly to Korean firms, and if the Koreans were unable to reverse-engineer it, they resorted largely to licensing. This strategy enabled Korean firms to acquire both tacit (training and supervision) and explicit (blueprints, product specifications, production manual, etc.) knowledge, which they assimilated in the shortest possible time.

When the technology was in the growing stage of its life cycle (transition stage, Figure 4-2) with unexpired patents, foreign firms were usually protective and unwilling to transfer it to Korean firms. Those with insufficient capability could not progress further, but some firms built enough expertise with the assistance of local government R&D institutes or smaller foreign firms to crack it through advanced reverse-engineering (Stage 3). Foreign firms often filed suit against Korean firms for infringement of intellectual property rights. Legal settlement eventually led to formal licensing.

When emerging technologies were involved (fluid stage, Figure 4-2), foreign firms were again protective and unwilling to transfer

Figure 9-1 Technology Transfer Strategy
Consumer Electronics Industry

	Low ⟶ Sophistication of Foreign Technology ⟶ High				
Supplier's Conditions	Simple and mature products, patent expired	Mature products, patented, or patent expired	Growing products, patented	Emerging products, patented	No products, capability to offer
Supplier's Strategy	Willing to transfer	Willing to transfer	Protective, unwilling to transfer	Protective, unwilling to transfer	Willing to cooperate
Recipient's Conditions	Sufficient capability	Insufficient capability	Sufficient capability	Insufficient capability	Capability to offer
Recipient's Strategy	Reverse engineering	Licensing, assimilation	Advanced reverse engineering	R&D outposts, merger and acquisition	Strategic alliance
Mode of Technology Transfer	Foreign products	Willing to license	Reluctant to license	Monitoring equity participation	Joint R&D, technology sharing
Stage	(1)	(2)	(3)	(4)	(5)
	Low ⟶ Level of Technological Capability of Recipients ⟶ High				

SOURCE: Consumer Electronics Industry

them to Koreans. Technology was so near the frontier that the latter firms could not learn from alternative R&D sources, and they found it difficult to develop sufficient competence to solve it. Some leading *chaebols* established R&D branches in the United States, Japan, and Europe to monitor the development of the emerging technology and bought equity stakes in foreign firms that possessed it. Hyundai's acquisition of AT&T-GIS for nonmemory chips, Samsung's investment in AST for personal computers, and LG's acquisition of Zenith for high-definition television gave them access to patents and other intellectual property rights, and each of them established R&D facilities in Silicon Valley.

Finally, Korean firms in advanced stages began to enter strategic alliances to develop technology. *Chaebol* affiliations include such leading firms as IBM, Apple, Intel, Fujitsu, Xerox, Microsoft, and Toshiba.

SUMMARY

This chapter draws conclusions on how Korean firms achieved and what factors are behind their phenomenal growth in technological learning. Most catching-up countries have tried to industrialize their economies, yet most have made little progress; only a few managed a significant stride in catching up. What conditions, then, make catching up possible? They may be diverse, and the Korean experience may be only one of them.

Korea's rapid technological learning may be attributed to the complex interactions of diverse factors: (1) the government's orchestrating role in directing *chaebols* and selectively allocating resources to them to achieve ambitious growth objectives in the early years and its supporting role in lowering corporate R&D costs; (2) entrepreneurs' can-do spirit exercised freely under restricted equity participation of multinationals; (3) *chaebols* that have advantages in mobilizing resources for technological learning; (4) well-trained, hardworking humans who were willing to learn; (5) to facilitate learning, the continuous inflow of foreign technology through formal and informal mechanisms; (6) competitive stimuli from the export market; (7) drastic increases in R&D investment, particularly in the private sector; and (8) government-imposed crises and top management-constructed crises as a major means to expedite technological learning in catching up. These factors have worked together to prompt Korean firms to learn and unlearn cumulatively and discontinuously, leading to their amazing growth.

In other words, a strong government with competent technocrats is an essential condition in the early stage of industrialization. Only after President Park and his competent economic advisors emerged and exercised strong leadership did the Korean economy get off the ground. Strong government alone, however, cannot be a sufficient condition. Many low-income countries that have authoritarian governments with competent economic advisers do not find it difficult to emulate public policy programs of successful catching-up countries, but they make little progress in industrialization. Major problems in these countries are the short supply of entrepreneurs and a skilled workforce that could implement national economic goals.

Similarly, other government programs cannot be effective without the presence of competitive firms. For example, a restrictive technology transfer policy worked well in Korea at the beginning only because there were independent-minded entrepreneurs and a relatively well-educated workforce determined to expedite technological learning through a reverse-engineering process. The export market is open to all catching-up countries, but only a few can take advantage because only a small number can develop the technological ability to tap it. Even crisis imposition or construction cannot lead to creative learning; it would be a disaster were it not for entrepreneurs and their hardworking labor force. Here sociocultural factors and education shape the mind-set and skills of people involved in the economy.

In short, successful technological learning cannot be explained by one or two factors. It requires an effective national innovation system, one that is an interactive, and therefore socially embedded, complex process of diverse formal and informal institutions in the situational and cultural contexts of a nation-state. Such a system should have an array of well-balanced public programs that create an economic environment conducive to the smooth inflow of foreign technology that reduces the cost of technological learning and is competitive enough to force firms to expedite that learning. The system should also bring about productive interaction not only between government programs and the private sector but also between suppliers and buyers. Here, sociocultural factors such as moral and social norms, customs, and traditions that shape habits and routines in an interactive learning process are as, if not more, important as formal institutions such as rules, laws, government agencies, banks, and technical support systems.

10 Korea's Technological Learning: Implications

As set forth in Chapter 1, Korea achieved phenomenal growth in three decades in the course of changing from a subsistent agricultural economy to an industrialized one. In 1960 the poorest of the newly industrialized countries, by 1995 it had become one of the most advanced. Behind this spectacular performance lies rapid technological learning in industry. The preceding chapters discussed the ways in which the Korean government, institutions within the country and abroad, sociocultural factors, and industry interacted in facilitating learning.

Chapter 9 offered an overview and drew conclusions regarding that experience. This chapter discusses the implications of Korea's background for both suppliers and recipients of technology, public policymakers, corporate managers, and Korea's future. It also presents connotations for other catching-up countries that may wish to emulate the Korean transformation.

IMPLICATIONS FOR SUPPLIERS OF TECHNOLOGY

The preceding chapters covered the way Korea expedited technological learning by acquiring foreign technologies through formal and informal mechanisms. Were it not for such foreign technologies, Korea's technological catching up would have been inordinately retarded. For this reason, some individuals in advanced countries argue that their firms should restrict technology transfer to catching-up countries in order to protect their own interests, that its long-term effect is negative. They argue that such transfers have boomerang effects, ultimately damaging their own international competitiveness. Therefore, should firms in advanced countries strive to stop transferring technology to catching-up countries? Can they stop it? The evidence presented here suggests that the answer to both questions is no.[1]

Any attempt to restrict technology transfer to catching-up countries through a first mode of market-mediated and active suppliers such as foreign direct investment (FDI), foreign licenses (FLs), and turnkey plants, as illustrated in Figure 4-4, results in negative consequences. Restricting FDI risks jeopardizing the global strategy of multinational firms, while restricting FLs risks shortening the economic life cycle of their technologies and products. If one supplier firm or nation refuses to transfer technology, a sophisticated buyer of technology in catching-up countries can usually turn to an alternative source. The astute buyer can also turn to advanced reverse-engineering or hire retired foreign experts as consultants.

Efforts to limit transfers through a second mode, market-mediated and passive suppliers, for example, standardized machinery transfer, could succeed only in limiting capital-goods trade, a self-defeating proposition. The evidence in Chapters 2 and 8 suggests that Korean firms, particularly those in the machinery industry, appear to have learned more from imported capital goods than from other types of technology transfer. A study offers useful insights into the way Korean firms innovate by taking advantage of locally available foreign products.[2]

The third transfer modes, nonmarket-mediated and active suppliers of, for instance, informal technical assistance, are similarly important means of economic activities for firms in advanced countries. Original equipment manufacturing in catching-up countries is a strategy of international sourcing of components and end products for firms in advanced countries to sustain price competitiveness in both domestic and international markets. Technical assistance from suppliers is simply an extra service needed to conclude sales.

Firms in advanced countries can do little to stop technology transfer through a fourth mode, nonmarket-mediated and passive suppliers such as reverse-engineering, observation, technical literature, and so on. These are the outcome of the absorptive capacity and entrepreneurship of firms and institutions in catching-up countries. Foreign technologies transferred through other means serve as important inputs for reverse engineering. For instance, the innovative and profitable Shinpoong Paper, described in Chapter 8, never entered collaborative arrangements with foreign partners but progressively reverse engineered foreign models in developing its most sophisticated, computerized papermaking line.

None of the technology transfer modes can be restricted by advanced country suppliers to reduce the boomerang effects from catching-up countries, and no firm or nation can maintain technological leadership through stringent controls of technology outflow. Witness the United Kingdom, which, in the nineteenth century, restricted the transfer of steam engines and the migration of skilled workers to catching-up countries. Transfers are likely to continue at a significant rate. On the supply side, alternative sources of technology are increasing and the firms that possess it may have to transfer it to expand sales and extend the economic life of their technologies to maximize their return. On the demand side, catching-up firms have developed increasing capabilities to exert strong bargaining power in acquiring foreign technologies, to master imported technologies, and to undertake R&D to create their own innovations. Only through continual innovations can technology suppliers in advanced countries maintain their position of leadership.

What then is the optimal strategic path for technology suppliers? Figure 10-1 schematically represents the preceding discussions and their implications for suppliers. In quadrant 2, where suppliers transfer technologies but catching-up firms do not have absorptive capacity, the suppliers enjoy technological power and recipients suffer from the syndromes of technological dependency. This represents the typical outcome of a zero-sum game. In contrast, no one gains in quadrant 4, where suppliers are unwilling to transfer their technology and catching-up firms do not have the skill to benefit from the existing technology.

It is in quadrants 1 and 3, where firms in catching-up countries have absorptive capacity, that technology suppliers in advanced countries worry about the backfiring effects of transfer. But regardless of whether or not a particular firm in an advanced country is willing to transfer technology through formal mechanisms, firms in catching-up countries in quadrants 1 and 3 would be able to acquire foreign technologies, either from alternative sources or through informal

Figure 10-1 Strategy for Suppliers of Technology

	Absorptive Capacity of Recipients	
	High	**Low**
Willingness of Suppliers to Transfer Technology to Recipients through Formal Mechanisms — Yes	Technology transfer takes place. Both suppliers and recipients gain. (1)	Technology transfer takes place. Suppliers gain but recipients become dependent. (2)
No	Technology transfer takes place. Suppliers lose but recipients gain. (3)	Technology transfer does not take place. Neither suppliers nor recipients gain. (4)

SOURCE: Adapted from Linsu Kim, "Pros and Cons of International Technology Transfer: A Developing Country View," in Tamir Agmon and Mary Ann von Glinow, *Technology Transfer in International Business* (New York: Oxford University Press, 1985), 223–239.

mechanisms. Then why do technology suppliers not take advantage of opportunities to expand their market through FDI and to extend the economic life of technologies through FLs? It is also in quadrant 1 that firms in catching-up countries do not end up technologically dependent on suppliers. That is, quadrant 1 is the best alternative for both suppliers and recipients.

IMPLICATIONS FOR RECIPIENTS OF TECHNOLOGY

The cases presented in this book offer several implications for firms in catching-up countries. First, is technology transfer a better strategy than in-house efforts in expediting technological learning? Foreign technology transfer should not be seen as a substitute for in-house efforts, or vice versa. Rather, the two strategies should be complementary. Transfer of foreign technology can provide new dimensions in raising knowledge levels and serve as a catalyst for technological change, enabling firms in catching-up countries to make a quantum jump in indigenous learning. The higher the tacit knowledge in a firm, the stronger the firm's bargaining power in transfer negotiations. Moreover, transferred information is easier to assimilate.

Second, is joint venture a good strategy for acquiring foreign technology? Fully owned FDI or a joint venture as a means of technology transfer may lead to either foreign dependency or conflicts. While these mechanisms definitely transfer production capability, they do not necessarily transfer investment or innovation capability, particularly when the parent company uses FDI or a joint venture to exploit a local market in catching-up countries. Prior to 1984 semiconductor manufacturing by multinational firms in Korea transferred only simple packaging technology. But that did not foster the skills, knowledge, and learning capabilities of the production workers or the engineering capabilities of the domestic economy. The comparative study of independent Hyundai and the Daewoo-GM joint venture in the automobile industry also shows that the local firm outperformed the multinational subsidiary in product development and market performance. While Hyundai maintained its management independence and acquired technologies from multiple sources to expedite learning, GM was inactive in technology transfer to its subsidiary and constrained Daewoo's investment in technological learning (see Chapter 5).[3]

When, then, should firms in catching-up countries operate independently or enter joint ventures with technology suppliers? For those which invest aggressively in technological learning to accumulate capability, particularly if they have a global vision, it is better to eschew foreign equity participation (quadrant 1, Figure 10-2). Even if such an interest is allowed, management should maintain its independence; Hyundai Motor is a good example. Otherwise, conflicts arise (quadrant 3) when the learning and marketing strategy of the subsidiary can be constrained by that of the parenty company. Daewoo Motor is a case in point. There is ample similar evidence in other Korean industries. But recipients of technology which are not aggressive in acquiring technological capabilities can definitely benefit from joint venture (quadrant 4); however, the parent company usually controls the pace of the learning. As a result, the recepients become dependent on the parent.

Third, what is the best way to use foreign licenses as a means to expedite technological learning? As with foreign direct investment, packaged FLs from a single source involve little risk to the recipient, as the supplier guarantees the performance of the transferred technology. However, it leads to the recipient's adopting a passive attitude toward the learning process. But when the recipient acquires technologies

Figure 10-2 Strategy for Recipients of Technology

	Strategy for Technological Learning	
	Aggressive	Unaggressive
Independent	Slow initial learning but dynamic long-run learning (1)	Slow learning throughout (2)
Joint Venture	Rapid initial learning but conflicts restrict dynamic long-run learning. (3)	Learning at the pace of the parent firm's strategy. Dependency (4)

(Row group label: Association with Foreign Firms)

from multiple sources, and assumes responsibility for integrating them into a workable system, it entails a major risk. This constructs a crisis, which forces, then motivates the recipient to expedite technological learning. For the recipient with adequate tacit knowledge, it is better to follow this path.

Fourth, how important are informal mechanisms in acquiring foreign technologies? Korea's experience proves that firms in catching-up countries can benefit greatly from such transfer. Its impact on Korea has not been quantified, but cases cited here and in many studies indicate clearly that it has been very important in Korea's acquisition of technology. This mode of transfer has clearly prevailed in innovative small firms and has for a long time been significant in broadening the capabilities of all exporters. The Korean experience indicates that most of the information required to solve technical problems in the early years of industrialization can be obtained free of charge through non-market-mediated informal mechanisms if catching-up firms have the local ability to undertake reverse engineering tasks.

The mode of technology transfer evolves over time in dynamic interactions between the conditions and strategy of the supplier and those of the recipient. A supplier's terms for the technological trajectory are relatively predictable. The transferability, mode, and price of foreign technology are thus determined largely by the recipient's absorptive capacity and its aggressive strategy. Independent firms in catching-up countries should invest heavily in gathering of technological expertise to minimize the cost of foreign transfer and maximize technological learning.

IMPLICATIONS FOR PUBLIC POLICY

Korea's experience also offers several implications for public policymakers responsible for education, trade, and industrial organization.

Education Policy

It is argued in Chapter 3 that ambitious investment for education not only at the primary level but also at the secondary and tertiary levels in the early decades played a decisive role in expediting imitative technological learning in Korea. The same chapter also argues that underinvestment in education, particularly at the tertiary level, is a major bottleneck in facilitating innovative technological learning in the 1990s.

There is a strong correlation between education and industrialization. Many studies support the same argument. William Baumol, Sue Blackman, and Edward Wolff conclude that industrialized market economies converge toward one another in terms of productivity and per capita income and that the quantity and quality of education are among the major influences determining whether the economy is rapidly narrowing the gap with advanced countries. They also found that even among catching-up countries, those with similar educational levels were consistently converging in terms of real per capita gross domestic product. Catching-up countries achieved parity with advanced countries in the percentage of children attending primary school. Provision of secondary and higher education explains differences in national wealth.[4]

Why is education so important? It builds an economy's ability to absorb new knowledge and technology. Education gives rise to individuals' initial tacit knowledge, an essential building block in technological learning. This knowledge is important in individual learning as it enables people to make sense of new explicit knowledge, which leads to creating new tacit knowledge, or allows them to attain a higher level of tacit knowledge through experience.

Initial tacit knowledge is equally important in organizational learning. This takes place in a spiral process of knowledge diffusion from one individual to others through conversions between tacit and explicit knowledge among organization members. For instance, the tacit knowledge of one individual may be transferred to another only when the latter has enough tacit knowledge to absorb it.

In short, education is a major factor in successful technological learning. The government should assume full responsibility for taking necessary measures. Proactive measures, as applied in Korea in the 1960s and 1970s, are expected to lay an important foundation for subsequent industrialization. But reactive measures, as applied in Korea in the 1980s and 1990s, could require a great deal of time before their effects bear fruit. A small cadre of highly educated elites is not sufficient for industrialization. Achieving rapid industrialization requires proactive measures to provide quality secondary and tertiary education to a country's populace.

Trade Policy

To facilitate effective technological learning in industry, the government should play another important role in creating a competitive market. While education supplies humans with high tacit knowledge, competitive markets create demand for it. As stated in Chapter 2, the demand side is as important as the supply side in bringing about effective technological learning.

Protection of local markets creates initial business opportunities, as occurred in Korea in the 1960s and 1970s, but prolonged protection fails to create competitive domestic markets and to stimulate technological learning in industry. The past experiences of India and communist economies support the argument that export-oriented strategy is more effective in creating competitive markets. As noted in earlier chapters, dynamic technological learning ensued when Korean industries turned to the export market. For this reason, export-oriented firms achieved technological learning more rapidly than import-substituting firms, and export-oriented economies grew faster than import-substituting ones.

An export-oriented strategy is one of the most effective means for creating market competition, and the government must play a decisive role in guiding an economy in the direction of export orientation.

Balanced Industrial Structure

Korea's advantage over other catching-up countries is the strength of its big businesses, while Taiwan's advantage is the strength of its dynamic small and medium-size enterprises (SMEs).[5] But these advantages also have weaknesses. As discussed in Chapter 8, Korea fails to support its dynamic SMEs stongly enough to make its large-scale assemblers innovative. As a result, *chaebols* have relied heavily on Japanese SMEs to supply critical components for automobiles and electronics. Taiwan, lacking large firms to challenge scale-intensive industries, is behind Korea in such industries as steel, automobile, and memory semiconductors. Its skewed industrial structure stemmed largely from the government's biased strategy. Korea deliberately promoted the formation and growth of large firms to bring about scale economies in the labor-intensive light industries, while Taiwan deliberately kept large businesses under state ownership for political reasons. These two economies belatedly recognized the importance of balanced industrial structure to sustain a healthy growth.

A desirable mix is well-balanced growth of both large and dynamic small firms, as in Japan and Germany. Governments in catching-up countries should promote such balanced structure to sustain long-term economic growth.

IMPLICATIONS FOR CORPORATE MANAGEMENT

The industry cases presented above also offer several implications for corporate management, including those for technological strategy, management of dynamic learning, and crisis construction.

Technological Strategy

Korea's industrialization evolved from duplicative to creative imitations. Most Korean industries still sustain their growth largely through imitative engineering. Is imitation a viable strategy for Korea and other countries?

Economic history provides ample evidence that imitation of both types has been and still is central to the process of late industrialization. Continental Europe and the United States caught-up with Great Britain in the nineteenth century through imitative development of British technologies. The earliest U.S. industrial success, for instance, stemmed largely from the country's ability to imitate, duplicatively and creatively, such British technologies as those for metallurgy and steam engines. By the first half of the nineteenth century, some American industries began to produce equipment which, in some sense, was superior to that of the British.[6]

So did Japan in the late nineteenth and early twentieth centuries. Japanese industrialization progressed through a similar pattern of evolution from duplicative to creative imitations. Industrial technology in the 1860s and onward consisted largely of faithful imitation of foreign products imported from advanced countries. Imported technologies included not only plant, machinery, and raw materials but foreign engineers and craftsmen to minimize trial and error in duplicative imitations. Assimilating the imported technologies, Japan progressively undertook creative imitations, rapidly catching up with other advanced countries.[7]

Even in industrially advanced countries today, creative imitation is not only more abundant than innovation but also a much more prevalent—and smarter—strategy for growth and profit. So why not encourage catching-up countries to take advantage of creative imitation?

Mastering creative imitation requires two essential components, strategic followership and learning by watching.[8] First, strategic followership, namely, a firm's decision to delay the adoption of a new product or practice, offers the greatest opportunity to succeed when small firms pioneer new markets. A small pioneer often finds it difficult to protect its lead in the absence of patents or when its patents can be circumvented. This is partly true when the pioneer is positioned at only one end of a market or the imitator can marshal greater financial muscle.[9]

Second, learning by watching refers to activities directed toward the acquisition, assimilation, and improvement of external knowledge. Japan as a catching-up country was more apt to focus on this component.[10] This way of creative imitation requires substantial investment in specialized R&D and related competencies. These are necessary to identify and acquire relevant external knowledge successfully through search, observation, and assimilation of new knowledge and translate that knowledge into creative new products and systems.

What distinguishes creative imitation from innovation is the way resources are allocated and expertise is involved in each strategy. Creative imitation as learning by watching requires organizationwide development of external linkages and substantial investments in formal and informal information systems to acquire generic, industry-specific knowledge. Learning-by-watching imitators zealously seek competitive information, undertaking widespread technology surveillance, hiring foreign specialists, and frequently calling on international trade shows and foreign suppliers. They also collect product catalogs and operating manuals from competitors, send engineers and managers to foreign universities and on observation tours in competitive countries, translate technical journals, and attend a growing number of professional meetings. Such competitive information may be translated into firm-specific knowledge through internal R&D.

Firms undertaking creative imitation benefit from relatively lower R&D costs and in turn lower prices, lower consumer education costs, and lower risk of market uncertainty. They also benefit from advantages in reading the growing market accurately, applying new technologies to strengthen product features, and entering markets at better times. Steven Schnaars introduces twenty-eight examples of creative imitations in advanced countries that surpassed the pioneers. Automated teller machines, CAT scanners, commercial jet aircraft, mainframe computers, microwave ovens, personal computers, and videocassette recorders are among them.

Japanese and Korean firms are relatively strong in these areas. American enterprises have been widely criticized for their NIH (not invented here) syndrome and their deficiency in creative imitation through learning by watching. These may be significant sources of U.S. competitive weaknesses.

The innovator, on the other hand, benefits from first-mover advantages that are unavailable to imitators. They include, among other things, image and reputation, brand loyalty, opportunity to pick the best market, technological leadership, opportunity to set product standards, access to distribution, experience effects, and opportunity to establish entry barriers of patents and switching costs. But critics contend that while first-mover advantages appear to be strong and immutable in theory, they prove to be weak and vulnerable to the invasion of creative and shrewd imitators.[11]

A few selected industries in Korea and other successful catching-up countries may compete neck and neck with those of advanced countries on the basis of innovation in frontier technologies. In other industries, the aspirants may have to trail the advanced countries on the basis of imitation. Nevertheless, as Japanese experience indicates, these catching-up countries can sustain economic growth as long as they remain effective followers by creatively imitating someone else's products in timely fashion.

Management of Dynamic Learning

How does a firm become dynamic? Some companies embark on building technological capability only when shocked by radical changes upstream in their supply chain or downstream in their markets. Others undertake systematic efforts to increase their production, investment, and innovation capabilities. The continuity of such systematic efforts distinguishes dynamic firms from less dynamic ones in catching-up countries.

My in-depth studies of more than 200 Korean firms show that

the dynamic companies have several characteristics: (1) they emphasize their own technological efforts in combination with foreign technological input; (2) they monitor development of the world technological frontier; (3) they are committed to training workers, thereby developing human resources; (4) entrepreneurs play a key role; and (5) they use crises as an effective means to expedite technological learning. Although all five characteristics were not necessarily present or conspicuous to the same degree in all the surveyed firms, most of the traits were clearly visible in every dynamic firm.

First, neither a firm that relied solely on foreign technological inputs nor one that relied exclusively on its own technological efforts was technologically the most dynamic; it was a firm that combined both. The dynamic firm thoroughly researched available foreign technologies and tapped them either through contractual agreement or informal mechanisms. It also combined or supplemented foreign technology, which it assimilated in the shortest possible time, with its indigenous technological efforts. Its increasing body of knowledge enabled the firm to strengthen its bargaining power in negotiating transfer contracts and to undertake further innovation.

Second, the dynamic firm vigorously monitored technological development in advanced countries through technical assistance agreements with foreign firms, short-term observation of foreign plants and exhibitions, short- and long-term training and education abroad, direct ties with local technical information centers, direct links with foreign research institutes, subscriptions to foreign technical journals, and R&D laboratories in advanced countries. All the firms did not avail themselves of all seven means; differences in industry and firm size accounted for the diversity. The larger, more sophisticated, and more dynamic the firm, the more resources it was likely to use. It appears that the least expensive tactics—subscriptions to foreign technical journals and short-term observation tours—were employed by all the firms.

Third, large firms were characteristically committed to training and developing their personnel. From the outset, they formulated and implemented sound strategies for developing staff; they established their own training institutes, offered programs ranging from foreign language and management training to job-specific technical training. Their overseas training is especially noteworthy—the majority of their engineers and leading technicians had benefited by it.

Fourth was the presence of the key entrepreneurs in large, dynamic, apprentice firms who forged ties with the developmental state but never relied completely on the government in venturing into challenging businesses. Rather, they created and managed crises successfully as a method of expediting technological learning. In small, dynamic, imitator firms, the entrepreneur took a pivotal champion role in directing technological development.[12] Possessing the most tacit knowledge within the firm, he had been the major source of ideas and ingenuity. When his tacit knowledge reached the limit of his scientific training, he recruited new technical personnel with university degrees and experience from other firms. Such an individual, as mentioned earlier, enabled the firm to take giant strides in technological capability. Even in technology-based small firms, such entrepreneurs played decisive roles in rapid technological learning.

Fifth, crisis construction has been a major path to opportunistic learning and a valuable facilitator of technological transformation at most Korean firms. Whenever dynamic firms were challenged by new technology, top management created crises as a means to marshal organizational efforts and expedite technological learning.

Firms that aspire to become dynamic must be able to tap multiple sources of foreign technologies, continually upgrade the tacit knowledge embodied in human resources, continually invest in R&D efforts to work on imported technologies and monitor technological changes in advanced countries, have an aggressive entrepreneur who orchestrates all imitation and innovation efforts, and construct and successfully manage crises. The absence of any of these factors is likely to retard the pace of technological learning.

Crisis Construction, Why Effective

The industry examples cited in this book show that crises were deliberately constructed to expedite technological learning. These cases suggest that to achieve this goal a fabricated crisis can be an even more effective tool than a naturally occurring one. Why?

A naturally evoked crisis creates a performance gap, a major discrepancy between how a firm is performing and what it ought to be performing, but it is subject to denial from those who refuse to believe it is real. This problem may stem from different perceptions and interpretations of environmental changes or from active resistance to maintaining the status quo and the inertia of adhering to existing norms and past practice. Consequently, the firm facing naturally evoked crises has to exert a significant portion of staff energy to educating coalitions and organizational members to agree to crisis management, mitigating resistance to change, and unlearning past practice. Varying perceptions of crises and diverse opinions about prescription also make it laborious for a firm to direct energy toward effective learning.

Constructed crises present an unclouded performance gap and an antidote to inertia. In contrast, to naturally evoked crises, top management can, if necessary, manipulate a performance gap to make constructed crises creative by keeping them from coming to a destructive end. Constructed crises also generate intense pressure to create mandates for change, enabling management coalitions to reach consensus on organizational goals and prompting members to accept them.

Constructed crises also increase the intensity of effort at both the individual and the organizational levels in searching for alternative courses of action to make the crises creative. Mandating change generates the volume of effort, while goal consensus and identification provide the direction for such effort, clearly focusing on expeditious learning for survival. Goal-focused effort to resolve crises also prompts members to search actively for information regarding new ways to respond to them and to expedite knowledge conversion and accumulation at the individual level. This intensifies interaction among them, giving rise to the same result at the organizational level.

Crisis construction may be more easily used as a means of expeditious learning in catching up than in pioneering, as learning goals may be more specific and clearer in the former than in the latter. In catching up, relevant knowledge in various forms is readily available elsewhere. A catching-up company can acquire prior knowledge through literature review, pirating new personnel, observation tours, and licensing technology. But a pioneering company has to employ strategic ambiguity that provides only a broad direction and leads to difficulty in identifying external sources of relevant knowledge.

Crisis construction, which may be an effective means of accelerating imitative technological learning in catching up, may not be a useful tool for innovative technological learning.

IMPLICATIONS FOR KOREA'S FUTURE

Can Korea sustain its phenomenal growth into the future? The preceding chapter showed that Korea achieved the highest average annual growth rate in the world in nations' R&D investment per gross domestic product (GDP), business R&D per GDP, Korean and U.S. patent registrations, number of scientific publications quoted by the *Science Citation Index,* and number of scientists and engineers.

However, total Korean R&D is merely about equal to that of a leading company in advanced countries. General Motors and Siemens alone spend as much for R&D as all of Korea does. The proportion of R&D to sales in Korean manufacturing is still less than half that of U.S. and Japanese manufacturers. As a result, Korea is squeezed between the advanced countries that have far stronger technological bases than it does and second-tier developing countries that are rapidly catching-up with it. Korea is indeed at a turning point in its modern history. What should the country do to sustain its growth?

First, Korea should institute major reform in educational systems, particularly at the tertiary level, to provide industries with a continuing inflow of well-trained personnel to build an adequate prior knowledge foundation. This includes developing strong basic research capabilities at universities to support industrial R&D. Without the availability of such high-level knowledge, R&D investment cannot be productive. The government is contemplating turning ten universities into research-oriented graduate universities with first-class research capabilities. But given the shortage of financial resources, the bureaucratic rigidity of the government, and the conservative culture of universities, it will take a great deal of time and effort before such an idea can be fully implemented. This is a major bottleneck in Korea's national innovation system.

Second, Korea should further intensify its R&D operations. Although Korea's business R&D investment per GDP showed the highest growth rate in the world, the intensity of manufacturing-sector R&D is still low compared with that of advanced countries. The government released a highly ambitious vision in which the proportion of R&D investment to gross national product would increase from 2.61 percent in 1994 to 3.6 percent by 2000 and 4 percent by 2010. The government believes that the proportion of high-technology industries in manufacturing can increase from 14.8 percent in 1995 to 31.6 percent by 2010. That eventuality remains to be seen.

Third, Korea should develop an environment in which more technology-based small and medium-size enterprises could emerge and grow successfully. Although many technological SMEs have emerged in the past decade, the number is not sufficiently large to support the size of industrialization in Korea. A strong surge of such SMEs requires research-intensive universities and R&D organizations that could incubate technical entrepreneurs. It also requires a creative financial services market such as an effective venture-capital industry, a dynamic over-the-counter secondary market, and loans based on a new product's potential rather than collateral. The absence of dynamic and innovative SMEs is a major weakness in Korea, resulting in shaky industrial networks between the formal and informal sectors. It cannot easily be corrected without these educational and financial changes to provide effective support for the birth of spin-off enterprises.

Fourth, Korea should intensify its network of technical support systems. Although it began developing a network of technical extension services in the 1980s, it has not been effective in helping SMEs. While mission-oriented, large national R&D projects might generate a leap in a selected number of technological areas, greater effort should be made in favor of technological diffusion in industry and more particularly in SMEs. Korea needs a systematic network of technical assistance offices countrywide or at least in industrial areas. Korea could emulate the effective network of supporting agencies in Germany or prefectural laboratories in Japan.[13]

Fifth, new environments require new institutions. For that reason, government R&D institutes (GRIs) established in the 1970s should adapt to drastic changes in the economic and technological environment in order to respond effectively to new technological challenges and competition.[14]

Sixth, Korea should make major changes in political and social conditions. Its society has been dominated by a small number of elites. Moreover, the liberalization of the economy has been strongly restrained by the centralization of power and regulations. Downsizing, decentralization, and democratization of the workplace are indispensable to sustaining the competitiveness of the Korean economy to cultivate creativity and initiative in the society as a whole. Such changes are slow to come, as they depend deeply on human behavior.

These five factors imply that Korea will be further squeezed between advanced and rapidly catching-up countries with narrower technological options. Koreans will not, however, succumb to economic crises. Rather, they will be most adaptable in making them creative through the Korean can-do spirit, as evidenced in Korea's history. Recent moves to reform educational institutions, ambitious R&D investment in both the public and private sectors, drastic measures being taken to create a conducive environment for SMEs, are expected to bring about significant results in the near future.

IMPLICATIONS FOR OTHER CATCHING-UP COUNTRIES

Many political leaders, economic planners, and corporate managers in other catching-up countries have shown keen interest in studying the Korean experience to determine whether they could duplicate in their own countries or firms the strategies that led to Korea's success.

The patterns presented in this book are not necessarily singular to Korea. Many studies conducted in other countries provide similar findings. For instance, Japanese industrialization evolved through a similar pattern. One study divides its hundred-year history into four stages: (1) the primitive stage with full reliance on imported technology and foreign engineers; (2) the transfer of industrial activity from the government to the private sector; (3) the assimilation of imported technology; and (4) catching up to advanced countries.[15]

Japan's industrial technology from the 1860s on depended wholly on technologies imported from Europe and North America. These included not only plant, machinery, and raw material, but also foreign engineers and craftsmen. In 1872 the Japanese government established the first textile mill with the aid of French technology and engineers. Such technology was diffused quickly throughout the country. By 1880 Japanese technicians, experienced in the government plant, were able to play a pivotal role in establishing private spinning mills.[16] The expansion of the textile industry resulted in the emergence of the textile machinery industry in Japan.

The Japanese automobile industry grew through a similar process. Although attempts were made to develop military trucks by reverse-engineering British and French models, the industry can be said to have started in the 1920s with an assembly operation of American Ford and GM passenger cars. Assimilation of foreign automobile technology through product design and manufacturing experience led Japan to introduce its own model eleven years later.[17] Through assimilation and improvement, Japan became one of the leading automobile exporters in the world.

In Japanese mechanical engineering industries such as steel and shipyards during 1900–1940, technological learning in Japan's early industrialization resembled that of Korea's more recent industrialization. The Japanese government, heavily involved in helping industries grow technologically, protected the local market for import substitution and provided local entrepreneurs with various financial and tax incentives. The government often took the initiative in starting new industries. Formal technology transfer from abroad, reverse-engineering foreign models, and the technical assistance of foreign experts were crucial inputs to technological learning. However, the long struggle to assimilate foreign technologies from various sources independently was the most effective learning method for Japan.[18]

In the face of World War II, the Japanese government strengthened its political leadership in industry, creating crises for firms to strengthen their efforts to upgrade technological capability. In the interwar and war periods, a series of crises imposed by the Japanese government on military arsenals, ammunition industries, and military R&D institutes forced them to expedite the acquisition of technological capability through intensified effort. After the dismantling of these organizations at the end of the war, tacit knowledge gained in this process was efficiently diffused to industries, enabling them to give significant rise to precision engineering capability.

Japan's postwar technological recovery was also built on imported technology. Terutomo Ozawa notes that Japan licensed a great number of foreign technologies. Its export competitiveness during the 1950s stemmed from successful assimilation of foreign technology, and in the 1960s further expansion of exports through enhanced competitiveness sprang from the improvement of acquired technologies through original R&D.[19]

Hiroyuki Odagiri and Akira Goto provide a strikingly similar account of Japanese technology and industrial development in the past century. After analyzing the process of technological development in such industries as textiles, steel, electrical and communication equipment, automobiles, shipbuilding and aircraft, and pharmaceutials, they conclude that "Japan has gradually built its capabilities through importing technological and other knowledge from overseas, adapting them to its own advantage, learning from trial and error, and, increasingly, making its own innovation efforts."[20]

To a certain extent, the United States went through a similar pattern a century ago. Reversing the sequence of research, development, and engineering (R,D&E), it started with practical technologies imported from European countries, then slowly evolved into its present position of affording substantial research.[21] For instance, U.S. imported steam engine technology from Great Britain in the late eighteenth century. But through assimilating it, Americans had developed excellent mechanical skills by the 1830s, and U.S. industry no longer relied on importing or imitating British models and techniques.[22] By World War I the United States had clearly seized leadership in mass-production industries and established the necessary infrastructure for new science-based industries coming into prominence. This led to its technological leadership after World War II.[23]

Evidence can also be found in other catching-up countries. Brazilian and Argentinean firms began manufacturing with assembly and packing and eventually expanded into more intricate operations. Engineering was the initiating portion of the R,D&E spectrum, leading gradually to more advanced development and research efforts.[24]

In short, the general pattern of technological learning, which proceeds, albeit at different speeds, from preparation to the acquisition of foreign technology to assimilation and eventually to improvement thereof to strengthen competitiveness, is evident in the history of manufacturing in a number of countries. However, many factors may account for variations in the pattern of technological learning. At the firm level, the availability of local entrepreneurs, successful crisis construction and management, and the capability of local engineers and technicians account for diversity. At the industry level, the characteristics of production technology and market structure may be sources of variation. At the national level, government policies on trade, foreign technology transfer, market structure, financial institutions, and education and sociocultural factors are important roots of difference.

So, can other catching-up countries emulate Korea's experience? Their present economic environment is so different from that of Korea in the past that it may not be easy for them to follow Korea's path. There are parts of Korea's experience that may be, parts that may not be, and parts that should not be emulated by these others.

Environmental Differences

Radical changes in the international economic environment will make it difficult for other catching-up countries to emulate Korea's experience and grow as fast as Korea did for a few reasons. First, the new order of international trade under the World Trade Organization (WTO) will make it difficult for them to protect their domestic markets for infant industry learning. Furthermore, new WTO regime pressure to liberalize domestic markets for product, service, and investment will make it more difficult for catching-up countries than it was for Korea to proceed independently of multinationals.

Second, intellectual property rights protection will preempt duplicative imitation of foreign technologies. It will be more difficult and costly for catching-up countries to reverse-engineer foreign products for cloning than it was for Korea in the 1960s and 1970s. China, for example, faces enormous pressure from the United States to honor intellectual property rights, which Japan, Korea, and Taiwan did not encounter in their early stages of industrialization.

Third, North American and European protectionist policy will hamper the export-oriented strategy of catching-up countries. Therefore, it will be more difficult for them to grow as rapidly as Korea did in the export market.

What May Be Emulated

Many parts of Korea's experience may be emulated. First, strong government leadership is an essential condition for catching-up countries to grow rapidly. Without transformational leadership with a vision and strong determination to make changes happen, no nation can grow effectively. The experience of Japan and the four East Asian tigers offers useful implications for other catching-up countries.

Second, aspiring countries can emulate various government programs that Korea used to facilitate technological learning. Some industrial and science and technology policy programs, presented in Chapter 2, may easily be adopted. Many formal institutions may be built to support effective learning in industry. Policies to open an economy to the international environment are particularly essential to facilitate rapid technological learning. It should be pointed out, however, that some may no longer be as effective as they were in Korea owing to changes in the international economic environment.

Third, as noted above, the expansion of educational systems, particularly at the secondary and tertiary levels, is one of the most important aspects of Korea's experience that may be copied as preparation for subsequent industrialization. In the initial stage of becoming industrialized, secondary-level education may play a remarkably powerful role, for it is adequate to assimilating labor-intensive mature technologies. But tertiary-level education becomes increasingly important to deepening technological capability in order to challenge increasingly complex technologies. Overinvestment in education is a misallocation of scarce resources, but it is still better than underinvestment.

Fourth, firms in catching-up countries can also emulate crisis construction to expedite technological learning, which Korea's experience proves is a useful strategy. Its effectiveness depends largely on such sociocultural factors as entrepreneurship and the work ethic of organization members.

What May Not Be Emulated

Other catching-up countries may be able to invest heavily in expanding and deepening education and introducing sundry programs, but their successful implementation may depend largely on whether members of firms, institutions, and society could exhibit behaviors compatible with the systems introduced. Thus, cultural and situational factors that shape and discipline individual and group behaviors are the most difficult to emulate.

First, the Korean War played the most decisive role in transforming Korea from a rigid, hermit, traditional class society to a dynamic, flexible, classless society. However, no catching-up country should launch a war to prepare its society for subsequent industrialization. War-caused chaos does not necessarily guarantee successful industrialization. Other essential factors should be present to turn such chaos into a dynamic social environment.

Second, not all catching-up countries can emulate the hardship imposed by Korea's physical conditions. The adversity imposed by severe climatic conditions, social competition caused by dense population, and adaptability acquired through frequent foreign invasions cannot, fortunately, be replicated by other countries.

Last, survival in spite of these hardships inculcated an entrepreneurial can-do spirit and hardworking trait in Koreans. These sociocultural factors cannot easily be duplicated.

What Should Not Be Emulated

Korea committed several mistakes that other catching-up countries should not emulate. Imbalanced promotion of *chaebols* at the cost of SMEs, underinvestment in education and basic research, heavy reliance on GRIs for advanced industrial R&D, and the lack of effective networks of technological assistance agencies for SMEs are major errors of the Korean government. Other aspiring countries should learn from Korean experience not to repeat them.

THE ICARUS PARADOX

Greek mythology offers an interesting paradox that still exists in industrial society. The fabled Icarus had powerful artificial wings that enabled him to fly so high, so close to the sun, that the wax wings melted and he plunged to his death. The paradox is that one's greatest asset can later become one's most serious liability.[25] The same paradox applies to many aspects of Korea's experience.

First, the strong Korean government was a major asset in Korea's early industrialization. The government nationalized all banks and monopolized all foreign savings to mobilize financial resources and allocate them for industrial projects according to national priorities. Then the government awarded to *chaebols* business licenses that allowed them to reach ambitious goals and become powerhouses. Such strong leadership pushed Korea's industrial locomotive far faster than its speed in the early decades, but it later became a major liability to bringing market mechanisms into the center of an innovation-oriented economy. The government strongly advocates the importance of private-sector-initiated market mechanisms, but what the government actually does in many aspects mirrors the role of the developmental state, hampering the proper working of the market mechanisms.

Second, *chaebols* had been an important asset in Korea's industrialization drive in the early decades. They played a major role in developing mass-production systems and exploring the export market on a massive scale and still play an important role in globalizing Korea's businesses. Their names are visible around the globe. However, the extreme economic concentration in a limited number of *chaebols* is a major liability in the Korean economy. It impedes the healthy growth of SMEs, constrains the government to bring about economic justice, and makes it difficult to eradicate corrupt business-government collusion.

Third, the nationalistic monoculture and monolanguage that had been Korea's strength in bringing about the internal cohesiveness of Korean society became a major liability in globalizing the Korean economy. The fact that Korea has a single race, single culture, and single language was an advantage in bringing people together to push for industrialization, but it has become a major detriment and obstacle in learning an international language and understanding different cultures. Such a disadvantage makes it difficult for Korean managers to manage and work harmoniously with workers from different cultures who speak different languages.

Fourth, Korea's militaristic organization, which had been an asset in the top-down-command march of industrialization, became a major liability in bringing about bottom-up innovation in recent decades. This organization is highly centralized and hierarchical but hardly formalized. It is quick to act and extremely efficient in carrying out decisions made at the top. The early rapid industrial growth is partly attributable to this type of action-oriented organizations in the government and in the private sector. Creative imitation and innovation, however, require more decentralized, flexible, and lateral bottom-up organizations. Korean firms are learning that transforming a large militaristic organization into a number of smaller, responsive organizations is extremely difficult.

In conclusion, Korea has dynamically achieved phenomenal growth in technological learning in the past three decades. But Korea, facing many problems of its own, is being squeezed between advanced countries and second-tier newly industrializing countries. As a result, Korea may not be able to grow as fast as it did in the past. But by turning future crises into creative learning, it is Korea's vision to join the industrially advanced community (G-7) by 2020.

NOTES

CHAPTER 1

1. The share of the manufacturing sector in gross domestic products (GDP) increased from 7.7 percent in 1953 to 28 percent in 1991, while that of the primary sector decreased from 48.6 percent to 8 percent during the same period.
2. The per capita GNP for Sudan was not reported in *World Development Report 1993*. It is, however, reported as $400 in the United Nations Development Programme, *Human Development Report, 1994*, 51.
3. *World Development Report* 1993 (Washington, D.C.: World Bank, 1993).
4. Ezra F. Vogel, *The Four Little Dragons: The Spread of Industrialization in East Asia* (Cambridge, Mass.: Harvard University Press, 1991), 65.
5. See, for example, "Korea Headed for High Tech's Top Tier," *Business Week*, July 31, 1995, 32.
6. See, for example, E. Denison, with J. Poullier, *Why Growth Rates Differ* (Washington, D.C.: Brookings Institution, 1967); Gene M. Grossman, *Innovation and Growth in the Global Economy* (Cambridge, Mass.: MIT Press, 1991); and M. Goldsmith, ed., *Technological Innovation and the Economy* (London: Wiley Science, 1970).
7. Linsu Kim, "Stages of Development of Industrial Technology in a Developing Country: A Model," *Research Policy* 9, no. 3 (1980): 254–277.
8. The concept of technological capability is similar to the concept of absorptive capacity used in Wesley M. Cohen and Daniel A. Levinthal, "Absorptive Capacity: A New Perspective on Learning and Innovation," *Administrative Science Quarterly* 35, no. 1 (1990): 128–152.
9. Ibid.
10. See Sang-Woon Jeon, *Science and Technology in Korea: Traditional Instruments and Techniques* (Cambridge, Mass.: MIT Press, 1974).
11. See Sang Chul Suh, *Growth and Structural Changes in the Korean Economy, 1910–1940* (Cambridge, Mass.: Council on East Asian Studies, Harvard University, 1978), for the analysis of Korea's industrial development during the Japanese colonial period.
12. Edward S. Mason, Mahn Je Kim, Dwight H. Perkins, Kwang Suk Kim, and David C. Cole, *The Economic and Social Modernization of the Republic of Korea* (Cambridge, Mass.: Council on East Asian Studies, Harvard University, 1980).
13. See Kwang-Suk Kim and Michael Roemer, *Growth and Structural Transformation* (Cambridge, Mass.: Council on East Asian Studies, Harvard University, 1979), for the analysis of Korea's economic growth in the 1960s and 1970s.
14. Linsu Kim, "Korea," in Surendra Patel, ed., *Technological Transformation in the Third World, Volume 1: Asia* (Aldershot, England: Avebury Publishers, 1993).

15. Kim and Roemer, *Growth and Structural Transformation*, 27.
16. Ibid., 36.
17. Mason et al., *The Economic and Social Modernization of the Republic of Korea*, 185.
18. Manuel Castells, "Four Asian Tigers with a Dragon Head: A Comparative Analysis of the State, Economy, and Society in the Asian Pacific Rim," in Richard Applebaum and Jeffrey Henderson, eds., *States and Development in the Asian Pacific Region* (Newbury Park, Calif.: Sage Publications, 1992), 33–70.
19. Sung Hwan Ban, Pal Yong Moon, and Dwight H. Perkins, *Rural Development in the Republic of Korea* (Cambridge, Mass.: Council on East Asian Studies, Harvard University, 1980).
20. Charles R. Frank, Kwang-Suk Kim, and Larry E. Westphal, *Foreign Trade Regimes and Economic Development: South Korea* (New York: National Bureau of Economic Research, 1975).
21. See John Sullivan and Roberta Foss, eds., *Two Koreas—One Future?* (Lanham, Md.: University Press of America, 1987), and Umesh C. Gulati, "The Foundations of Rapid Economic Growth: The Case of the Four Tigers," *American Journal of Economics and Sociology* 51, no. 2 (April 1992).
22. Mason et al., *The Economic and Social Modernization of the Republic of Korea*.
23. NICs include dynamically growing East Asian countries such as Korea, Taiwan, Singapore, Hong Kong, and such Latin American countries as Brazil, Mexico, and Argentina. Thailand, Malaysia, and the coastal area of China are often categorized as second-tier NICs.
24. Edwin Mansfield, "R&D and Innovation," in Zvi Griliches, ed., *R&D, Patents, and Productivity* (Chicago: University of Chicago Press, 1984), 142–143.
25. This and the following paragraphs draw heavily on Steven P. Schnaars, *Managing Imitation Strategy: How Later Entrants Seize Markets from Pioneers* (New York: Free Press, 1994), 5–14.
26. Richard R. Nelson and Sidney G. Winter, *An Evolutionary Theory of Economic Change* (Cambridge, Mass.: Belknap Press, Harvard University Press, 1982), 123–124.
27. Michele K. Bolton, "Imitation versus Innovation," *Organizational Dynamics* (Winter 1993): 34.
28. Joseph Schumpeter, *The Theory of Economic Development* (Cambridge, Mass.: Harvard University Press, 1934).
29. Nelson and Winter, *An Evolutionary Theory of Economic Change*, 124.
30. This ranking is based on 1993 figures. In shipbuilding, Korea moved from second position for a decade to first position in 1993 in terms of new orders received but slipped back to second position in 1994. See Korea Development Bank, *Korean Industry in the World, 1994* (Seoul: Korea Development Bank, 1994).
31. The data here are based on the global 500 published in "The World's Largest Industrial Corporations," *Fortune*, July 26, 1993, 188–234.
32. Michael Porter, *The Competitive Advantage of Nations* (New York: Free Press, 1990).

33. Linsu Kim, "Korea's Acquisition of Technological Capability for Internationalization: Macro and Micro Factors," *Business Review of Korea University* 22, no. 1 (1988): 183–197.
34. Peter Clark and Neil Staunton, *Innovation in Technology and Organization* (London: Routledge, 1990), 45–46.
35. Monographs on Korea's economic development include Lee-Jay Cho and Yoon-Hyung Kim, eds., *Economic Development in the Republic of Korea: A Policy Perspective* (Honolulu: East-Wester Center, University of Hawaii Press, 1992); Lee-Jay Cho and Yoon-Hyung Kim, eds., *Korea's Political Economy: An Institutional Perspective* (Boulder, Colo.: Westview Press, 1994); Byung-Nak Song, *The Rise of the Korean Economy* (Hong Kong: Oxford University Press, 1990); Il Sakong, *Korea in the World Economy* (Washington, D.C.: Institute for International Economics, 1993); Soon Cho, *The Dynamics of Korean Economic Development* (Washington, D.C.: Institute of International Economics, 1994); Dilip K. Das, *Korean Economic Dynamism* (London: Macmillan, 1992); World Bank, *The East Asian Miracle: Economic Growth and Public Policy* (New York: Oxford University Press, 1993); A. Chowdhury and I. Islam, *The Newly Industrializing Economies of East Asia* (London: Routledge, 1993); Sung Moon Pae, *Korea Leading Developing Nations: Economy, Democracy, and Welfare* (Lanham, Md.: University Press of America, 1992); T. W. Kang, *Is Korea the Next Japan? The Structure, Strategy, and Tactics of America's Next Competitor* (New York: Free Press, 1988); and Jung-En Woo, *Race to the Swift: State and Finance in Korean Industrialization* (New York: Columbia University Press, 1991).
36. Works include Richard M. Steers, Yoo Keun Shin, and Gerardo R. Ungson, *The Chaebols: Korea's New Industrial Might* (Grand Rapid, Mich.: Harper & Row, 1989); Choong Soon Kim, *The Culture of Korean Industry: An Ethnography of Poongsan Corporation* (Tucson: University of Arizona Press, 1992); Roger L. Janelli, *Making Capitalism: The Social and Cultural Construction of a South Korean Conglomerate* (Palo Alto: Stanford University Press, 1993); J. L. Enos and W. H. Park, *The Adoption and Diffusion of Imported Technology: The Case of Korea* (London: Croom Helm, 1988); and Robert P. Kearney, *The Warrior Worker: The Challenge of the Korean Way of Working* (New York: Henry Holt, 1991).
37. I was the coauthor of this micro study when we jointly undertook a project for the World Bank in 1981–1985. See Alice H. Amsden, *Asia's Next Giant: South Korea and Late Industrialization* (New York: Oxford University Press, 1989).

CHAPTER 2

1. "Developmental state" is the term Chalmers Johnson coined in his analysis of Japan's economic transformation to describe the orchestrating role of the state in Japanese industrialization. See Chalmers Johnson, *MITI and the Japanese Miracle: The Growth of Industrial Policy, 1925–1975*, (Stanford: Stanford University Press, 1982).
2. See, for example, World Bank, *The East Asian Miracle: Economic Growth and*

Public Policy (New York: Oxford University Press, 1993); Kiwhan Kim and Danny Leipziger, "Korea: A Case of Government-led Development: Lessons from East Asia, a Country Studies Approach," (Washington, D.C.: World Bank, 1993); and Robert Hassink, "South Korea: Economic Miracle by Policy Miracle?" a Maastricht Economic Research Institute on Innovation and Technology mimeograph, 1994.

3. Among monographs, the most comprehensive may be Lee-Jay Cho and Yoon-Hyung Kim, eds., *Economic Development in the Republic of Korea: A Policy Perspective* (Honolulu: East-West Center, University of Hawaii Press, 1992). Others include Alice H. Amsden, *Asia's Next Giant: South Korea and Late Industrialization* (New York: Oxford University Press, 1989); Dilip K. Das, *Korean Economic Dynamism* (London: Macmillan, 1992); World Bank, *The East Asian Miracle: Economic Growth and Public Policy* (New York: Oxford University Press, 1993); A. Chowdhury and I. Islam, *The Newly Industrializing Economies of East Asia* (London: Routledge, 1993). Informative articles include Robert Wade, "Industrial Policy in East Asia: Does It Lead or Follow the Market?" in Gary Gereffi and Donald L. Wyman, eds., *Manufacturing Miracles: Paths of Industrialization in Latin America and East Asia* (Princeton: Princeton University Press, 1990), 231–266; Manuel Castells, "Four Asian Tigers with a Dragon Head: A Comparative Analysis of the State, Economy, and Society in the Asian Pacific Rim," in Richard Applebaum and Jeffrey Henderson, eds., *States and Development in the Asian Pacific Region* (Newbury Park, Calif.: Sage Publications, 1992), 33–70.

4. The discussions in this and subsequent paragraphs draw heavily on Linsu Kim and Carl J. Dahlman, "Technology Policy and Industrialization: An Integrative Framework and Korea's Experience," *Research Policy* 21 (1992): 437–452.

5. On the other hand, he created and used the Korean CIA to oppress his dissidents.

6. Low wages in civil service and strong power given to bureaucrats in allocating business licenses and financial resources led to serious corruption.

7. Ezra F. Vogel, *The Four Little Dragons: The Spread of Industrialization in East Asia* (Cambridge, Mass.: Harvard University Press, 1991), 93.

8. Ibid., 49.

9. A study undertaken in 1993 by the International Exchange Foundation of Japan revealed that Korea had the largest number (820,000) studying Japanese, followed by China (250,000), Australia (170,000), Indonesia (73,000), and the United States (50,000). "Segye ileo hakseopja jeolbani hankookin." (Koreans comprise half the students of Japanese), *Kookmin Ilbo*, (Korea daily, Seoul), February 21, 1995, 5.

10. Alice H. Amsden, "The Specter of Anglo-Saxonization Is Haunting South Korea," in Lee-Jay Cho and Yoon Hyung Kim, eds., *Korea's Political Economy: An Institutional Perspective* (Boulder, Colo.: Westview Press, 1994), 87–126.

11. Vogel, *The Four Little Dragons*, 54. He, however, rightly criticizes Koreans' copying the Japanese institutions they learned during the Japanese occupation in the 1930s and 1940s rather than more recent variants.

12. Trade policy is also included here.
13. Richard M. Steers, Yoo Keun Shin, and Gerardo R. Ungson, *The Chaebols: Korea's New Industrial Might* (New York: Harper & Row, 1989), 34.
14. For excellent discussions of how the government promoted the growth of chaebols, see Seok-Ki Kim, *Business Concentration and Government Policy,* D.B.A. diss., Harvard Business School, 1987.
15. The data here are based on "The World's Largest Industrial Corporations," *Fortune,* July 26, 1993, 188–234.
16. The 1994 global 100 included only Daewoo among Korean *chaebols.* Unlike the 1992 list, the 1994 global 100 included not only manufacturing but also service firms. Consequently, Ssangyong and Sunkyung were pushed out, and Samsung, like Hyundai and LG, did not reveal its group revenue.
17. Amsden, *Asia's Next Giant.*
18. Chung-Yum Kim, *Hankuk Kyungje Jungchek 30 Nyunsa* (Korea's thirty-year economic policy history), Seoul: Chung-Ang Ilbo Press, 1990.
19. Linsu Kim, "Toward Reinventing Korea's National Management System in the Changing Global Environment," Institute report, East Asian Institute, Columbia University, October 1993.
20. For example, Samsung began as a small trader, Hyundai as one of 3,000 small construction subcontractors, LG as a primitive face cream producer, and Daewoo was a small spin-off from a trading company.
21. H. Chenery, S. Robinson, and M. Syrquin, *Industrialization and Growth: A Comparative Study* (New York: Oxford University Press, 1986), as quoted in Amsden, *Asia's Next Giant.*
22. The import-substitution policy refers to a mechanism that provides high protection to local markets in attempts to substitute foreign imports.
23. See Chapters 5, 6, and 8 for discussions of these industries.
24. Linsu Kim, "Korea," in Surendra Patel, ed., *Technological Transformation in the Third World, Volume 1: Asia* (Aldershot, England: Avebury Publishers, 1993).
25. Kwang-Suk Kim, "The 1964–1965 Exchange Rate Reform, Export-Promotion Measures, and Import-Liberalization Program," in Cho and Kim, *Economic Development in the Republic of Korea.*
26. Mason et al., *Economic and Social Modernization,* 265.
27. Linsu Kim, "National System of Industrial Innovation: Dynamics of Capability Building in Korea," in Richard Nelson, ed., *National Innovation Systems: A Comparative Analysis* (New York: Oxford University Press, 1993), 357–383.
28. For a more detailed discussion of export incentives see Kwang-Suk Kim, "Dynamics of Industrial Policy: Export-oriented Industrialization," paper presented at Korea's State-Guided Modernization Conference at East West Center, Honolulu, August 9–12, 1994.
29. World Bank, *World Bank Atlas,* various years.
30. For a detailed discussion of HCIs, see Suk-Chae Lee, "The Heavy and Chemical Industries Promotion Plan (1973–1979)," in Cho and Kim, *Economic Development in the Republic of Korea,* 431–472. From Lee's Table 17.11 (p. 452), total

HCI investment of W 6,166 billion is divided by the exchange rate of W 484 per dollar.

31. T. Watanabe, "Economic Development in Korea: Lessons and Challenges," in Toshio Shishido and Ryuzo Sato, eds., *Economic Policy and Development: New Perspectives* (Dover, Del.: Auburn House, 1985), quoted from Robert Wade, "Industrial Policy in East Asia: Does It Lead or Follow the Market?" in Gary Gereffi and Donald L. Wyman, eds., *Manufacturing Miracles: Paths of Industrialization in Latin America and East Asia* (Princeton: Princeton University Press, 1990), 231–266.
32. Walden Bello and Stephanie Rosenfeld, *Dragons in Distress: Asia's Miracle Economies in Crisis* (San Francisco: Institute for Food and Development Policy, 1992), 58.
33. Paul Samuelson, "Truths, Hard Truths, for Korea," *Dateline*, March 1990: 4–7.
34. For excellent discussions of labor subordination in Korea and other East Asian countries, see Frederic C. Deyo, ed., *Beneath the Miracle: Labor Subordination in the New Asian Industrialism* (Berkeley: University of California Press, 1989). For Korea, see Jang-Jip Choi, *Labor and Authoritarian State: Labor Unions in South Korean Manufacturing Industries, 1961–1980* (Seoul: Korea University Press, 1989).
35. Bello and Rosenfeld, *Dragons in Distress.*
36. Robert P. Kearney, *The Warrior Worker: The Challenge of the Korean Way of Working* (New York: Henry Holt, 1991), 25.
37. Byung-Nak Song, *The Rise of the Korean Economy* (Hong Kong: Oxford University Press, 1990).
38. There are two types of affiliates: *jahoisa* (child company) and *gyeyulsa* (affiliate companies). See "Largest Business Groups Continue Affiliate Expansion," *Korea Economic Weekly,* September 5, 1994, 26.
39. *Chaebols* divided some of their affiliates to give them to other family members.
40. A 1994 survey conducted by the Korea Economic Research Institute shows that of the thirty largest *chaebols*, six are owned and managed predominantly by the founders and their family groups and nine are managed by the mother firm, also managed by the founders and their family members. In other words, half the thirty largest *chaebols* are still run traditionally, but they are relatively smaller ones. The larger firms have significantly dispersed their ownership and modernized management style. See "KERI Report Reveals *Chaebol's* Ownership, Management Structure," *Korea Economic Weekly,* August 15, 1994, 18.
41. Net export subsidies represent the sum of direct cash subsidies, export dollar premium, direct tax reductions for exporters, and interest preference for exporters. See Kwang Suk Kim, "Industrial Policy and Trade Regimes," in Cho and Kim, *Korea's Political Economy,* 531–555.
42. The Korean government protects the local market from such Japanese imports as electronic goods and automobiles in an attempt to control trade imbalance with Japan.
43. Denise Chai, "Skeletons in the Closet," *Asia Money* 4, no. 7 (September 1993): 67–69.

44. Korea submitted its formal membership application to OECD in March 1995. However, it takes at least a year for a final decision to be made.
45. "Learning the Soft Way," *Far Eastern Economic Review*, December 3, 1992, 54–56.
46. "Korea Draws Legal Lines to Protect Property Rights," *Korea Business World*, September 1987, 84–87.
47. "Jijaekwon bumjae 5nyunse 5bae" (The number of violations of intellectual property rights quintupled in five years), *Chosun Ilbo* (Seoul daily), April 10, 1995, 39.
48. In a private conversation, Alice Amsden claimed that the Korean state, compared with that of other countries, is still relatively powerful in the marketplace.
49. For brevity of presentation, linking mechanisms are also included in this section.
50. My earlier examination of foreign license contract agreements through the end of the 1960s shows that all licensers that demanded payment above the 3 percent royalty ceiling later agreed to that figure.
51. Korea Exchange Bank, "Direct Foreign Investment in Korea," *Monthly Review*, October 1987, 18–19.
52. Dong-Sae Cha, *Weja Doipeo Hyogwa Boonsuk* (The effects of direct foreign investment) (Seoul: Korean Institute of Economics and Trade Press, 1983).
53. Linsu Kim and Youngbae Kim, "Innovation in a Newly Industrializing Country: A Multiple Discriminant Analysis," *Management Science* 31, no. 3 (1985): 312–322.
54. Larry E. Westphal, Linsu Kim, and Carl J. Dahlman "Reflections on the Republic of Korea's Acquisition of Technological Capability," in Nathan Rosenberg and C. Frischtak, eds., *International Technology Transfer: Concepts, Measures, and Comparisons* (New York: Praeger, 1985), 167–221.
55. The automatic approval system expedites foreign investors' applications by okaying them unless an applicant is otherwise notified within fifteen days in principle and within forty-five days if the application requires the evaluation of environmental effects and diversification of farmland.
56. "Foreign Investment Soars 43% in First Seven Months," *Korea Economic Weekly*, September 12, 1994, 6.
57. The current system stipulates that reporting to the appropriate ministry is necessary for the licensing of foreign technology with a fixed royalty of more than $300,000 or a running royalty of more than 3 percent of sales and a down payment of $50,000.
58. Even in the reporting system, the government often exercised its veto power by refusing to accept a report. For instance, until 1995 it refused to accept the reporting of Samsung's technology licensing agreement with Nissan as a way to block Samsung's entry into the automobile industry.
59. "Firms Receive 23 Percent More Foreign Technology," *Korea Economic Weekly*, September 11–18, 1995, 8.
60. Linsu Kim and Jeffrey B. Nugent, "Korean SMEs and Their Support Mecha-

nisms: An Empirical Analysis of the Role of Government and Other Nonprofit Organizations," paper presented at the World Bank Conference "Can Intervention Work? The Role of Government in SME Success," Washington, D.C., February 9, 1994.
61. This institution was renamed the Korea Advanced Institute of Science and Technology in 1980.
62. Ministry of Science and Technology, Korea, *1994 Report on the Survey of Research and Development in Science and Technology* (Seoul: MOST, December 1994).
63. The only exception may be the Pohang University of Science Technology, founded by the Pohang Iron and Steel Company.
64. The government originally set a goal to reach G-7 status by 2001, but revised the target date to 2020.
65. Ministry of Science and Technology, Korea.
66. National Defense College, "Gukbang yungu gebalkwa mingan yungu gebaleo gwange ganghwa bangane kwanhan yungu" (A proposal to strengthen the link between military and industrial R&D) (Seoul: KIST Center for Science and Technology Policy, 1990).
67. Korea Industrial Technology Association, *Sanup Gisul Baegseo* (Industrial technology white paper), *1994* (Seoul: KITA Press, December 1994), Table 2–39, 109.
68. Korea Trade Promotion Corporation, *World Class Korean Products* (Seoul: KOTRA, no date).
69. IMD generated 381 indicators, some based on objective data and others on the opinions of 2,851 executives in forty-four countries, in eight major categories of international competitiveness. See Samsung Economic Research Institute, *1994 Segye Jooyogukbyul Gyungjaengryuk Bikyo* (International comparison of competitiveness among selected countries) (Seoul: Samsung Economic Research Institute, September 1994).
70. IMD, in cooperation with the World Economic Forum, has undertaken an annual survey of international competitiveness since 1980. In 1994, it studied 16,500 executives in forty-four countries and reported indicators related to various aspects of international competitiveness.
71. These include Korea Economic Research Institute and Korea Institute of Economy and Trade.

CHAPTER 3

1. Ezra F. Vogel, *The Four Little Dragons: The Spread of Industrialization in East Asia* (Cambridge, Mass.: Harvard University Press, 1991), 65.
2. Charles Cooper, "Are Innovation Studies on Industrialized Economies Relevant to Technology Policy in Developing Countries?" Institute of New Technology, United Nations University Working Paper No. 3, June 1991, 6.
3. Michael E. Porter, *The Competitive Advantage of Nations* (New York: Free Press, 1990).
4. Noel F. McGinn, Donald R. Snodgrass, Yung Bong Kim, Shin-Bok Kim, and

Quee-Young Kim, *Education and Development in Korea* (Cambridge, Mass.: Council on East Asian Studies, Harvard University, 1980).
5. Frederick Harbison and Charles A. Myers, *Education, Manpower, and Economic Growth* (New York: McGraw-Hill, 1964).
6. Office of Statistics, *Tonggyero bon Hankukeo Baljachiu* (Korea's Progress in statistics) (Seoul: Office of Statistics, 1995).
7. The average tertiary enrollment ratio among Organization for Economic Cooperation and Development countries was 47 percent in 1991. See United Nations Development Programme (UNDP), *Human Development Report, 1994,* (New York: Oxford University Press, 1994), 153, 184.
8. The other three countries are Portugal, Columbia, and Panama, which all began at a significantly higher level of the human development index (HDI) in 1960 and reached a lower level in 1992. HDI includes not only knowledge level but also longevity and standard of living. See United Nations Development Programme, *Human Development Report, 1994* (New York: Oxford University Press, 1994), 91, 96, 105.
9. Other developing countries that show a high ratio are Cuba (19.8) and Singapore (18.7). See Ibid., 138.
10. Ministry of Science and Technology, *1994 Report on the Survey of Research and Development in Science and Technology* (Seoul: MOST, December 1994), 75.
11. Alice H. Amsden, *Asia's Next Giant: South Korea and Late Industrialization* (New York: Oxford University Press, 1989), Table 7.6, 171.
12. "Kyo Yuk Gehyuk: igushi moonje" (Education reform: this is the problem), *Kookmin Ilbo* (Korean daily), March 14, 1995, 1.
13. Beginning in 1945, Korea received approximately $6 billion in economic aid and another $7 billion in military assistance from the United States. See Edward S. Mason, Mahn Je Kim, Dwight H. Perkins, Kwang Suk Kim, and David C. Cole, *The Economic and Social Modernization of the Republic of Korea* (Cambridge, Mass.: Council on East Asian Studies, Harvard University, 1980), Preface.
14. Ibid., 342–378.
15. Larry E. Westphal, Linsu Kim, and Carl J. Dahlman, "Reflections on Korea's Acquisition of Technological Capability," in Nathan Rosenberg and Claudio Frischtak, eds., *International Technology Transfer: Concepts, Measures, and Comparisons* (New York: Praeger, 1985), 167–221.
16. The numbers are China, 44,381, Japan, 43,770, Taiwan, 37,581, and India, 34,796. Canada (22,655), Hong Kong (13,752), Malaysia (13,718), Indonesia (11,744), and Thailand (9,537) follow Korea. It is noteworthy that Canada is the only non-Asian representative among the largest ten countries. See "Mi Daehak Hankookin Yuhak" (Koreans studying in American universities), *Joong-Ang Ilbo* (Korean daily), January 5, 1995, 8, quoting statistics from the Institute of International Education.
17. The number of foreign students by country of origin was China, 21,801, Korea, 12,947, Taiwan, 6,207, Malaysia, 2,105, Indonesia, 1,206, the United

States, 1,192, Thailand, 992, Bangladesh, 581, the Philippines, 528, Hong Kong, 520, and other countries, 4,326, a total of 52,405 as of May 1993. Of them, 6,408 received Japanese government scholarships. See Ministry of Education (Japan), *Educational Policy of Japan* (Tokyo: Ministry of Education, Japan, 1993).

18. "Eoikuk baksa 12,000 myong numeo" (Foreign P.h.Ds exceed 12,000), *Chosun Ilbo*, March 11, 1996, 38.
19. Harriet A. Hentges, "The Repatriation and Utilization of High-Level Manpower: A Case Study of the Korea Institute of Science and Technology," Ph.D. diss., Johns Hopkins University, 1975.
20. Bang-Soon L. Yoon, "Reverse Brain Drain in South Korea: State-led Model," *Studies in Comparative International Development* 27, no. 1 (1992): 4–26.
21. About 42 percent of them stayed less than a year on short-term assignments, 22 percent for as long as two years.
22. No statistics are available as to the percentage of Koreans who studied abroad, then returned home. However, from my experience in the United States, I believe that most Koreans who study in the States aspire to return to Korea, where, given rapid economic development, attractive opportunities are growing accordingly. An indicator is that in leading Korean universities, more than 90 percent of faculty members who hold Ph.D.'s received them at American universities, the rest at Japanese or European universities.
23. For an earlier study, see Herman Kahn, *World Economic Development: 1979 and Beyond* (London: Croom Helm, 1979). For a more recent argument, see Geert Hofstede and Michael Bond, "The Confucius Connection: From Cultural Roots and Economic Growth," *Organizational Dynamics*, Spring 1988, 4–21.
24. See, for example, Joseph Levenson, *Confucian China and Its Modern Fate* (Berkeley: University of California Press, 1958).
25. Official statistics report that Buddhism accounts for almost 23 percent of the Korean population. Buddhists are not as committed as Protestants to attending regular religious services and activities.
26. Wei-Ming Tu, *Confucian Ethics Today—The Singapore Challenge* (Singapore: Federal Publications, 1984).
27. Ibid., 110.
28. This paragraph is based largely on Byung-Nak Song, *The Rise of the Korean Economy* (Hong Kong: Oxford University Press, 1989), 51–55.
29. Myung-Sook Kim, "Study of Public Expenditures on Education," *Korea Development Review*, December 1986, quoted by Song, *The Rise of the Korean Economy*, 51.
30. Despite Hofstede's report that Korea's score is significantly higher than Japan's in his collectivism-individualism measure of IBM employees, many other studies indicate that Koreans stand somewhere between the United States and Japan in collectivism. See Geert Hofstede, *Culture's Consequences: International Differences in Work Related Values* (Beverly Hills,: Sage Publications, 1980). For other studies, see, for instance, Chan-Sup Chang, "Comparative Analysis of Management Systems: Korea, Japan, and the United States," *Korea Manage-*

ment Review 13, no. 1 (1983): 77–89, and Lane Kelley, Arthur Whatley, Reginald Worthley, and Harry Lie, "The Role of the Ideal Organization in Comparative Management: A Cross-cultural Perspective of Japan and Korea," *Asia and Pacific Journal of Management* 3, no. 2 (1986): 59–70.
31. Vogel, *The Four Little Dragons*, 84.
32. Ibid., 48.
33. Professor Glenn Page of the University of Hawaii delivered this speech on March 1, 1972, to a group of Korean students at the East-West Center in commemoration of Korea's independence movement from the Japanese occupation.
34. Tai K. Oh, Thomas E. Maher, and Cheong Han, "Codependency, Asian-style: The Impact of Confucian Values on the Korean Labor Force," School of Business Administration and Economics, California State University, Fullerton, 1991, mimeographed.
35. See B. De Mente, *Korean Etiquette and Ethics in Business* (Lincolnwood, Ill: NTC Business Books, 1988), and Jae-Un Kim, *The Koreans: Their Mind and Behavior* (Seoul: Kyobo Book Center, 1991).
36. Small city-states such as Hong Kong, Singapore, Barbados, Bahrain, Mauritius, and the Maldives have a higher population density than Korea. See UNDP, *Human Development Report*, 176.
37. Sookon Kim, "Employment Policy and Labor Management Relations in State-guided Modernization of Korea," paper presented at the conference "Korea's State-guided Modernization," Honolulu, Hawaii, August 8–12, 1994, 4.
38. *U.S. News and World Report*, February 27, 1989, 36, quoted from Oh et al., "Codependency," 14.
39. *Joong-Ang Ilbo* (Korean daily), February 23, 1990, quoted from Oh et al., "Codependency," 14–15.
40. A study released by the government, reported in *Joong-Ang Ilbo*, December 10, 1994.
41. Joon-Shik Shin, *Jaseng ryuki dangshineul chiryo handa* (Self-generating power heals your illness) (Seoul: Maeil Kyungje Shinmoonsa, 1992), 35–36.
42. See "Entrepreneurs and Ethnicity," *Fortune*, October 3, 1994, 23.
43. Even among Asians, Korean men have almost nine times the self-employment rate of their Laotian counterparts.
44. Books on Korean entrepreneurs include Donald Kirk, *Korean Dynasty: Hyundai and Chung Ju Yung* (Armonk, N.Y.: M. E. Sharpe, 1994); Byung-Chull Lee, *Ho-Am Jajun* (Ho-Am autobiography) (Seoul: Joong-Ang Ilbo, 1986); and Woo-Choong Kim, *Sesangeon Nulbgo Halileon Mantta* (World is wide and a lot to be done) (Seoul: Kimyoungsa, 1989).
45. Vogel, *The Four Little Dragons*, 61–62.
46. See Linsu Kim, "Stages of Development of Industrial Technology in a Developing Country: A Model," *Research Policy* 9, no. 3 (1980): 254–277.
47. More than 2 million North Koreans migrated to South Korea during the Korean War.
48. Leroy Jones and Il Sakong, *Government, Business, and Entrepreneurship in*

Economic Development: The Korean Case (Cambridge, Mass.: Council on East Asian Studies, Harvard University, 1980).

49. Vogel, *The Four Little Dragons*, 98–99.
50. It can be said, however, that the Japanese military culture rather than the American had the most influence on the military leaders in the Korean armed forces and those who took political power in 1961, as they had been trained by the Japanese during World War II. It is also true that organizational culture in the Korean military is closer to that of the Japanese military in World War II than that of the Americans.
51. Sung-Hwan Ban, "Economic Growth and Equitable Development Problems in Korea," paper presented at the International Conference on the Economic Development, Korean Economics Association, August 1984.
52. Sookon Kim, "Ijik yul oi kukje bikyo wha yoin boonsuk" (International comparison of separation rates and analysis of their determinants), *Korea Development Review* 3, no. 3 (1981).
53. Song, *The Rise of the Korean Economy*, 47.
54. Vogel, *The Four Little Dragons*, 45.
55. The Recruit Company undertakes a yearly survey to report the best employers selected by college students. No foreign firm has ever appeared on the list. The conclusion that few graduates from leading universities join foreign companies is based on the statistics of Korea University, where I teach.
56. The Recruit Company surveyed 1,216 students studying in the United States in 1994. See "Migook yoohak 59% gooknae chwiup hwimang" (59% of Korean students in the United States want to find jobs in Korea), *Kookmin Ilbo* (Seoul daily), December 2, 1994, 6.
57. Robert P. Kearney, *Warrior Worker: The Challenge of the Korean Way of Working* (New York: Henry Holt, 1991), 123.
58. Walden Bello and Stephanie Rosenfeld, *Dragons in Distress: Asia's Miracle Economies in Crisis* (San Francisco: Institute for Food and Development Policy, 1992), 40–43.
59. Mario F. Bognanno, "Korea's Industrial Relations at the Turning Point," Korea Development Institute Working Paper No. 8816, December 1988, 46.
60. "Balancing Workers' Interests against the Nations," *Business Korea*, February 1990, 31.
61. "Older, but Wiser," *Business Korea* 12, no. 1 (July 1994): 24–25. See also Ronald A. Rodgers, "The Role of Industrial Relations in Recent National and Enterprise Level Industrial Strategies in the Republic of Korea," in Lawrence B. Krause and Fun-Koo Park, eds., *Social Issues in Korea: Korean and American Perspectives* (Seoul: Korea Development Institute, 1993), 67–110.
62. Yoo-Keun Shin and Heung-Gook Kim, "Individualism and Collectivism in Korean Industry," in Gene Yoon and Sang-Chin Choi, eds., *Psychology of the Korean People: Collectivism and Individualism* (Seoul: Doug-A Publishing, 1994), 189–208.
63. Business Environment Risk Intelligence, *Labor Force Evaluation Measures*, 1992, quoted in Jae-Won Kim, *Jungyo Gyeongjaenggookeo Geonro Hyuntae Bigyo* (A

comparative study of labor behavior among major competitors) (Seoul: Korea Chamber of Commerce, 1995), 162.
64. Kearney, *Warrior Worker,* 244–245.
65. A statistical analysis shows that they show high competitiveness, high self-reliance, and internal locus of control that reflect the can-do spirit. They also reveal, at the individual level, professionalism through growth of self-confidence, ability, efficiency, competitiveness, and egocentrism, but they are not as individualistic as Western people. See Nam-Guk Cho, "The Emergence of Individualism in Korean Organizations," in Yoon and Choi, *Psychology of the Korean People,* 209–232.

CHAPTER 4

1. See William J. Abernathy and James M. Utterback, "Patterns of Industrial Innovation," *Technology Review,* June/July 1978, 41–48. For similar discussions, see Richard R. Nelson and Sidney Winter, *An Evolutionary Theory of Economic Change* (Cambridge, Mass.: Belknap Press, Harvard University Press, 1982), and Giovanni Dosi, "Technological Paradigms and Technological Trajectories: A Suggested Interpretation of the Determinants and Directions of Technical Change," *Research Policy* 11 (1992): 147–162.
2. This and the subsequent two paragraphs draw heavily on Abernathy and Utterback, "Patterns of Industrial Innovation," 41–48, and James M. Utterback, *Mastering the Dynamics of Innovation* (Cambridge, Mass.: Harvard Business School Press, 1994).
3. See James M. Utterback and Linsu Kim, "Invasion of Stable Business by Radical Innovations," in Paul R. Kleindorfer, ed., *Management of Productivity and Technology in Manufacturing* (New York: Plenum Press, 1985), 113–151; Arnold Cooper and Dan Schendel, "Strategic Responses to Technological Threat," *Business Horizons* 19 (1976): 61–69; and Philip Anderson and Michael Tushman, "Technological Discontinuities and Dominant Designs: A Cyclical Model of Technological Change," *Administrative Science Quarterly* 35 (1990): 604–633.
4. See Yosunori Baba, "Japanese Color TV Firms: Decision-making from the 1950s to the 1980s: Oligopolistic Corporate Strategy in the Age of Microelectronics," D.Phil. diss., University of Sussex, 1985.
5. Christopher Freeman and Carlota Perez, "Structural Crises of Adjustment, Business Cycles, and Investment Behavior," in Giovanni Dosi, Christopher Freeman, Richard Nelson, Gerald Silverberg, and Luc Soete, eds., *Technical Change and Economic Theory* (London: Pinter Publishers, 1988), 38–66.
6. See Linsu Kim, "Stages of Development of Industrial Technology in a Developing Country: A Model," *Research Policy* 9, no. 3 (1980): 254–277.
7. This paragraph summarizes the seminal article by Jinjoo Lee and his associates. See Jinjoo Lee, Zong-Tae Bae, and Dong-Kyu Choi, "Technology Development Processes: A Model for a Developing Country with a Global Perspective," *R&D Management* 18, no. 3 (1988): 235–250.
8. Perez and Soete provide a useful discussion of four entry barriers associated

with four different phases of technological trajectory and conditions for imitators to enter and effectively catch up at each phase. Their Phase III appears to correspond with the early stage of the specific state and their Phase IV with the later stage of the specific state. See Carlota Perez and Luc Soete, "Catching Up in Technology: Entry Barriers and Windows of Opportunity," in Dosi et al., *Technical Change and Economic Theory*, 458–479.
9. This progressive pattern of technological trajectory in developing countries may be attributed to the fact that such countries lack resources to overcome entry barriers and in turn fail to take advantage of windows of opportunity, as suggested by Perez and Soete, in the early stage of technological trajectory in advanced countries. See ibid., 475–478.
10. See ibid., 458–479.
11. Wesley M. Cohen and Daniel A. Levinthal, "Absorptive Capacity: A New Perspective on Learning and Innovation," *Administrative Science Quarterly* 35, no. 1 (1990): 128–152.
12. Ibid, 128–152.
13. Linsu Kim and Youngbae Kim, "Innovation in a Newly Industrializing Country: A Multiple Discriminant Analysis," *Management Science* 31, no. 3 (1985): 312–322.
14. Nelson and Winter, *An Evolutionary Theory of Economic Change*.
15. Wesley M. Cohen and Daniel A. Levinthal, "Innovation and Learning: The Two Factors of R&D," *Economic Journal* 99 (1989): 469–596.
16. Herbert Simon, "What We Know about the Creative Process," in R. L. Kuhn, ed., *Frontiers in Creative and Innovative Management* (Cambridge, Mass.: Ballinger, 1985), 3–20.
17. Linsu Kim, "Organizational Innovation and Structure," *Journal of Business Research* 8, no. 2 (1980): 225–245.
18. Charles Cooper, "Are Innovation Studies on Industrialized Economies Relevant to Technology Policy in Developing Countries?" Institute of New Technology, United Nations University, Working Paper No. 3, June 1991, 6.
19. Burton Klein, *Dynamic Economics* (Cambridge, Mass.: Harvard University Press, 1977).
20. Robert B. Duncan and Andrew Weiss, "Organizational Learning: Implications for Organizational Design," in B. Staw, ed., *Research in Organizational Behavior* 1 (1978): 75–123.
21. His migratory knowledge, embodied in individuals who migrate from one organization or country to another, includes tacit knowledge. See Joseph L. Badaracco, Jr., *The Knowledge Link: How Firms Compete through Strategic Alliances* (Boston: Harvard Business School Press, 1991), 33–47.
22. See Ikujiro Nonaka, "The Knowledge-creating Company," *Harvard Business Review* (November–December 1991): 96–104. For more theoretical discussions, see Ikujiro Nonaka, "A Dynamic Theory of Organizational Knowledge Creation," *Organization Science* 5, no. 1 (1994): 14–37. See also Ikujiro Nonaka and Hirotaka Takeuchi, *The Knowledge-creating Company* (New York: Oxford University Press, 1995).

23. Nelson and Winter, *An Evolutionary Theory of Economic Change*, 134.
24. Patricia W. Meyers "Nonlinear Learning in Large Technological Firms: Period Four Implies Chaos," *Research Policy* 19 (1990): 97–115.
25. Nonaka, "A Dynamic Theory of Organizational Knowledge Creation," 28.
26. Martyn Pitt, "Crisis Modes of Strategic Transformation: A New Metaphor for Managing Technological Innovation," in R. Loveridge and M. Pitt, eds., *The Strategic Management of Technological Innovation* (Chichester, England: John Wiley & Son, 1990), 253–272.
27. Pitt introduces the concept of incipient, ignored, and negotiated crises in addition to imposed and constructed crises. See Pitt, 263–265.
28. Alice H. Amsden, *Asia's Next Giant: South Korea and Late Industrialization* (New York: Oxford University Press, 1989), 3–10.
29. Amsden argues in her seminal work on Korea's late industrialization that, squeezed between the state and the salaried engineers, entrepreneurs' usefulness appears much reduced compared with entrepreneurial histories in the late eighteenth century. See ibid., 9.
30. Ikujiro Nonaka, "Toward Middle-Up-Down Management: Accelerating Information Creation," *Sloan Management Review* 29, no. 3 (1988): 9–19.
31. Linsu Kim, "Pros and Cons of International Technology Transfer: A Developing Country View," in Tamir Agmon and Mary Ann von Glinow, eds., *Technology Transfer in International Business* (New York: Oxford University Press, 1991), 223–239. The idea of the two dimensions originated with Martin Fransman, "Conceptualizing Technical Change in the Third World in the 1980s: An Interpretive Survey," *Journal of Development Studies*, (July 1985).
32. Kim and Kim, "Innovation in a Newly Industrializing Country."
33. Kim, "Pros and Cons of International Technology Transfer."
34. Linsu Kim, "National System of Industrial Innovation: Dynamics of Capability Building in Korea," in Richard R. Nelson, ed., *National Innovation Systems: A Comparative Analysis* (New York: Oxford University Press, 1993), 357–383.

CHAPTER 5

1. "Automotive Industry: An Industry in Suspension," *Far Eastern Economic Review*, August 13, 1992.
2. Based on *Market Data Book,* published by the U.S.-based automobile magazine *Automotive News.* See "Korea Edges Past Canada to Become the Fifth Largest Auto Manufacturer," *Korea Economic Weekly,* June 12, 1995, 16.
3. Of $3.17 billion in exports, assembled cars account for 89.4 percent, motorcycles for 0.7 percent, and parts and components for 9.7 percent. See Korea Auto Industries Cooperatives Association, *Jadongcha Gongup Pyonram 1993* (Automobile industry manual 1993) (Seoul: KAICA, 1993), 12.
4. "Korea's Big American Push," *Business Week,* December 23, 1985, 38.
5. See Wonchul Oh, "Sanup Junryak goondansa" (History of industrial strategy corps), *Hankook Kyungje Shinmoon* (Korean economic daily), September 27, 1993, 10.
6. SKD refers to the assembly operation of foreign-designed automobiles on

the basis of semi-assembled foreign parts and components. The number of operations is small and technical tasks are relatively simple. Parts and components are designed and supplied by foreign automobile producers, and there is virtually no room for local adaptation. This is the usual type of operation adopted by developing countries in the initial stage of their automobile production.

7. *Hankook Kyungje Shinmoon* (Korean economic daily), September 28, 1993, 20.
8. Daewoo is the successor to the Saenara Motor Company. Shinjin Motor Company, a joint venture with Toyota, took over Saenara when it was forced to shut down during the 1963 foreign exchange crisis. In 1972 Toyota pulled out of Korea to comply with China's demand that Japanese companies end all relationships with Korean firms before they enter business with mainland Chinese firms. Then Shinjin formed a joint venture with General Motors. In 1978 Daewoo acquired Shinjin's share of the company, and when it assumed management of the joint venture in 1982, it changed its name to Daewoo Motor Company. Daewoo became an independent firm after divorcing from General Motors in 1992.
9. A. Altshuler, M. Anderson, D. Jones, and J. Womack, *The Future of the Automobile* (Cambridge, Mass.: MIT Press, 1984).
10. CKD refers to the assembly of foreign-designed automobiles with completely knocked-down parts and components. The number of operations is significantly large compared with SKD, and technical tasks are relatively more complex, as the assembler is responsible for making the cars operative. Under CKD arrangements, the domestic content ratio can be raised with a significant degree of local adaptation.

    The statistics can be found in Korea Institute of Economics and Trade, *Problems and Promotional Direction of the Automobile Industry* (Seoul: KIET, 1982).
11. Although Chung Joo Young, the chairman of Hyundai, had automobile repair experience in the 1940s, setting up and managing an efficient production system was an entirely new task.
12. Hyundai signed the agreement with Ford subsidiaries in the United States, the United Kingdom, and West Germany, as they provided various inputs to Hyundai.
13. Hyundai Motor Company, *Hyundai Jadongcha Sa* (History of Hyundai Motor) (Seoul: HMC, 1992), 274–287.
14. This and the subsequent discussion of comparative analysis draws heavily on Alice H. Amsden and Linsu Kim, "Comparative Analysis of Local and Transnational Corporations in the Korean Automobile Industry," in Dong-Ki Kim and Linsu Kim, eds., *Management behind Industrialization: Readings in Korean Business* (Seoul: Korea University Press, 1989), 579–596.
15. Tetsuro Nakaoka, "Lessons from the Experience of Auto Industries in Korea, Mexico, and Japan: For the Technological Capability Building of the Developing Countries in the 1990s," paper presented at the Korea Development Institute, June 25–27, 1992.

16. Kia, based on a Mazda model, developed a Brisa in 1974, a year ahead of Hyundai's Pony, with a 60 percent local-content ratio. Kia's history book does not, however, contain as detailed a record of its development process as Hyundai's on Pony. It is also difficult to identify interviewees who could provide a comprehensive outline of Brisa development, which took place twenty years ago. See Kia Motor Company, *Kia 50 Nyunsa* (Kia's fifty-year history) (Seoul: Kia Motor Company, 1995), 209–213.
17. Front wheel drive vehicles consume 20 percent less fuel, provide more interior space, are more comfortable and safe, and make less noise than those with conventional rear wheel drive.
18. Mitsubishi's initial equity participation of 10 percent was later increased to 12 percent.
19. This and subsequent paragraphs on FF development draw heavily on Hyundai Motor Company, *Hyundai Jadongcha Sa* (History of Hyundai Motor) (Seoul: HMC, 1992), 491–636.
20. Young-Suk Hyun and Jinjoo Lee, "Can Hyundai Go It Alone?" *Long Range Planning* (1989): 66.
21. A Hyundai manager complained, "Mitsubishi stopped transferring its passenger car technology a long time ago." See "Car Manufacturers Consider Revising Partnerships Seeking More Technology," *Korea Economic Weekly,* February 20, 1995, 8.
22. "Korea's Automakers Take On the World (Again)," *Fortune,* March 6, 1995, 74–80.
23. Ibid., 77.
24. Young-Suk Hyun, "The Road to Self-reliance: New Product Development at Hyundai Motor Company," paper presented at the International Motor Vehicle Program Annual Sponsors Meeting, Toronto, June 4–7, 1995.
25. Ibid.
26. "Hyundai Motor Introduces Three Versions of 'Beta' Engine," *Korea Economic Weekly,* March 20, 1995, 8.
27. "Korea's Automakers Take On the World."
28. Ibid. reports that Hyundai models have competed well in price but not much else; all four 1994 cars—Sonata, Elantra, Excel, and Scope—ranked almost at the bottom of the heap in terms of maintenance problems, and Elantra received the lowest grade in crash tests.
29. "Hyundai Auto Exports Top Historic 3 Million Mark," *Korea Economic Weekly,* October 17, 1994, 8.
30. Hyun and Lee, "Can Hyundai Go It Alone?" 64.
31. Hyundai Motor Company, *Hyundai Jadongcha Sa,* 1111.
32. "Hyundai Stakes Billions on Green Car Breakthrough," *Australian,* June 26, 1995, 17.
33. Sookon Kim, "Ijikyul oi kukjebikyo wha yoinboonsuk" (The international comparison of separation rates and their determinants), *Korea Development Review* 3, no. 3 (1981): 66–85.
34. Martyn Pitt, "Crisis Modes of Strategic Transformation: A New Metaphor for

Managing Technological Innovation," in R. Loveridge and M. Pitt, eds., *The Strategic Management of Technological Innovation* (Chichester, England: John Wiley & Son, 1990), 253–272.

CHAPTER 6

1. This is based on a study of the production of electronic goods released by Elsevier, a British research organization, in 1994. According to the report, the United States produced $240.8 billion, followed by Japan ($215.1 billion), Germany ($43.7 billion), and Korea ($33.4 billion). However, Korea's Electronics Industry Association states that Korea produced $41.8 billion in 1994. See "Hankook Jeonja Sanup Segye 3wui Jubgeon" (Korea's electronics industry approaching world third place), *Joong-Ang Ilbo,* (Korean daily), May 14, 1995, 20.
2. *Yearbook of World Electronics Data,* 1991.
3. It has often been argued that multinational corporations have a giant share of production and exports of the Korean electronics industry. Multinational corporations have played a significant role in the rapid growth of Korea's giant consumer electronics producers as technology suppliers and product distributors, but their contributions to production are insignificant.
4. LG Electronics was originally GoldStar Company, a member of the Lucky-GoldStar chaebol, which changed its name to LG in 1995.
5. Daewoo Electronics was established in 1974 as a small-scale audio products manufacturer. But when it acquired Taehan Electric Wire's electronics division, in 1983, Daewoo became a full-scale electronics industry producer.
6. The Electronics Industry Promotion Act of 1969 provided a legal basis to promote the industry as a strategic export sector. The government, in consultation with private producers, also introduced a series of long-term development plans every three or four years as guidelines for future investment.
7. Garage production refers to rudimentary operations in a small firm. This term was coined by those who investigated the technology-based small firms that often spin off from research laboratories of existing firms or universities. Roberts and his associates undertook a series of studies on the spin-off process and the characteristics of these firms. See Edward B. Roberts and H. A. Wainer, "New Enterprises on Route 128," *Science Journal* (1968).
8. GoldStar Company, *Keumsung Sa 35 Neon Sa* (Thirty-five-year history of GoldStar Co.) (Seoul: GoldStar Co., 1993).
9. Linsu Kim, "Stages of Development of Industrial Technology in a Developing Country: A Model," *Research Policy* 9 (1980): 254–277.
10. This and subsequent paragraphs on Samsung's microwave oven development draw heavily on Ira C. Magaziner and Mark Patinkin, "Fast Heat: How Korea Won the Microwave War," *Harvard Business Review* (January–February, 1989): 83–93.
11. Samsung Electronics Company, *Samsung Jeonja 20 Nyonsa* (Twenty-year history of Samsung Electronics) (Seoul: Samsung Electronics, 1989), 335.

12. Magaziner and Patinkin "Fast Heat," 89.
13. Ibid., 88.
14. This and the following paragraph draw heavily on Linsu Kim, Jangwoo Lee, and Jinjoo Lee, "Korea's Entry into the Computer Industry and Its Acquisition of Technological Capability," *Technovation* 6 (1987): 277–293.
15. "Research and Innovation: Russian Bargains," *Far Eastern Economic Reviewer*, April 15, 1993, 44.
16. Linsu Kim and Jeffrey Nugent, "Korean SMEs and Their Support Mechanisms: An Empirical Analysis of the Role of Government and Other Nonprofit Organizations," paper presented at the World Bank Conference "Can Intervention Work? The Role of Government in SME Success," Washington, D.C., February 9, 1994.
17. "Next Generation LCD Screen Development Draws Attention of Domestic Industry," *Korea Economic Weekly*, September 19, 1994, 20.
18. Liquid crystal display may be categorized into two matrices: passive and active. Passive matrix includes twisted nematic LCDs, which are used in watches and calculators, and super-twisted nematic LCDs, which are largely used in notebook computers. Active matrix LCDs include thin film transistor LCDs, which are expected to replace existing display technology in notebook computers, television sets, and multimedia devices.
19. This and the following paragraphs are based on Hyundai Electronics Industries, *Hyundai Jeonja 10 Neonsa* (Ten-year history of Hyundai Electronics) (Seoul: HEI, 1994, 205–206, 297–300, 430–432).
20. The development of Korean semiconductor technology is discussed in Chapter 7.

CHAPTER 7

1. See "Korea: Headed for High Tech's Top Tier," *Business Week*, July 31, 1995, 32–38.
2. This part draws heavily on Samsung Semiconductor and Telecommunications Company, *Samsung Bandoche Tongshin 10 Nyunsa* (Ten-year history of Samsung Semiconductor and Telecommunications) (Seoul: Samsung Semiconductor and Telecommunications Company, February 15, 1987); Samsung Electronics Company, *Samsung Jeonja 20 Nyunsa* (Twenty-year history of Samsung Electronics) (Seoul: Samsung Electronics Company, November 1, 1989); and Hyundai Electronics Company, *Hyundai Jeonja 10 Nyunsa* (Ten-year history of Hyundai Electronics) (Seoul: Hyundai Electronics Company, February 23, 1994).
3. Changrok Suh, "The Political Economy of Competitiveness: The Case of the Korean Semiconductor Industry," paper presented at the conference Redefining Korean Competitiveness in an Age of Globalization, University of California at Berkeley, April 24, 1993.
4. Korea Semiconductor Company was a joint venture with Integrated Circuits International, Inc., an American company, where Dr. Kang had worked pre-

viously. ICII's American engineers also played an important role in extending technical assistance to Samsung, which later bought out ICII's equity share of KSC.
5. Jinjoo Lee, "Urinara Giupeo Changeojuk Gisulgyebal Sunggongsarae" (Successful cases of creative technological development in Korea), Korea Advanced Institute of Science and Technology, October 1993, mimeographed, 5.
6. Samsung Semiconductor and Telecommunications Co., *Samsung Bandoche Tongshin 10 Nyonsa*, 204.
7. The working good die is a functionally operating wafer (at about 99 percent level) before packaging and reliability testing.
8. Suh, "The Political Economy of Competitiveness."
9. Byung-Moon Byun and Byong-Hun Ahn, "Growth of the Korean Semiconductor Industry and Its Competitive Strategy in the World Market," *Technovation* 9 (1989): 635–656.
10. Martin Bloom, *Technological Change in the Korean Electronics Industry* (Paris: Office for Economic Cooperation and Development, Development Center, 1992), 79.
11. Ibid., 87.
12. This part also draws heavily on the histories of Samsung Semiconductor, Samsung Electronics, and Hyundai Electronics. See note 2.
13. Linsu Kim, "National System of Industrial Innovation: Dynamics of Capability Building in Korea," in Richard R. Nelson, ed., *National Innovation Systems: A Comparative Analysis* (New York: Oxford University Press, 1993), 357–383.
14. When a joint research project is successful and its outcome is commercialized, the companies involved refund government R&D subsidies.
15. Bloom, *Technological Change in the Korean Electronics Industry*, 64.
16. The stack and trench structures are methods of increasing storage capacitors on wafers. The former stacks capacitors on wafers while the latter etches wafers in a trench shape.
17. Kee-Young Kim and Ji-Dae Kim, "The Korean Electronics Industry," College of Commerce and Economics, Yonsei University, 1993, mimeographed.
18. "Samsung Electronics Jumps Ahead of Competition in Memory Chip Output," *Korea Economic Weekly*, January 16, 1995, 10.
19. "Samsung Announces First Ever 256M DRAM Chip Prototype Development," *Korea Economic Weekly*, September 5, 1994, 8.
20. "Samsung Inks Semiconductor Tech Tie-up Contract with U.S. Company," *Korea Economic Weekly*, October 3, 1994, 10.
21. "Semiconductor Applications Dominate Patent Filings in Korea," *Korea Economic Weekly*, February 6, 1995, 12.
22. "Korea: Headed for High Tech's Top Tier," *Business Week*, July 31, 1995, 37.
23. "Symbios Logic to Dominate Nonmemory Market," *Korea Times*, March 25, 1995, 5.
24. "Daewoo Electronics Signs with David Sornoff Research to Develop Nonmemory Semiconductors," *Korea Economic Weekly*, July 17, 1995, 6.

25. "Non-memory Capacity Expansion by Chip Makers Leads to Higher Sales," *Korea Economic Weekly,* August 14, 1995, 9.
26. "Making Fortunes in Silicon Chips," *Korea Money,* March 1995, 39.
27. Boston Consulting Group introduced the concept of a two-by-two matrix: cash cows, stars, question marks, and dogs. A cash cow refers to a business that enjoys the largest market share in a stagnant industry, requiring no new investment but siphoning off cash to other businesses. A star refers to a business that enjoys the largest market share in a rapidly growing industry, requiring a substantial amount of new investment to retain that share. A question mark refers to a business that suffers from a small market share in a growing industry. A successful push may transform it into a star. A dog refers to a business that suffers from a small market share in a stagnant industry, offering little hope for the future.
28. For an excellent discussion of the state role in the development of the Korean semiconductor industry, see Jeong-Ro Yoon, "The State and Private Capital in Korea: The Political Economy of the Semiconductor Industry, 1965–1989," Ph.D. diss., Harvard University, 1989.

CHAPTER 8

1. Linsu Kim, "Entrepreneurship and Innovation in a Rapidly Developing Country," *Journal of Development Planning* 18 (1988): 183–194.
2. Firms may be categorized into four groups by two variables: size of firm and dynamism. Large firms with low dynamism may be called static large firms; large firms with high dynamism, dynamic large firms; small firms with low dynamism, traditional petty firms. Last, small firms with high dynamism may have two groups: traditional dynamic small firms and technology-based small firms. The former is dynamic in the mature technology area, the latter in the high technology area.
3. Linsu Kim and Jeffrey B. Nugent, "Korean SMEs and Their Support Mechanisms: An Empirical Analysis of the Role of Government and Other Nonprofit Organizations," a report submitted to the World Bank, 1994. Nugent, in his earlier statistical analysis, argues that the reversed trend should be attributable to the relative importance of exports, trade liberalization, the development of credit markets, and a variety of technological considerations, all of which have a strong association with government policy. See Jeffrey Nugent, "Variations in the Size Distribution of Korean Manufacturing Establishments across Sectors and Over Time," Working Paper #8932, Korea Development Institute, Seoul, Korea, 1989.
4. See note 2 for the definition of these two types of small firms.
5. In 1979 the government introduced a policy designed to facilitate the development of industrial technology in the industry. Specifically, in 1979 and 1980 the government designated eighty-six capital goods developed by the seventy firms as newly developed innovative machines and offered special incentives to the producers and purchasers. See Linsu Kim and Youngbae Kim, "Innova-

tion in a Newly Industrializing Country: A Multiple Discriminant Analysis," *Management Science* 31, no. 2 (1985): 312–322.
6. I met these engineers during one of my several visits to Shinpoong's second and third plants.
7. Korea Machinery Corporation, privatized in 1968 and acquired by the Daewoo *chaebol* in 1976, is now Daewoo Heavy Industries.
8. Rolling mills are exceedingly simple: a pair of cylindrical rollers made of iron and steel rotate in opposite directions with a gap between them smaller than the cross section of the piece to be rolled. Hot rolling is carried out at temperatures of about 1,000 degrees centigrade for mild steel and 450 degrees centigrade for aluminum. Cold rolling is carried out at room temperature and has the effect of hardening the metal.
9. This section draws heavily on Medison Company, *Medison Moonhwa* (Medison culture) (Seoul: Medison Company, 1995). I conducted a number of interviews with core members of Medison to supplement the literature.
10. See Chapter 2 for a more detailed discussion of the state's role in creating the venture-capital industry in Korea.
11. Written comments from Professor Mark Dodgson on an earlier draft of this book.

CHAPTER 9

1. Studies covering these firms include, among others, Linsu Kim, "Stages of Development of Industrial Technology in a Developing Country: A Model," *Research Policy* 9, no. 3 (1980): 254–277; Linsu Kim and Youngbae Kim, "Innovation in a Newly Industrializing Country: A Multiple Discriminant Analysis," *Management Science* 31, no. 3 (1985): 312–322; Alice H. Amsden and Linsu Kim, "Technological Perspective on the General Machinery Industry in the Republic of Korea," in Martin Fransman, ed., *Machinery and Economic Development,* (London: Macmillan, 1986), 93–123; Linsu Kim, Jangwoo Lee, and Jinjoo Lee, "Korea's Entry into the Computer Industry and Its Acquisition of Technological Capability," *Technovation* 6, no. 4 (1987): 277–293; Youngbae Kim, Linsu Kim, and Jinjoo Lee, "Innovation Strategies of Local Pharmaceutical Firms in Korea: A Multivariate Analysis," *Technology Analysis and Strategic Management* 1, no. 1 (1989): 29–49; Alice H. Amsden and Linsu Kim, "Comparative Analysis of Local and Transnational Corporations in the Korean Automobile Industry," in Dong-Ki Kim and Linsu Kim, eds., *Management behind Industrialization: Readings in Korean Business* (Seoul: Korea University Press, 1989); and Linsu Kim and James M. Utterback, "The Evolution of Organizational Structure and Technology in a Developing Country," *Management Science* 29, no. 10 (1983): 1185–1197.
2. These figures underestimate the number of Korean scientific publications, as most Korean academic journals, in the Korean language, are not included in the Science Citation Index. Only 6 English-language journals are listed, compared with 1,235 American, 690 British, 291 Dutch, 269 German, and 80 Japanese journals.

3. The 1973 and 1980 rankings could not be identified. It is not surprising to find Korea ranking far below most developing countries in these years. When Korea published 27 articles in 1973, Argentina, Egypt, Turkey and Thailand published 764, 683, 149, and 117, respectively, and when Korea published 171 articles in 1980, these countries published 1,716, 1,358, 376, and 344, respectively. See Linsu Kim and Jinjoo Lee, *Gisul Hyukshin eo Kwajung kwa Jungcheck* (Technological innovation: process and policy) (Seoul: Korea Development Institute Press, 1982).
4. Organization for Economic Cooperation and Development, *Reviews of National Science and Technology Policy: Republic of Korea* (Paris: OECD, 1996), 135–191.
5. World Bank, "Korea Technology Development Project: Staff Appraisal Report" (Washington, D.C.: Industrial Projects Department, World Bank 3707-KO, February 25, 1982).
6. Linsu Kim, "Pros and Cons of International Technology Transfer: A Developing Country View," in Tamir Agmon and Mary Ann von Glinow, eds., *Technology Transfer in International Business* (New York: Oxford University Press, 1991), 223–239.
7. James M. Utterback, "The Role of Applied Research Institutes in the Transfer of Technology in Latin America," *World Development* 3, no. 9 (1975): 665–673.
8. See Henry Ergas, "Does Technology Policy Matter?" in Harvey Brooks and Bruce Guile, eds., *Technology and Global Industry* (Washington, D.C.: National Academy Press, 1987), 191–245.
9. For detailed discussions of this category and associated characteristics, see Joan Woodward, *Industrial Organization: Theory and Practice* (London: Oxford University Press, 1965).
10. See Chapter 1 for the definition of these three capabilities.
11. See Alice H. Amsden, *Asia's Next Giant: South Korea and Late Industrialization* (New York: Oxford University Press, 1989), 291–318. Amsden and I jointly took this case study of Pohang Iron and Steel Company.
12. A new term coined here to refer to Korean firms' strategy of reverse engineering highly sophisticated foreign products with valid patents as a way to receive licenses to use them legally after foreign patent holders refuse to share them.
13. Department of Industry, Science, and Technology, Australia, *Australian Science and Innovation Resources Brief 1994* (Canberra: Australian Government Publishing Service, 1994), 21.
14. Industrial property applications include those for patents, utilities, designs, and trademarks. It is noteworthy that only about 30 percent of patent applications are registered.
15. Kwang Koo Ahn, "Teukhuh robon hankukeo doone" (Korean intellect in patent registration), *Wolgan Chosun* (monthly magazine), January 1995, 424–429.
16. See National Technical Information Service, *Industrial Patent Activity in the United States: Part I, Time Series Profile by Company and Country of Origin,*

1969–1992 (Washington, D.C.: Patent and Trademark Office, July 1993), A1-1.
17. Stephen Haggard, "The East Asian NICs in Comparative Perspective," *Annals of the American Academy of Political and Social Sciences* 505 (1989): 158.
18. The term "conservation-of-power rationality" was coined by Klein to describe firms that manipulate the rules of a game to make its environment completely predictable in order to survive. See Burton Klein, *Dynamic Economics* (Cambridge, Mass.: Harvard University Press, 1977).
19. Having undertaken a series of empirical research, diagnosing and prescribing organizational culture of many *chaebols*, I consistently arrive at the same conclusion.
20. "The Corporate Culture," *Fortune*, October 17, 1983, 15–26.
21. T. E. Deal and A. A. Kennedy, *Corporate Cultures—The Rites and Rituals of Corporate Life* (Reading, Mass.: Addison-Wesley, 1982).
22. Michael Porter, *The Competitive Advantage of Nations* (New York: Free Press, 1990).
23. For electronics, see Kim, "Stages of Development of Industrial Technology in a Less Developed Country," 254–277. For shipbuilding and steel, see Amsden, *Asia's Next Giant*, and Alice H. Amsden and Linsu Kim, "The Acquisition of Technological Capability in Korean Industries," mimeograph, World Bank, 1985. For the machinery industry, see Amsden and Kim, "Technological Perspective on the General Machinery Industry in the Republic of Korea."

CHAPTER 10

1. This and subsequent paragraphs draw heavily on Linsu Kim, "Pros and Cons of International Technology Transfer: A Developing Country's View," in Tamir Agmon and Mary Ann von Glinow, eds., *Technology Transfer in International Business* (New York: Oxford University Press, 1991), 223–239.
2. See Linsu Kim and Youngbae Kim, "Innovation in a Newly Industrializing Country: A Multiple Discriminant Analysis," *Management Science* 31, no. 3 (1985): 312–322.
3. Alice H. Amsden and Linsu Kim, "A Comparative Study of Local and Transnational Corporations in the Korean Automobile Industry," in Dong-ki Kim and Linsu Kim, eds., *Management behind Industrialization: Readings in Korean Business* (Seoul: Korea University Press, 1989), 579–596.
4. William J. Baumol, Sue A. Blackman, and Edward N. Wolff, *Productivity and American Leadership* (Cambidge, Mass.: MIT Press, 1991), 195–210.
5. Gary Gereffi and Donald L. Wyman, eds., *Manufacturing Miracles: Paths of Industrialization in Latin America and East Asia* (Princeton: Princeton University Press, 1990).
6. See Richard R. Nelson, "U.S. Technological Leadership: Where Did It Come From and Where Did It Go? *Research Policy* 19, no. 4 (1990): 117–132. See also Nathan Rosenberg, *Technology and American Economic Growth* (Armonk, N.Y.: M. E. Sharpe, 1976).
7. For the prewar period, see Tetsuro Nakaoka, "On Technological Leaps of Japan

as a Developing Country, 1900–1940," *Osaka City University Economic Review* 22 (1987): 1–25. For the postwar period, see Terutomo Ozawa, *Japan's Technological Challenge to the West, 1950–1974: Motivation and Accomplishment* (Cambridge, Mass.: MIT Press, 1974). For NICs, see Linsu Kim, "Stages of Development of Industrial Technology in a Developing Country: A Model," *Research Policy* 9, no. 3 (1980): 254–277. See also Jorge Katz and Nestor A. Bercovich, "Science, Technology, and Socioeconomic Restructuring: The Case of Argentina," in Richard R. Nelson, ed., *National Innovation Systems: A Comparative Analysis* (New York: Oxford University Press, 1993), 451–475.

8. Michele K. Bolton, "Imitation versus Innovation: Lessons to be Learned from the Japanese," *Organizational Dynamics* (Winter 1993): 32.
9. Steven P. Schnaars, *Managing Imitation Strategy* (New York: Free Press, 1994), 228–231.
10. Discussions in this and the following paragraphs draw heavily from Bolton, "Imitation versus Innovation," 30–45.
11. Schnaars, *Managing Imitation Strategy*, 15–18.
12. The term "champion" is frequently used in the management of technology literature to describe one who generates an idea and commits all his or her efforts to developing it. That person is often referred to as an idea or technical champion.
13. Organization for Economic Cooperation and Development, *Reviews of National Science and Technology Policy: Republic of Korea* (Paris: OECD, 1996), 134–191.
14. Mark Dodgson and John Bessant, *Effective Innovation Policy* (London: Routledge, 1996).
15. T. Shishido, *"Japanese Policies for Science and Technology,"* Nikko Research Center, Japan, 1972, mimeographed.
16. Ibid., 18.
17. Taizo Yakushiji, "Dynamics of Policy Interventions: Government and Automobile Industry in Japan, 1900–1960," Ph.D. diss., MIT, Cambridge, Mass., 1977.
18. This and the following two paragraphs are based on Professor Nakaoka's work on technological development in the Meiji period. See Tetsuro Nakaoka, "On Technological Leaps of Japan as a Developing Country in 1900–1940," *Osaka City University Economic Review* 22, (1987): 1–25. See also Tetsuro Nakaoka, "Technology in Japan: From the Opening of Ports to the Start of Postwar Economic Growth," paper presented at Hosei University's Sixteenth International Symposium, "Technological Development and Economic Systems: Japanese Experiences and Lessons," Tokyo, October 1–2, 1994.
19. Ozawa, *Japan's Technological Challenge to the West.*
20. Hiroyuki Odagiri and Akira Goto, *Technology and Industrial Development in Japan* (Oxford, England: Clarendon Press, 1996), 296.
21. National Academy of Science, *U.S. International Firms and R,D&E in Developing Countries* (Washington, D.C.: National Academy of Sciences, 1973).
22. Nathan Rosenberg, *Perspectives on Technology* (New York: Cambridge University Press, 1976).
23. For an interesting discussion of American technological transformation, see

Nathan Rosenberg, *Technology and American Economic Growth* (New York: Harper Torchbooks, 1972), and Nelson, "U.S. Technological Leadership."

24. For Latin American countries in general, see Jack Baranson, "The Drive toward Technological Self-sufficiency in Developing Countries," paper presented at the Conference on Latin America–United States Economic Interactions: Conflict, Accommodation, and Policies for the Future," University of Texas at Austin, March 19, 1973. For Brazil, see Carl J. Dahlman and Claudio R. Frischtak, "National Systems Supporting Technical Advance in Industry: The Brazilian Experience," in Nelson, *National Innovation Systems,* 414–450. For Argentina, Katz and Bercovich, "Science, Technology and Socioeconomic Restructuring," 451–475.

25. The legend of Icarus and its application to modern companies can be found in Danny Miller, *The Icarus Paradox: How Exceptional Companies Bring about Their Own Downfall* (New York: Harper Business, 1990).

REFERENCES

Abernathy, William, and James M. Utterback. "Patterns of Industrial Innovation." *Technology Review* (June/July 1978): 41–48.
Agmon, Tamir, and Mary Ann von Glinow, eds. *Technology Transfer in International Business*. New York: Cambridge University Press, 1991.
Ahn, Kwang Koo, "Tukhuh robon hankookdo doonae" (Korean intellect in terms of patent registration). *Wolgan Chosun* (monthly magazine), January 1995, 424–429.
Altshuler, A., M. Anderson, D. Jones, and J. Womack *The Future of the Automobile* Cambridge, Mass.: MIT Press, 1984.
Amsden, Alice H. *Asia's Next Giant: South Korea and Late Industrialization*. New York: Oxford University Press, 1989.
———. "The Specter of Anglo-Saxonization Is Haunting South Korea." In Cho and Kim, *Korea's Political Economy*, 87–126.
Amsden, Alice H., and Linsu Kim. "The Acquisition of Technological Capability in Korean Industries." The World Bank, 1985. Mimeographed.
———. "Technological Perspective on the General Machinery Industry in the Republic of Korea." In Fransman, *Machinery and Economic Development*, 93–123.
———. "Comparative Analysis of Local and Transnational Corporations in the Korean Automobile Industry." In Kim and Kim, *Management behind Industrialization*, 579–596.
Anderson, Phillip, and Michael Tushman. "Technological Discontinuities and Dominant Designs: A Cyclical Model of Technological Change." *Administrative Science Quarterly* 35 (1990): 604–633.
Applebaum, Richard, and Jeffrey Henderson, eds. *States and Development in the Asian Pacific Region*. Newbury Park, Calif.: Sage Publications, 1992.
"Automotive Industry: An Industry in Suspension." *Far Eastern Economic Review*, August 13, 1992.
Baba, Yosunori. "Japanese Colour TV Firms: Decision-making from the 1950s to the 1980s: Oligopolistic Corporate Strategy in the Age of Micro-electronics." D. Phil. diss., University of Sussex, 1985.
Badaracco, Joseph L., Jr. *The Knowledge Link: How Firms Compete through Strategic Alliances*. Boston: Harvard Business School Press, 1991, 33–47.
"Balancing Workers' Interest against the Nations'." *Business Korea*, February 1990, 31.
Ban, Sung Hwan. "Economic Growth and Equitable Development Problems in Korea." Paper presented at the International Conference on Economic Development, Korean Economics Association, August 1984.

Ban, Sung Hwan, Pal Yong Moon, and Dwight H. Perkins, *Rural Development in the Republic of Korea*. Cambridge, Mass.: Council on East Asian Studies, Harvard University, 1980.

Baranson, Jack. "The Drive toward Technological Self-sufficiency in Developing Countries." Paper presented at the Conference on Latin America–United States Economic Interactions: Conflict, Accommodation, and Policies for the Future, University of Texas at Austin, March 19, 1973.

Baumol, William J., Sue A. Blackman, and Edward N. Wolff. *Productivity and American Leadership*. Cambridge, Mass.: MIT Press, 1991.

Bello, Walden, and Stephanie Rosenfeld. *Dragons in Distress: Asia's Miracle Economies in Crisis*. San Francisco: Institute for Food and Development Policy, 1992, 58.

Bloom, Martin. *Technological Change in the Korean Electronics Industry*. Paris: Office for Economic Cooperation and Development, Development Center, 1992, 79.

Bognanno, Mario F. "Korea's Industrial Relations at the Turning Point." Korea Development Institute Working Paper No. 8816, December 1988, 46.

Bolton, Michele K. "Imitation versus Innovation." *Organizational Dynamics* (Winter 1993): 34.

Business Environment Risk Intelligence. *Labor Force Evaluation Measures, 1992*. Quoted from Jae-Won Kim. *Jungo Gyeongjaenggookeo Geonro Hyungtae Bigyo* (A comparative study of labor behavior among major competitors). Seoul: Korea Chamber of Commerce, 1995, 162.

Byun, Byung-Moon and Byong-Hun Ahn. "Growth of the Korean Semiconductor Industry and Its Competitive Strategy in the World Market." *Technovation* 9 (1989): 635–656.

"Car Manufacturers Consider Revising Partnerships Seeking More Technology." *Korea Economic Weekly*, February 20, 1995, 8.

Castells, Manuel. "Four Asian Tigers with a Dragon Head: A Comparative Analysis of the State, Economy, and Society in the Asian Pacific Rim." In Applebaum and Henderson, *States and Development in the Asian Pacific Region*, 33–70.

Cha, Dong-Sae. *Weja Doipeo Hyogwa Boonsuk* (The effects of direct foreign investment). Seoul: Korea Institute of Economics and Trade Press, 1983.

Chai, Denise. "Skeletons in the Closet." *Asia Money* 4, no. 7 (September 1993): 67–69.

Chang, Chan-Sup. "Comparative Analysis of Management Systems: Korea, Japan, and the United States." *Korea Management Review* 13, no. 1 (1983): 77–89.

Chenery, H., S. Robinson, and M. Syrquin. *Industrialization and Growth: A Comparative Study*. New York: Oxford University Press, 1986. Quoted from Amsden, *Asia's Next Giant*, 112.

Cho, Lee-Jay, and Yoon-Hyung Kim, eds. *Economic Development in the Republic of Korea: A Policy Perspective*. Honolulu: East-West Center, University of Hawaii Press, 1992.

———. *Korea's Political Economy: An Institutional Perspective.* Boulder, Colo.: Westview Press, 1994.

Cho, Nam-Guk. "The Emergence of Individualism in Korean Organizations." In Yoon and Choi, *Psychology of the Korean People,* 209–232.

Cho, Soon, *The Dynamics of Korean Economic Development.* Washington, D.C.: Institute of International Economics, 1994.

Choi, Jang-Jip. *Labor and the Authoritarian State: Labor Unions in South Korean Manufacturing Industries, 1961–1980.* Seoul: Korea University Press, 1989.

Chowdhurry, A., and I. Islam, *The Newly Industrializing Economies of East Asia.* London: Routledge, 1993.

Clark, Peter, and Neil Staunton. *Innovation in Technology and Organization.* London: Routledge, 1990, 45–46.

Cohen, Wesley M., and Daniel A. Levinthal. "Absorptive Capacity: A New Perspective on Learning and Innovation." *Administrative Science Quarterly* 35, no. 1 (1990): 128–152.

———. "Innovation and Learning: The Two Factors of R&D." *Economic Journal* 99 (1989): 469–596.

Cooper, Arnold, and Dan Schendel. "Strategic Responses to Technological Threat." *Business Horizons* 19 (1976): 61–69.

Cooper, Charles. "Are Innovation Studies on Industrialized Economies Relevant to Technology Policy in Developing Countries?" Institute of New Technology, United Nations University, Working Paper No. 3, June 1991, 6.

"The Corporate Culture." *Fortune,* October 17, 1983, 15–26.

"Daewoo Electronics Signs with DSRC to Develop Nonmemory Semiconductors." *Korea Economic Weekly,* July 17, 1995, 6.

Dahlman, Carl J., and Claudio R. Frischtak. "National Systems Supporting Technical Advances in Industry: The Brazilian Experience." In Nelson, *National Innovation Systems,* 414–450.

Das, Dilip K. *Korean Economic Dynamism.* London: Macmillan, 1992.

Deal T. E., and A. A. Kennedy. *Corporate Cultures—The Rites and Rituals of Corporate Life.* Reading, Mass.: Addison-Wesley, 1982.

De Mente, B. *Korean Etiquette and Ethics in Business.* Lincolnwood, Ill.: NTC Business Books, 1988.

Denison, E., with J. Poullier. *Why Growth Rates Differ.* Washington, D.C.: Brookings Institution, 1967.

Department of Industry, Science, and Technology (Australia). *Australian Science and Innovation Resources Brief 1994.* Canberra: Australian Government Publishing Service, 1994.

Deyo, Frederic C., ed. *Beneath the Miracle: Labor Subordination in the New Asian Industrialism.* Berkeley: University of California Press, 1989.

Dodgson, Mark, and John Bessant. *Effective Innovation Policy.* London: Routledge, 1996.

Dosi, Giovanni. "Technological Paradigms and Technological Trajectories:

A Suggested Interpretation of the Determinants and Directions of Technical Change." *Research Policy* 11 (1992): 147–162.

Dosi, Giovanni, Christopher Freeman, Richard Nelson, Gerald Silverberg, and Luc Soete, eds. *Technical Change and Economic Theory.* London: Pinter Publishers, 1988.

Duncan, Robert B., and Andrew Weiss. "Organizational Learning: Implications for Organizational Design." In B. Staw, ed. *Research in Organizational Behavior* 1 (1978): 75–123.

Enos, J. L., and W. H. Park. *The Adoption and Diffusion of Imported Technology: The Case of Korea.* London: Croom Helm, 1988.

"Entrepreneurs and Ethnicity." *Fortune*, October 3, 1994, 23.

"Eoikuk baksa 12,000 myong numeo" (Foreign P.h.Ds exceed 12,000). *Chosun Ilbo* (Seoul daily), March 11, 1996, 38.

Ergas, Henry. "Does Technology Policy Matter?" In Harvey Brooks and Bruce Guile, eds. *Technology and Global Industry.* Washington, D.C.: National Academy Press, 1987, 191–245.

"Firms Receive 23 Percent More Foreign Technology." *Korea Economic Weekly,* September 11–18, 1995, 8.

"Foreign Investment Soars 43% in First Seven Months." *Korea Economic Weekly,* September 12, 1994, 6.

Frank, Charles R., Kwang-Suk Kim, and Larry E. Westphal. *Foreign Trade Regimes and Economic Development: South Korea.* New York: National Bureau of Economic Research, 1975.

Fransman, Martin, ed. *Machinery and Economic Development:* London: Macmillan, 1986.

Freeman, Christopher, and Carlota Perez. "Structural Crises of Adjustment, Business Cycles, and Investment Behavior." In Dosi et al., *Technical Change and Economic Theory*, 38–66.

Gereffi, Gary, and Donald L. Wyman, eds. *Manufacturing Miracles: Paths of Industrialization in Latin America and East Asia.* Princeton: Princeton University Press, 1990.

Goldsmith, M., ed. *Technological Innovation and the Economy.* London: Wiley Science, 1970.

GoldStar Company. *Keumsung Sa 35 Neon Sa* (Thirty-five-year history of GoldStar). Seoul: GoldStar Company, 1993.

Grossman, Gene M. *Innovation and Growth in the Global Economy.* Cambridge, Mass.: MIT Press, 1991.

Gulati, Umesh C. "The Foundations of Rapid Economic Growth: The Case of the Four Tigers." *American Journal of Economics and Sociology* 51, no. 2 (April 1992).

Haggard, Stephen. "The East Asian NICs in Comparative Perspective." *Annals of the American Academy of Political and Social Sciences* 505 (1989): 158.

"Hankook jeonja sanup segye samui jeopkeun" (Korea's electronics industry approaching world third place). *Joong-Ang Ilbo* (Korean daily), May 14, 1995, 20.

Hankook Kyungje Shinmoon (Korean economic daily), September 28, 1993, 20.

Harbison, Frederick, and Charles A. Myers. *Education, Manpower, and Economic Growth.* New York: McGraw-Hill, 1964.

Hassink, Robert. "South Korea: Economic Miracle by Policy Miracle?" Maastricht Economic Research Institute on Innovation and Technology, 1994. Mimeographed.

Hentges, Harriet A. "The Repatriation and Utilization of High-Level Manpower: A Case Study of the Korea Institute of Science and Technology." Ph.D. diss., Johns Hopkins University, 1975.

Hofstede, Geert. *Culture's Consequences: International Differences in Work Related Values.* Beverly Hills: Sage Publications, 1980.

Hofstede, Geert and Michael Bond. "The Confucius Connection: From Cultural Roots and Economic Growth." *Organizational Dynamics* (Spring 1988): 4–21.

Hyun, Young-suk. "The Road to Self-reliance: New Product Development of Hyundai Motor Company." Paper presented at the International Motor Vehicle Program Annual Sponsors Meeting, Toronto, June 4–7, 1995.

Hyun, Young-Suk, and Jinjoo Lee. "Can Hyundai Go It Alone?" *Long Range Planning* (1989): 66.

"Hyundai Auto Exports Top Historic 3 Million Mark." *Korea Economic Weekly,* October 17, 1994, 8.

Hyundai Electronics Industries. *Hyundai Jeonja 10 Neonsa* (Ten-year history of Hyundai Electronics). Seoul: HEI, 1994, 205–206, 297–300, 430–432.

Hyundai Motor Company. *Hyundai Jadongcha Sa* (History of Hyundai Motor). Seoul: HMC, 1992, 274–287.

"Hyundai Stakes Billions on Green Car Breakthrough." *Australian,* June 26, 1995, 17.

Janelli, Roger L. *Making Capitalism: The Social and Cultural Construction of a South Korean Conglomerate.* Palo Alto: Stanford University Press, 1993.

Jeon, Sang-Woon. *Science and Technology in Korea: Traditional Instruments and Techniques.* Cambridge, Mass.: MIT Press, 1974.

"Jijaekwon bumjae 5nyunse 5bae" (The number of violations of intellectual property rights quintupled in five years). *Chosun Ilbo* (Seoul daily), April 10, 1995, 39.

Johnson, Chalmers. *MITI and the Japanese Miracles: The Growth of Industrial Policy, 1925–75.* Palo Alto: Stanford University Press, 1982.

Jones, Leroy, and Il Sakong. *Government, Business, and Entrepreneurship in Economic Development: The Korean Case.* Cambridge, Mass.: Council on East Asian Studies, Harvard University, 1980.

Joong-Ang Ilbo (Korean daily), February 23, 1990.

———. December 10, 1994.

Kahn, Herman. *World Economic Development: 1979 and Beyond.* London: Croom Helm, 1979.

Kang, T. W. *Is Korea the Next Japan? The Structure, Strategy, and Tactics of America's Next Competitor.* New York: Free Press, 1988.

Katz, Jorge, and Nestor A. Bercovich. "Science, Technology and Socio-economic Restructuring: The Case of Argentina." In Nelson, *National Innovation Systems,* 451–475.

Kearney, Robert P. *The Warrior Worker: The Challenge of the Korean Way of Working.* New York: Henry Holt, 1991.

Kelley, Lane, Arthur Whatley, Reginald Worthley, and Harry Lie. "The Role of the Ideal Organization in Comparative Management: A Cross Cultural Perspective of Japan and Korea." *Asia and Pacific Journal of Management* 3, no. 2 (1986): 59–70.

"KERI (Korea Economic Research Institute) Report Reveals *Chaebol's* Ownership, Management Structure." *Korea Economic Weekly,* August 15, 1994, 18.

Kia Motor Company. *Kia 50 Nyunsa* (Kia's fifty-year history). Seoul: Kia Motor Company, 1995, 209–213.

Kim, Choong Soon. *The Culture of Korean Industry: An Ethnography of Poongsan Corporation.* Tucson: University of Arizona Press, 1992.

Kim, Chung-Yum. *Hankuk Kyungje Jungchek 30 Nyunsa* (Korea's thirty-year economic policy history). Seoul: Chung-Ang Ilbo Press, 1990.

Kim, Dong-Ki, and Linsu Kim, eds. *Management behind Industrialization: Readings in Korean Business.* Seoul: Korea University Press, 1989.

Kim, Gyun. "A Study of the Development of Technological Capability of Korea in the 1980s." Ph.D. diss., Department of Economics, Seoul National University, 1994.

Kim, Jae-Un. *The Koreans: Their Mind and Behavior.* Seoul: Kyobo Book Center, 1991.

Kim, Jae-Won. *Jungyo Gyeongjaenggookeo Geonro Hyungtae Bigyo* (A comparative study of labor behavior among major competitors). Seoul: Korea Chamber of Commerce, 1995, 162.

Kim, Kee-Young, and Ji-Dae Kim. "The Korean Electronics Industry." College of Commerce and Economics, Yonsei University, 1993. Mimeographed.

Kim, Kiwhan, and Danny Leipziger. "Korea: A Case of Government-led Development: Lessons from East Asia, A Country Studies Approach." Washington, D.C.: World Bank, 1993.

Kim, Kwang-Suk. "The 1964–1965 Exchange Rate Reform, Export-Promotion Measures, and Import-Liberalization Program." In Cho and Kim, *The Economic Development in the Republic of Korea,* 101–134.

———. "Industrial Policy and Trade Regimes." In Cho and Kim, *Korea's Political Economy,* 531–555.

———. "Dynamics of Industrial Policy: Export-oriented Industrialization." Paper presented at Korea's State-guided Modernization Conference, East-West Center, Honolulu, August 9–12, 1994.

Kim, Kwang-Suk, and Michael Roemer, *Growth and Structural Transformation.* Cambridge, Mass.: Council on East Asian Studies, Harvard University, 1979.

Kim, Linsu. "Enterpreneurship and Innovation in a Rapidly Developing Country." *Journal of Development Planning* 18 (1988): 183–194.

———. "Korea." In Surendra Patel, ed. *Technological Transformation in the Third World, Volume 1: Asia.* Aldersot, England: Avebury Publishers, 1993.

———. "Korea's Acquisition of Technological Capability for Internationalization: Macro and Micro Factors." *Business Review of Korea University* 22, no. 1 (1988): 18.

———. "National System of Industrial Innovation: Dynamics of Capability Building in Korea." In Nelson, *National Innovation Systems.*

———. "Organizational Innovation and Structure." *Journal of Business Research* 8, no. 2 (1980): 225–245.

———. "Pros and Cons of International Technology Transfer: A Developing Country View." In Agmon and von Glinow, *Technology Transfer in International Business,* 223–239.

———. "Stages of Development of Industrial Technology in a Developing Country: A Model." *Research Policy* 9, no. 3 (1980): 254–277.

———. "Toward Reinventing Korea's National Management System in the Changing Global Environment." Institute report, East Asian Institute, Columbia University, October 1993.

Kim, Linsu, and Carl J. Dahlman. "Technology Policy and Industrialization: An Integrative Framework and Korea's Experience." *Research Policy* 21 (1992): 437–452.

Kim, Linsu, and Youngbae Kim. "Innovation in a Newly Industrializing Country: A Multiple Discriminant Analysis." *Management Science* 31, no. 3 (1985): 312–322.

Kim, Linsu, and Hosun Lee, "Patterns of Technological Change in a Rapidly Developing Country: A Synthesis." *Technovation* 6, no. 4 (1987): 261–276.

Kim, Linsu, and Jinjoo Lee. *Gisul Hyunksin eo Gwajungkwa Jungchek* (Technology innovation: process and policy). Seoul: Korea Development Institute Press, 1982, 112–114.

Kim, Linsu, Jangwoo Lee, and Jinjoo Lee, "Korea's Entry into the Computer Industry and Its Acquisition of Technological Capability." *Technovation* 6 (1987): 277–293.

Kim, Linsu, and Jeffrey B. Nugent. "Korean SMEs and Their Support Mechanisms: An Empirical Analysis of the Role of Government and Other Nonprofit Organizations." Paper presented at the World Bank Conference "Can Intervention Work? The Role of Government of SME Success," Washington, D.C., February 9, 1994.

Kim, Linsu, and James M. Utterback. "The Evolution of Organizational Structure and Technology in a Developing Country. *Management Science* 29, no. 10 (1983): 1185–1197.

Kim, Myung-Sook. "Study of Public Expenditures on Education." *Korea Development Review*, (December 1986.)
Kim, Seok-Ki. "Business Concentration and Government Policy." D.B.A. diss., Harvard Business School, 1987.
Kim, Sookon. "Ijik yul oi kukje bikyo wha yoin boonsuk" (International comparison of separation rates and analysis of their determinants). *Korea Development Review* 3, no. 3 (1981).
———. "Employment Policy and Labor-Management Relations in State-guided Modernization of Korea." Paper presented at the conference "Korea's State-Guided Modernization," at Honolulu, August 8–12, 1994, 4.
Kim, Woo-Choong. *Sesangeon Nulbgo Halileon Mantta* (World is wide and a lot to be done), Seoul: Kimyoungsa, 1989.
Kim, Youngbae, Linsu Kim, and Jinjoo Lee. "Innovation Strategies of Local Pharmaceutical Firms in Korea: A Multivariate Analysis." *Technology Analysis and Strategic Management* 1, no. 1 (1989): 29–49.
Kirk, Donald. *Korean Dynasty: Hyundai and Chung Ju Yung*. Armonk, N.Y.: M. E. Sharpe, 1994.
Klein, Burton. *Dynamic Economics*. Cambridge, Mass.: Harvard University Press, 1977.
Kleindorfer, Paul R., ed. *Management of Productivity and Technology in Manufacturing*. New York: Plenum Press, 1985.
Korea Auto Industries Cooperative Association. *Jadongcha Gongup Pyungram 1993* (Automobile industry manual, 1993). Seoul: KAICA, 1993, 12.
Korea Development Bank. *Korean Industry in the World, 1994*. Seoul: Korea Development Bank, 1994.
"Korea Draws Legal Lines to Protect Property Rights." *Korea Business World*, September 1987, 84–87.
"Korea Edges Past Canada to Become the Fifth Largest Auto Manufacturer." *Korea Economic Weekly*, June 12, 1995, 16.
Korea Exchange Bank. "Direct Foreign Investment in Korea." *Monthly Review*, October 1987, 18–19.
"Korea Headed for High Tech's Top Tier." *Business Week*, July 31, 1995, 32.
Korea Industrial Technology Association. *Sanup Gisul Baegseo* (Industrial technology white paper, 1994). Seoul: KITA Press, December 1994, 1, Table 2–39.
Korea Institute of Economics and Trade. *Problems and Promotional Direction of the Automobile Industry*. Seoul: KIET, 1982.
Korea Trade Promotion Corporation. *World Class Korean Products*. Seoul: KOTRA, no date.
"Korea's Automakers Take On the World (Again)." *Fortune*, March 6, 1995, 74–80.
"Korea's Big American Push." *Business Week*, December 23, 1985, 38.
Krause, Lawrence B., and Fun Koo Paik, eds. *Social Issues in Korea: Korean and American Perspectives*. Seoul: Korea Development Institute, 1993.

Kuhn, R. L., ed. *Frontiers in Creative and Innovative Management.* Cambridge, Mass.: Ballinger, 1985.
"Kyo Yuk Gehyuk: igushi moonje" (Education reform: this is the problem). *Kookmin Ilbo* (Korean daily), March 14, 1995, 1.
"Largest Business Groups Continue Affiliate Expansion." *Korea Economic Weekly,* September 5, 1994, 26.
"Learning the Soft Way." *Far Eastern Economic Review,* December 3, 1992, 54–56.
Lee, Byung-Chull. *Ho-Am Jajun (Ho-Am autobiography).* Seoul: Joong-Ang Ilbo, 1986.
Lee, Jinjoo. "Urinara Giupeo Changeojuk Gisulgyebal Sunggongsarae" (Successful cases of creative technological development in Korea). Korea Advanced Institute of Science and Technology, October 1993, 5. Mimeographed.
Lee, Jinjoo, Zong-Tae Bae, and Dong-Kyu Choi. "Technology Development Processes: A Model for a Developing Country with a Global Perspective." *R&D Management* 18, no. 3 (1988): 235–250.
Lee, Suk-Chae. "The Heavy and Chemical Industries Promotion Plan (1973–1979)." In Cho and Kim, *The Economic Development in the Republic of Korea,* 431–472.
Levenson, Joseph. *Confucian China and Its Modern Fate.* Berkeley: University of California Press, 1958.
Loveridge R., and M. Pitt, eds. *The Strategic Management of Technological Innovation.* Chichester, England: John Wiley & Son, 1990.
McGinn, Noel F., Donald R. Snodgrass, Yung Bong Kim, Shin-Bok Kim, and Quee-Young Kim. *Education and Development in Korea.* Cambridge, Mass.: Council on East Asian studies, Harvard University, 1980.
Magaziner, Ira C., and Mark Patinkin. "Fast Heat: How Korea Won the Microwave War." *Harvard Business Review* (January–February 1989): 83–93.
"Making Fortunes in Silicon Chips." *Korea Money,* March 1995, 39.
Mansfield, Edwin. "R&D and Innovation." In Zvi Griliches, ed. *R&D, Patents, and Productivity.* Chicago: University of Chicago Press, 1984, 142–143.
Mason, Edward S., Mahn Je Kim, Dwight H. Perkins, Kwang Suk Kim, and David C. Cole. *The Economic and Social Modernization of the Republic of Korea.* Cambridge, Mass.: Council on East Asian Studies, Harvard University, 1980.
Medison Company. *Medison Moonhwa* (Medison culture). Seoul: Medison Company, 1995.
Meyers, Patricia W. "Nonlinear Learning in Large Technological Firms: Period Four Implies Chaos." *Research Policy* 19 (1990): 97–115.
"Mi Daehak Hankookin Yuhak" (Koreans studying in American universities). *Joong-Ang Ilbo* (Korean daily), January 5, 1995, 8, quoting Institute of International Education statistics.
"Migook yoohak 59% gooknae chwiup hwimang" (Fifty-nine percent of Korean students in the United States want to find jobs in Korea). *Kookmin Ilbo* (Korean daily), December 2, 1994, 6.

Miller, Danny. *The Icarus Paradox: How Exceptional Companies Bring about Their Own Downfall.* New York: Harper Business, 1990.

Ministry of Education (Japan). *Educational Policy of Japan.* Tokyo: Ministry of Education, Japan, 1993.

Ministry of Science and Technology (Korea). *1994 Report on the Survey of Research and Development in Science and Technology.* Seoul: MOST, December 1994.

Nakaoka, Tetsuro. "Lessons from the Experience of Auto Industries in Korea, Mexico, and Japan: For the Technological Capability Building of the Developing Countries in the 1990s." Paper presented at the Korea Development Institute, June 25–27, 1992.

———. "On Technological Leaps of Japan as a Developing Country, 1900–1940." *Osaka City University Economic Review* 22 (1987): 1–25.

———. "Technology in Japan: From the Opening of Ports to the Start of the Postwar Economic Growth." Paper presented at Hosei University's 16th International Symposium, "Technological Development and Economic Systems: Japanese Experiences and Lessons," Tokyo, October 1–2, 1994.

National Academy of Science (United States). *U.S. International Firms and R,D,&E in Developing Countries.* Washington, D.C.: National Academy of Science, 1973.

National Defence College (Korea). "Gukbang yungu gebalkwa mingan yungu gebaleo gwange ganghwa bangane kwanhan yungu" (A proposal to strengthen the link between military and industrial R&D). Seoul: Korea Institute of Science and Technology, Center for Science and Technology Policy, 1990.

National Technical Information Service (United States). *Industrial Patent Activity in the United States: Part I, Time Series Profile by Company and Country of Origin, 1969–1992.* Washington, D.C.: Patent and Trademark Office, July 1993, A1–1.

Nelson, Richard R. *National Innovation Systems: A Comparative Analysis.* New York: Oxford University Press, 1993.

———. "U.S. Technological Leadership: Where Did It Come From and Where Did It Go?" *Research Policy* 19, no. 4 (1990): 117–132.

Nelson, Richard R., and Sidney G. Winter. *An Evolutionary Theory of Economic Change.* Cambridge, Mass.: Belknap Press, Harvard University Press, 1982, 123–124.

"Next Generation LCD Screen Development Draws Attention of Domestic Industry." *Korea Economic Weekly,* September 19, 1994, 20.

Nonaka, Ikujiro. "A Dynamic Theory of Organizational Knowledge Creation." *Organization Science* 5, no. 1 (1994): 14–37.

———. "The Knowledge-Creating Company." *Harvard Business Review* (November–December 1991): 96–104.

———. "Toward Middle-Up-Down Management: Accelerating Information Creation." *Sloan Management Review* 29, no. 3 (1988): 9–19.

Nonaka, Ikijiro, and Hirotaka Takeuchi. *The Knowledge-Creating Company.* New York: Oxford University Press, 1995.

"Nonmemory Capacity Expansion by Chip Makers Leads to Higher Sales." *Korea Economic Weekly*, August 14, 1995, 9.

Nugent, Jeffrey. "Variations in the Size Distribution of Korean Manufacturing Establishments across Sectors and Over Time." Working Paper No. 8932. Seoul: Korea Development Institute, 1989.

Odagiri, Hiroyuki, and Akira Goto. *Technology and Industrial Development in Japan.* Oxford, England: Clarendon Press, 1996.

Office of Statistics. *Tonggyero bon Hankukeo Baljachiu* (Korea's progress in statistics). Seoul: Office of Statistics, 1995.

Oh, Tai K., Thomas E. Maher, and Cheong Han. "Codependency, Asian-style: The Impact of Confucian Values on the Korean Labor Force." School of Business Administration and Economics, California State University, Fullerton, 1991. Mimeographed.

Oh, Wonchul. "Sanup Junryak goondansa" (History of industrial strategy corps). *Hankook Kyungje Shinmoon* (Korean economic daily), September 27, 1993, 10.

"Older, but Wiser." *Business Korea* 12, no. 1 (July 1994): 24–25.

Organization for Economic Cooperation and Development. *Reviews of National Science and Technology Policy: Republic of Korea.* Paris: OECD, 1996, 135–191.

Ozawa, Terutomo. *Japan's Technological Challenge to the West, 1950–1974: Motivation and Accomplishment.* Cambridge, Mass.: MIT Press, 1974.

Pae, Sung Moon. *Korea Leading Developing Nations: Economy, Democracy, and Welfare.* Lanham, Md.: University Press of America, 1992.

Perez, Carlota, and Luc Soete. "Catching Up in Technology: Entry Barriers and Windows of Opportunity." In Dosi et al., *Technical Change and Economic Theory,* 458–479.

Pitt, Martyn. "Crisis Modes of Strategic Transformation: A New Metaphor for Managing Technological Innovation." In Loveridge and Pitt, *The Strategic Management of Technological Innovation,* 253–272.

Porter, Michael. *The Competitive Advantage of Nations.* New York: Free Press, 1990.

———. *Competitive Strategy.* New York: Free Press, 1980.

"Research and Innovation: Russian Bargains." *Far Eastern Economic Review,* April 15, 1993, 44.

Roberts, Edward. *Entrepreneurs in High Technology.* New York: Oxford University Press, 1991.

Roberts, Edward B. and H. A. Wainer. "New Enterprises on Route 128." *Science Journal* (1968).

Rodgers, Ronald A. "The Role of Industrial Relations in Recent National and Enterprise Level Industrial Strategies in the Republic of Korea." In Krause and Park, *Social Issues in Korea,* 67–110.

Rosenberg, Nathan. *Perspectives on Technology.* New York: Cambridge University Press, 1976.

———. *Technology and American Economic Growth.* New York: Harper Torchbooks, 1972.

Rosenberg, Nathan, and C. Frischtak, eds. *International Technology Transfer: Concepts, Measures, and Comparisons*. New York: Praeger, 1985.

Sakong, Il. *Korea in the World Economy*. Washington, D.C.: Institute for International Economics, 1993.

"Samsung Announces First Ever 256M-DRAM Chip Prototype Development." *Korea Economic Weekly*, September 5, 1994, 8.

Samsung Economic Research Institute. "*1994 Segye Jooyokukbyul Gyungjaengryuk Bikyo* (International comparison of competitiveness among selected countries). Seoul: Samsung Economic Research Institute, September 1994.

Samsung Electronics Company. *Samsung Jeonja 20 Nyonsa* (Twenty-year history of Samsung Electronics). Seoul: Samsung Electronics, 1989, 335.

"Samsung Electronics Jumps Ahead of Competition in Memory Chip Output." *Korea Economic Weekly*, January 16, 1995, 10.

"Samsung Inks Semiconductor Tech Tie-up Contract with U.S. Company." *Korea Economic Weekly*, October 3, 1994, 10.

Samsung Semiconductor and Telecommunications Company. *Samsung Bandoche Tongshin 10 Nyunsa* (Ten-year history of Samsung Semiconductor and Telecommunications). Seoul: Samsung Semiconductor and Telecommunications Company, February 15, 1987.

Samuelson, Paul. "Truths, Hard Truths, for Korea." *Dateline*, March 1990, 4–7.

Schnaars, Steven P. *Managing Imitation Strategy: How Later Entrants Seize Markets from Pioneers*. New York: Free Press, 1994, 5–14.

Schumpeter, Joseph, *The Theory of Economic Development*. Cambridge, Mass.: Harvard University Press, 1934.

"Segye ileo hakseopja jeolbani hankookin" (Koreans comprise half the students of Japanese). *Kookmin Ilbo* (Korean daily), February 21, 1995, 5.

"Semiconductor Applications Dominate Patent Filings in Korea." *Korea Economic Weekly*, February 6, 1995, 12.

Shin, Joon-Shik. *Jaseng ryuki dangshineul chiryo handa* (Self-generating power heals your illness). Seoul: Maeil Kyungje Shinmoonsa, 1992, 35–36.

Shin, Yoo-Keun, and Heung-Gook Kim. "Individualism and Collectivism in Korean Industry." In Yoon and Choi, *Psychology of the Korean People*, 189–208.

Shishido T. "Japanese Policies for Science and Technology." Nikko Research Center, Japan, 1972. Mimeographed.

Shishido T., and R. Sato, eds. *Economic Policy and Development: New Perspectives*. Dover, Del.: Auburn House, 1985.

Simon, Herbert. "What We Know about the Creative Process." In Kuhn, *Frontiers in Creative and Innovative Management*, 3–20.

Song, Byung-Nak. *The Rise of Korean Economy*. Hong Kong: Oxford University Press, 1990.

Steers, Richard M., Yoo Keun Shin, and Gerardo R. Ungson. *The Chaebols: Korea's New Industrial Might*. Grand Rapid, Mich.: Harper and Row, 1989.

Suh, Changrok. "The Political Economy of Competitiveness: The Case of the

Korean Semiconductor Industry." Paper presented at the conference Redefining Korean Competitiveness in an Age of Globalization, University of California at Berkeley, April 24, 1993.

Suh, Sang Chul. *Growth and Structural Changes in the Korean Economy, 1910–1940.* Cambridge, Mass.: Council on East Asian Studies, Harvard University, 1978.

Sullivan, John, and Roberta Foss, eds. *Two Koreas—One Future?* Lanham, Md.: University Press of America, 1987.

"Symbios Logic to Dominate Nonmemory Market." *Korea Times*, March 25, 1995, 5.

Tu, Wei-Ming. *Confucian Ethics Today—The Singapore Challenge.* Singapore: Federal Publications, 1984.

United Nations Development Programme. *Human Development Report, 1994.* New York: Oxford University Press, 1994.

U.S. News and World Report, February 27, 1989, 36.

Utterback, James M. *Mastering the Dynamics of Innovation: How Companies Can Seize Opportunities in the Face of Technological Change.* Cambridge, Mass.: Harvard Business School Press, 1994.

———. "The Role of Applied Research Institutes in the Transfer of Technology in Latin America." *World Development* 3, no. 9 (1975): 665–673.

Utterback, James M., and Linsu Kim. "Invasion of Stable Business by Radical Innovations." In Kleindorfer, *Management of Productivity and Technology in Manufacturing*, 113–151.

Vogel, Ezra F. *The Four Little Dragons: The Spread of Industrialization in East Asia.* Cambridge, Mass.: Harvard University Press, 1991.

Wade, Robert, *Governing the Market.* Princeton: Princeton University Press, 1990.

———. "Industrial Policy in East Asia: Does It Lead or Follow the Market?" In Gereffi and Wyman, *Manufacturing Miracles*, 231–266.

Watanabe, T. "Economic Development in Korea: Lessons and Challenges." In Shishido and Sato, *Economic Policy and Development*, 95–111.

Westphal, Larry E., Linsu Kim, and Carl J. Dahlman. "Reflections on the Republic of Korea's Acquisition of Technological Capability." In Rosenberg and Frischtak, *International Technology Transfer,* 167–221.

Woo, Jung-Eun. *Race to the Swift: State and Finance in Korean Industrialization.* New York: Columbia University Press, 1991.

Woodward, Joan. *Industrial Organizations: Theory and Practice.* London: Oxford University Press, 1965.

World Bank. *The East Asian Miracle: Economic Growth and Public Policy.* New York: Oxford University Press, 1993.

———. "Korea Technology Development Project: Staff Appraisal Report." Washington, D.C.: Industrial Projects Department, World Bank 3707-KO, February 25, 1982.

———. *World Bank Atlas.* Various years.

———. *World Development Report 1993.* Washington, D.C.: World Bank, 1993.

"The World's Largest Industrial Corporations." *Fortune*, July 26, 1993, 188–184.

Yakushiji, Taizo. "Dynamics of Policy Interventions: Government and the Automobile Industry in Japan, 1900–1960." Ph.D. diss., MIT, 1977.

Yoon, Bang-Soon L. "Reverse Brain Drain in South Korea: State-led Model." *Studies in Comparative International Development* 27, no. 1 (1992): 4–26.

Yoon, Gene, and Sang-Chin Choi. *Psychology of the Korean People: Collectivism and Individualism.* Seoul: Dong-A Publishing, 1994.

Yoon, Jeong-Ro. "The State and Private Capital in Korea: The Political Economy of the Semiconductor Industry, 1965–1989." Ph.D. diss., Harvard University, 1989.

INDEX

Abernathy, William, 86, 88, 90
Acquisitions, 143–144, 147, 212. *See also* Joint ventures
Advanced countries
　as source of technology transfer, 91–93, 102, 221–224
　technological innovation in, 86–88, 89, 90–91, 168
　See also Germany; Japan; United States
Advanced Engineering and Research Institute, 119–120
Advanced Micron Devices, 156
A. F. Ioffe Physico-Technical Institute, 144
Ahn, Byong-Hun, 264n. 9 (157)
Ahn, Kwang Koo, 267n. 15 (213)
Akira, Goto, 238
Alfa Romeo, 117
Alliances. *See* Joint ventures
Aloka, 185
Alps Electric, 145
Altshuler, A., 260n. 9 (107)
American Bureau of Ships (ABS), 179
American Pulp and Paper Technical Institute, 174
AMI, 151
Amsden, Alice, 17, 26, 116, 248n. 3 (21), 249n. 17 (28), 250n. 48 (39), 253n. 11 (64), 259n. 28, 29 (100), 260n. 14 (114), 266n. 1 (194), 267n. 11 (209), 268n. 23 (215), 268n. 3 (225)
Anderson, M., 260n. 9 (107)
Anderson, Philip, 257n. 3 (87)
Antitrust policies, 34–35, 195
Apple Computer, 144, 218
Apprentices, imitation versus, 208–209

Argentina, 43, 66, 238–239
ARM, 164, 166
Array Microsystem, 164, 167
Asia Motor, 107, 116
AST Research, 144, 218
AT&T-GIS, 166
Automobile industry, 29
　comparison of Hyundai and Daewoo in, 114–118
　imitation in, 106, 110
　　of assembly operation, 110–112
　　of car development, 112–114
　innovation in, 119–124
　sequence of, 124–127
　production and exports in, 14, 105–106, 108–109, 169
　promoting technological learning in, 209, 210, 211, 229
　success of Hyundai in, 127–129
Automobile Industry Long-term Promotion Plan (1973), 112–113
Automotive Industry Promotion Law (1962), 107
Automotive News, 109
Axil Computer, 143

Baba, Yosunori, 257n. 4 (87)
Badaracco, Joseph, 96
Ban, Sung Hwan, 246n. 19 (9), 256n. 51 (74)
Banks, commercial, 25, 27, 36–37
Baranson, Jack, 270n. 24 (239)
Basic Research Promotion Law (1989), 50
Baumol, William, 227
Bello, Walden, 250n. 32 (32), 250n. 35 (33), 256n. 58 (76)

INDEX

Bercovich, Nestor A., 268n. 7 (230), 270n. 24 (239)
Bern Convention on copyrights, 38
Bessant, John, 269n. 14 (236)
Biotechnology industry, 13, 184–188, 189
Blackman, Sue, 227
Bloom, Martin, 264n. 10 (159), 264n. 11 (161), 264n. 15 (162)
Bognanno, Mario F., 256n. 59 (76)
Bolton, Michele K., 269n. 8 (230)
Brain Pool, 67
Brazil, 42, 43, 66, 238–239
Bright Microelectronics, 163
British Leyland, 114, 127
Byte Computer, 187
Byun, Byung-Moon, 264n. 9 (157)

Capital goods imports
   government regulation of, 40–41, 43, 45, 57
   in promoting technological learning, 101, 102, 199, 201
Castells, Manuel, 246n. 18 (9), 248n. 3 (21)
Catching-up countries. *See* Newly industrializing countries
Central Intelligence Agency (CIA), 33
Cha, Dong-Sae, 251n. 52 (42)
Chaebols, 56, 67, 76, 99
   antitrust and trade laws affecting, 34–35
   effects of, on industrial development, 15, 16, 241, 242
   government policies promoting, 24, 26, 27–29, 57
   in promoting technological learning, 195, 196–198, 202, 203, 209, 214–215, 218
   See also names of specific chaebols
Chai, Denise, 250n. 43 (36)
Chang, Chan-Sup, 254n. 30 (69)
Chemical industry, 26, 31–32, 51

Chenery, H., 249n. 21 (28)
China, 6–7, 213, 239. *See also* Confucian education
Cho, Lee-Jay, 247n. 35 (16), 248n. 3 (21)
Cho, Nam-Guk, 257n. 65 (78)
Cho, Soon, 247n. 35 (16)
Choi, Jang-Jip, 250n. 34 (33)
Chowdhury, A., 247n. 35 (16), 248n. 3 (21)
Chrysler, 119, 120, 122
Chung, Il-Hong, 173–176
Clark, Peter, 247n. 34 (16)
Clones, 11–12. *See also* Duplicative imitation
Cohen, Wesley M., 245n. 8, 9 (4), 258n. 11, 12 (91), 258n. 15 (93)
Cole, David C., 245n. 12 (8), 246n. 17 (9), 253n. 13, 14 (66)
Colleges. *See* Universities
Colony Inc., 145
Commercial Vehicle R&D Center, 119–120
Companies. *See Chaebols*; Firms; Small and medium-size enterprises
Compaq, 144
Completely knocked-down (CKD) assembly plants, 110, 112
Compulsory Lending Ratio, 37
Computer industry
   innovation in, 14, 140–141
   mergers and acquisitions in, 143–144
   See also Electronics industry; Semiconductor industry
Confucian education, 7, 25, 204
   effects of, on work ethic, 72, 73, 80
   evolution of, 68–69
Conglomerates. *See Chaebols*; *names of specific chaebols*
Consumer electronics products. *See* Electronics industry; Microwave oven technology; Television industry

Continuous-process production, 205, 206, 207
Control Data, 151
Cooper, Arnold, 257n. 3 (87)
Cooper, Charles, 252n. 2 (59), 258n. 18 (93)
Copyright (intellectual), 38, 239. *See also* Imitation; Protectionism
Counterfeits, 11–12. *See also* Imitation
Creative imitation, 11, 12–13, 14, 229–231
Crisis, 16
    effectiveness of constructing, 233–234, 240
    Hyundai's construction of, 111–112, 113, 128
    in promoting technological learning, 98–100, 200, 215–216, 218, 219, 226
Culture. *See* Socioculture

Daewoo *chaebol*, 15, 27, 179
    in semiconductor development, 153, 156–157, 166, 167
Daewoo Electronics, 132–133, 139, 141, 143, 169
Daewoo Motor, 106, 107, 110, 112
    partnership of GM and, 114–117, 118
Dahlman, Carl J., 5, 248n. 4 (22), 251n. 54 (43), 253n. 15 (66), 270n. 24 (239)
Das, Dilip K., 247n. 35 (16), 248n. 3 (21)
Dasso Aerospace, 118
David Sarnoff Research, 167
Deal, T. E., 268n. 21 (215)
De Mente, B., 255n. 34 (70)
Denison, E., 245n. 6 (4)
Developing countries. *See* Korea; Newly industrializing countries
Deyo, Frederic C., 250n. 34 (33)
Discontinuous learning, 98–99, 100

DNV, 179
Dodgson, Mark, 269n. 14 (236)
Domestic companies. *See* Firms
Dong-Ah, 152
Dosi, Giovanni, 257n. 1 (87)
DRAM technology
    development of integrated circuits, 152–153
    development of 64K chip, 153–157
    development of 256K chip, 157–160
    development of 1M chip, 160–161
    development of 4M chip, 162–163
    development of 64M and 256M chips, 163–165
    production and exports of, 149–152, 167–170
Duncan, Robert B., 258n. 20 (96)
Duplicative imitation, 11–13, 14, 229, 239
Dynamic learning process. *See* Knowledge
Dynamic random-access memory chips. *See* DRAM technology

Education
    acquired from Chinese, 6–7
    acquired from Japanese, 7–10, 25–26
    acquired in foreign countries, 65–67, 232
    effects of, on corporate technology, 92, 93, 94–95
    effects of, on work ethic, 70–71
    effects of Confucianism on, 68–69
    effects of nationalism on, 75–76
    growth and development in, 60–63
    introduced by Americans, 10, 26
    Korean commitment to, 15–16, 59–60, 79–80, 240
    in promoting technological learning, 195, 198–199, 204, 219, 227–228

for research in universities, 49–50
vocational and tertiary, 63–65
See also Socioculture
Electronic Industry Promotion Fund, 133
Electronics and Telecommunications Research Institute (ETRI), 140–141, 162, 163
Electronics industry
  development and growth of, 14, 131–133, 146–147, 169
  government in promoting, 29, 32, 51
  imitation in, 133–135
    of microwave ovens, 136–140
    of TV, 135–136
  innovation in, 140–141
    of flat panel displays, 144–146
    research and development for, 141–144
  promoting technological learning in, 212, 216, 229
Electronics Industry Promotion Act (1969), 133
Elementary education, 60, 61, 62
Employees
  education and development of, 60–63
  effects of labor disputes on, 76–79
  mobility and networking of, 74–75
  nationalism of, 75–76
  See also Human resources; Work ethic
Engineering research centers (ERCs), 50
Engineering Service Promotion Law (1973), 45
Enos, J.L., 247n. 36 (16)
Entrepreneurship
  for crisis promotion, 99, 100, 232–233
  fostered by Korean work ethic, 72–73

government in promoting *chaebol*, 27–29, 218
  of small and medium-size enterprises, 172–176, 180, 181, 184
  See also Management
Ergas, Henry, 267n. 8 (203)
Explicit knowledge, 154
  in auto industry, 110–111
  nature of, 96–97, 99
  in promoting technological learning, 209, 227–228
Export-oriented industries (EOI), 31
Exports
  in auto industry, 106, 116–118, 123–124
  effects of Western protectionism on, 33–34
  in electronics industry, 131–132, 133–134
  government policies promoting, 15, 16, 26, 29–31, 35–36
  from 1960s to 1990s, 2
  in promoting technological learning, 199–200
  in semiconductor industry, 149–150
  in small and medium-size enterprises, 179, 182, 186, 187–188

Fairchild, 67, 151, 155
Fairlie, Robert, 72
Fair Trade Act (1980), 34
Fiat, 107
Firms (private sector)
  discipline and socioculture within, 73–74
  framework for technology transfer in, 100–102
  as source of technological learning, 92, 93–95, 103
  technological learning process within, 95–100, 203

apprentices versus imitation in, 208–209
building capability in, 205–208
phases of, 209–212
First Economic Development Plan, 28, 107, 177
Five Year Economic Development Plan, 177
Flat panel display (FPD) development, 144–146
Ford, 105, 107, 117, 155, 237
assembly agreement with Hyundai, 110–112, 127
Foreign direct investment (FDI)
in catching-up countries, 101, 102, 222
government regulation of, 40–42, 43, 57, 199, 201
Foreign licensing
in catching-up countries, 101, 102, 222, 225
in electronics industry, 135, 136, 137, 139, 146
government regulation of, 39–44, 57, 199, 200, 201
in promoting technological learning, 207, 209, 211, 212
in semiconductor industry, 153–155, 157
in small and medium-size enterprises, 174, 175
Foss, Roberta, 246n. 21 (10)
France, auto industry in, 106, 108–109
Frank, Charles R., 246n. 20 (10)
Fransman, Martin, 101
Freeman, Christopher, 257n. 5 (88)
Frischtak, Claudio R., 270n. 24 (239)
Frohling, Josef, 183
Fujitsu, 151, 164, 165, 166, 218

General Electric (GE), 138–139, 185
General Instrument, 163, 164

General Motors (GM), 105, 111, 118, 120, 122, 234, 237
partnership with Daewoo, 114–118
Gereffi, Gary, 268n. 5 (228)
Germany, 213
in aiding Korean small business, 179, 180, 181, 183, 184
auto industry in, 105, 106, 108–109, 113, 117
electronics industry in, 131, 134–135
GKN, 117
Global technology environment
in advanced countries, 86–87
in catching-up countries, 88–90
integration of, 90–91
Korean competitiveness and policy in, 56–57
nature of, 85–86, 102, 193
Goldsmith, M., 245n. 6 (4)
GoldStar. *See* LG Electronics
Government
demand side policies of, 26–27, 57
antitrust and fair trade regulations promoting, 34–35
in facilitating technological development, 21–24, 57–58, 94, 194–196, 199, 201–204, 215–126, 218–219
imitation versus innovation in, 38–39
1980s shift in, 33–34
in promoting big business, 27–29, 196–198
in promoting exports, 29–31, 35–36
in promoting heavy and chemical industries, 31–32
in repressing labor unions, 32–33, 76–77
future role of, in public policy, 227–229
globalization policy of, 56–57

in learning from Japanese rule,
  24–26
in promoting education, 64–65,
  198–199
in promoting small and medium-size
  enterprises, 37, 171–172, 175,
  176–177, 184–186
in regulating auto industry, 107,
  110, 112–113, 116
in regulating electronics industry,
  133–134, 140–141, 147
in regulating semiconductor industry, 152, 162–163, 170
role in industrial development,
  15–16, 241–242
supply side policies of, 39, 57–58
  in promoting indigenous research, 47–54
  in promoting research investment, 54–56
  in technology diffusion, 44–47
  in technology transfer, 39–44,
    200–201
Government R&D institutes (GRIs)
  in aiding auto firms, 120
  in aiding electronics firms, 136,
    140–141
  in aiding semiconductor firms, 152,
    162, 163, 170
  in aiding small business, 184–186,
    189
  development of, 46, 47, 48–49
  nature of, 50–51
  in promoting technological capability, 92, 93, 195, 201–204,
    236
  role in education, 66–67
Gross national product (GNP)
  chaebol influence on, 28, 34
  comparison of research expenses to,
    54–55, 212
  influence of exports on, 31
  influence of foreign direct investments on, 40, 42

from 1950s to 1990s, 1–3, 9
ratio of education expenditure to,
  65, 68 79, 100
Grossman, Gene M., 245n. 6 (4)
G-7 Project, 50, 51
Gulf Oil, 179

Haggard, Stephen, 268n. 17 (213)
Han, Cheong, 255n. 34 (70)
Hangul, 75
Hanjin Heavy Industries, 176–179
Hanjin Shipping, 176
Han psyche, 70, 78, 204
Hanyang University, 141
Harbison, Frederick, 62
Hassink, Robert, 248n. 2 (21)
Heavy and chemical industries (HCIs),
  152
  government promotion of, 31–32,
    215–216
Hentges, Harriet A., 254n. 19 (66)
Hermit Kingdom Korea, 74
Hewlett Packard, 163
Highly Advanced National R&D Project,
  50, 51
  See also G-7 Project
High school education, 61, 62–63, 227,
  240
Hitachi, 135, 139, 151, 153, 161, 163,
  165
HMS, 166
Hofstede, Geert, 254n. 30 (69)
Hollomon, Herbert, 72
Honda, 105, 118, 122–123
Honeywell, 154
Hsinchu, 49
Human resources
  education and development of,
    60–63
  in evolution from imitation to innovation, 15–16
  See also Employees; Work ethic
Hyun, Young-suk, 125, 261n. 20 (117),

INDEX 291

261n. 24, 25 (122), 261n. 30 (124)
Hyundai American Technical Center, Inc., 120
Hyundai *chaebol*, 15, 27, 179
  in semiconductor development, 151, 155–156, 159, 161, 162–163, 165, 166, 167
Hyundai Electronics, 133, 141, 143–144, 145
Hyundai Motor Company, 155
  in car development, 113–114
  comparison of Daewoo-GM partnership with, 114–118
  initial assembly plants of, 110–112
  original designs of, 119–124
  promoting technological learning at, 209, 210, 211
  sequencing product development at, 124–127
  technological success of, 127–129
Hyundai Styling Studio, 120

IBM, 67, 118, 144, 151, 154, 163, 218
Icarus paradox, 241–243
IgT, 166
Illiteracy rate, 61
Image Quest Technology, 143, 145
Imitation
  in auto industry, 106, 110–114
  duplicative and creative, 11–13, 229–231
  effects of copyright and patent laws on, 34, 38
  in electronics industry, 133–140
    of microwave ovens, 136–140
    of TV sets, 135–136
  evolution to innovation, 14–16, 193–194, 208–209
  in semiconductor industry, 151–152
    of integrated circuits, 152–153
    of 64K DRAM chips, 153–157
    of 256K DRAM chips, 157–160
    of 1M DRAM chips, 160–161
  in small and medium-size enterprises, 172
    Korea Shipbuilding and Engineering, 176–179
    Korea Steel Pipe, 179–182
    Shinpoong Paper, 172–176
    Wonil Machinery Work, 182–184
  See also Innovation
Immos, 159
Imports
  government regulation of capital goods, 39–44
  government regulation of technology diffusion, 44–47
  government substitution policy on, 29, 31, 140, 147, 199–200
  1980s liberalized policy on, 35–36
Import-substituting industries (ISI), 31
India, 43, 66
Industrial Advancement Administration, 46, 47
Industrial Generic Technology Development Project (IGTDP), 50
Industrial policy
  creation of heavy and chemical industries, 31–32
  exports promotion, 29–31, 35–36
  government in promoting, 26–27, 34–37, 57, 193
  nature of, 22–24
  promoting *chaebols*, 27–28
  repression of labor unions, 32–33
  small and medium-size enterprises, 37
Industrial Promotion Act (1986), 39
Industrial Technology Information Center, 46
Innovation
  in advanced and catching-up countries, 85–91
  in auto industry, 119–127
  capability, 4, 5, 6, 102–103, 206–208
  effects of education on, 64–65

in electronics industry, 141–146
evolution from imitation to, 14–16,
    193–194, 230
at firm level, 95–100
in institutional environment, 91–95
research and development in, 13–14
in semiconductor industry, 161–167
in small and medium-size enter-
    prises, 171–172, 229, 235–236
Medison Company, 184–188
technology transfer for, 100–102
See also Imitation
Inspections and Testing Institutes, 46
Institute of Advanced Engineering, 141
Institutional technology environment
effects of domestic community on,
    92, 93
effect of international community
    on, 91–93
factors influencing interaction in,
    94–95
at firm level, 92, 93–94
nature of, 102–103
Integrated circuits. *See* DRAM technol-
    ogy
Intel, 67, 151, 154, 161
Intellectual property rights, 38, 239. *See
    also* Imitation; Protectionism
International companies
as source of technology transfer,
    91–93, 102
technological learning in, 86–88, 89,
    90–91
See also Advanced countries
International Management Develop-
    ment (IMD), 56, 57
Investment capability, 5–6, 206–208
ISD, 164, 166
Islam, I., 247n. 35 (16), 248n. 3 (21)
Italdesign, 113, 114, 117, 127
Italy, auto industry in, 108–109, 113,
    114, 117
Itochu, 107

Janelli, Roger L., 247n. 36 (16)
Japan, 2, 7, 213
in aiding Korean small business, 173,
    174, 175, 176, 177–179,
    180–181, 182–183, 229
auto industry in, 105–106, 107,
    108–109, 113, 114, 117, 120,
    122–123, 128
electronics industry in, 131, 134,
    135, 136, 137, 138, 139, 140,
    144, 145, 146
expenditure for education in, 68
government influence on business
    in, 28, 30, 32, 37, 38
industrialization in, 229–230, 231,
    237–238
Korea under rule of, 7–8, 9–10, 75
learning acquired from, 25–26, 193
semiconductor industry in, 149,
    153, 154, 155, 157, 158,
    159–160, 161, 162, 163–164,
    166, 167, 168
in technological innovation, 90, 212
in transferring technology, 40–41,
    44, 215
work ethic in, 69, 71, 74
Japanese Military Academy, 26
J. C. Penny, 138
Jeon, Sang-Woon, 7
Johnson, Chalmers, 247n. 1 (21)
Joint ventures, 41, 212, 225
between Daewoo and GM, 114–117
government policy on, 41–42
in electronics industry, 143–144,
    145, 147
in semiconductor industry, 156, 167
Jones, D., 260n. 9 (107)
Jones, Leroy, 255n. 48 (72)
Josef Frohling, 183

Kahn, Herman, 254n. 23 (68)
Kang, Ki-Dong, 152, 155

Kang, T.W., 247n. 35 (16)
Katz, Jorge, 268n. 7 (228), 270n. 24 (239)
Kawasaki, 177, 179
KDW, 179
Kearney, Robert P., 247n. 36 (16), 250n. 36 (33), 256n. 57 (76), 257n. 64 (78)
Kelley, Lane, 254n. 30 (69)
Kennedy, A.A., 268n. 21 (215)
Kia Motor, 106, 107, 112, 113, 115, 116, 117
Kim, Chang Soo, 165
Kim, Choong Soon, 247n. 36 (16)
Kim, Chung-Yum, 249n. 18 (28)
Kim, Gyun, 126
Kim, Heung-Gook, 78, 256n. 62 (78)
Kim, Jae-Un, 255n. 35 (70)
Kim, Ji-Dae, 264n. 17 (162)
Kim, Kee-Young, 264n. 17 (162)
Kim, Kiwhan, 248n. 2 (21)
Kim, Kwang Suk, 245n. 12, 13 (8), 246n.15 (8), 246n. 16, 17 (9), 246n. 20, 21 (10), 249n. 25, 26 (30), 249n. 28 (31), 250n. 41 (36), 253n. 13, 14 (66)
Kim, Linsu, 5, 101, 116, 207, 224, 245n. 7 (4), 245n. 7 (8), 247n. 33 (16), 249n. 19 (28), 249n. 24 (29), 249n. 27 (30), 251n. 53 (42), 251n. 54 (43), 251n. 60 (43), 253n. 15 (66), 255n. 46 (72), 257n. 1 (87), 257n. 6 (88), 258n. 13 (93), 258n. 17 (93), 259n. 31 (101), 259n. 32, 33, 34 (102), 260n. 14 (114), 262n. 9 (136), 263n. 14 (140), 263n. 16 (144), 265n. 1 (171), 265n. 3 (172), 265n. 5 (175), 266n. 1 (194), 267n. 3 (199), 268n. 21 (215), 268n. 23 (215), 268n. 1, 2 (222), 268n. 3 (225), 268n. 7 (228)

Kim, Mahn Je, 245n. 12 (8), 246n. 17 (9), 246n. 21 (10), 249n. 26 (30), 253n. 13, 14 (66)
Kim, Myung-Sook, 254n. 29 (68)
Kim, Quee-Young, 61, 252n. 4 (62)
Kim, Seok-Ki, 249n. 14 (27)
Kim, Shin-Bok, 61, 252n. 4 (62)
Kim, Sookon, 255n. 37 (71), 256n. 52 (74), 261n. 33 (128)
Kim, Woo-Choong, 255n. 44 (72)
Kim, Yoon-Hyung, 247n. 35 (16), 248n. 3 (21)
Kim, Youngbae, 258n. 13 (93), 259n. 32 (102), 265n. 5 (175), 266n. 1 (194), 268n. 2 (222)
Kim, Yung Bong, 61, 252n. 4 (62)
Kirk, Donald, 255n. 44 (72)
Klein, Burton, 258n. 19 (96), 268n. 18 (214)
Knockoffs (clones), 11–12. *See also* Duplicative imitation
Knowledge
  absorption of, 97–98
  dynamic learning in building, 95–96, 231–233
  effects of crises on learning and, 98–100
  framework for transfer of, 100–102, 110–111, 135, 152, 154
  importance of, for technological learning, 227–228
  types and dimensions of, 96–97, 209, 211
Korea
  changes in social organization of, 74–75
  comparing catching-up countries with, 236–241
  duplicative and creative imitation of, 11–13
  dynamics of technological learning in, 16–17

294 INDEX

effects of Japanese rule and civil war on, 7–10
evolution from imitation to innovation in, 14–16
future of growth in, 234–236, 242–243
implications of corporate management in, 229–234
implications of public policy in, 227–229
implications of technology transfer in, 221–227
industrial transformation in, 1–4, 241–242
neo-Confucianism of, 68–69
research and development in, 13–14
technological capabilities of, 4–6
work ethic in, 69–74
See also Newly industrializing countries
Korea Academy of Industrial Technology, 46, 47
Korea Advanced Institute of Science and Technology (KAIST), 49, 65, 120, 141, 152, 184, 185, 186, 187
Korea Automotive Industry Cooperation, 106
Korea Development Bank, 132, 150, 158
Korea Economic Weekly, 164
Korea Institute of Electronic Technology (KIET), 140, 152, 156
Korea Institute of Industrial Design and Packaging, 46
Korea Institute of Science and Technology (KIST), 48, 66–67, 136, 140, 201, 202
Korea International Medical Equipment Show, 185
Korea Machinery Corporation, 180
Korea Multimedia Communication, 187

Korean Airlines, 176
Korean War, 73, 176
economic and societal effects of, 8–9, 10, 14, 74, 204–205, 241
Korea Productivity Center, 46
Korea Semiconductor Co., 152
Korea Shipbuilding and Engineering Corporation (KSEC), 172, 176–179
Korea Standards Association, 46
Korea Steel Pipe (KSP) Company, 172, 179–182, 183
Korea Steel Pipe Machinery (KSPM) Company, 181–182
Korea Technology Development Corporation, 185
Korea Trade Promotion Corporation, 37
Korea University, 141
Kukje, 152

Labor unions
democratization and disputes of, 76–79
government in repressing, 26–27, 32–33
Laserbyte Corp., 143
Learning. *See* Knowledge; Technological learning
Lee, Byung-Chull, 255n. 44 (72)
Lee, Hosun, 207
Lee, Jangwoo, 263n. 14 (140), 266n. 1 (194)
Lee, Jinjoo, 89, 90, 261n. 20 (117), 261n. 30 (124), 263n. 14 (140), 264n. 5 (153), 266n. 1 (194), 267n. 3 (199)
Lee, Min-Hwa, 184
Lee, Sang-Joon, 155
Lee, Suk-Chae, 249n. 30 (32)
Leipziger, Danny, 248n. 2 (21)
Levinson, Joseph, 254n. 24 (68)

INDEX 295

Levinthal, Daniel A., 245n. 8, 9 (4), 258n. 11, 12 (91), 258n. 15 (93)
LG (Lucky-Goldstar) *chaebol*, 15, 27, 28, 35
   in semiconductor development, 151, 152, 156, 162, 163, 164–165, 166, 167
LG Electronics, 132, 134, 139, 169, 209
   in producing flat panel displays, 145–146
   in producing TV sets, 135–136, 218
   research and development at, 141, 142, 143
LG North American Laboratory, 142, 143
LG Technology, 142, 143
Lie, Harry, 254n. 30 (69)
Liquid crystal display (LCD) development, 144–145
Long-term Electronics Industry Promotion Plan, 133
Lotte, 152
Lucky-Goldstar. *See* LG *chaebol*

Machinery industry, 172, 182–184
Magaziner, Ira, 137, 139
Maher, Thomas E., 255n. 34 (70)
Management
   of crisis construction, 233–234
   of dynamic learning, 95, 99, 100, 231–233
   effects of, on technological capability, 95, 99, 100, 213–215
   technological strategy of, 229–231
   See also Entrepreneurship
Mansfield, Edwin, 246n. 24 (10)
Manufacturing Technology Center, 120
Market-mediated technology transfer, 100–102, 222
Marshall Plan, 10

Mason, Edward S., 245n. 12 (8), 246n. 17 (9), 249n. 26 (30), 253n. 13, 14 (66)
Mass-production systems, 205, 206, 207
Mazda, 107
McGinn, Noel F., 61, 252n. 4 (62)
Medidas, 187
Medison Company, 172, 184–188, 189
Memory chips. *See* DRAM technology
Mergers, 143–144, 147, 212. *See also* Joint ventures
Meridian, 187
Meritocratic elites, 25
Metaflow, 143, 166
Meta Software, 165
Mexico, 1, 16, 43, 66
Meyer, Bruce, 72
Meyers, Patricia W., 259n. 24 (99)
Micron Technology, 151, 153, 154, 158, 159, 164
Microsoft, 218
Microwave oven technology, 136–140, 169, 212
Migratory knowledge, 96
Military technology
   compulsory service and, 73, 80
   research and development in, 51–52, 242
   U.S. influence on, 66, 73
Miller, Danny, 270n. 25 (239)
Ministry of Education, 50, 61
Ministry of Labor, 77
Ministry of Science and Technology (M.O.S.T.), 50, 54
Ministry of Trade and Industry, 30, 50, 112
Mitsubishi, 107, 113, 117, 118, 119, 120, 127, 151, 164, 165, 176
Moller and Neumann, 183
Monthly Trade Promotion Conference, 30
Moon, Pal Yong, 246n. 19 (9)

Mosaid, 163
Mostek, 154
Motorola, 151, 152, 153
Myers, Charles, 62

Nakaoka, Tetsuro, 260n. 15 (115), 268n. 7 (230), 269n. 18 (237)
National Administration Information System (NAIS), 140
National Industrial Technology Institute, 46, 47
Nationalism, 75–76, 78
National R&D Project (NRP), 50, 51
National Road and Motorist Association of Australia, 123
National Semiconductors, 154
NEC, 151, 164
Nelson, Richard R., 13, 97, 246n. 26 (12), 246n. 29 (13), 257n. 1 (87), 258n. 14 (93), 259n. 23 (97), 268n. 6 (225)
Neo-Confucianism, 68–69, 78, 80
Networking, 74–75
Newly industrializing countries (NICs)
 future of growth in, 227, 228, 229, 236–241
 global technology environment of, 88–90
 institutional technology environment of, 91–95
 neo-Confucianism and education in, 66, 68–69, 80
 promoting big business in, 27–29
 technology development and learning in, 4, 5, 10, 168, 202, 219, 227, 228, 229, 231
 within firms, 95–100
 technology transfer and imports in, 42–43, 100–102, 221–227
 work hours and vacation in, 78, 79
New Technology Commercialization Program, 53
Nissan, 105, 107, 118

Nixon, Richard, 31
Nonaka, Ikujiro, 96, 97, 100, 258n. 25 (99)
Nonmemory semiconductor technology, 166–167
NTN, 117
Nugent, Jeffrey B., 251n. 60 (45), 263n. 16 (144), 265n. 3 (172)

Odagiri, Hiroyuki, 238
Oh, Tai K., 255n. 33 (70)
Oh, Wonchul, 259n. 5 (107)
Oprex, 145
Organization for Economic Cooperation and Development (OECD), 2, 16, 37
Organizations. *See Chaebols;* Firms; Small and medium-size enterprises
Ovonic Battery, 124
Ozawa, Terutomo, 238, 268n. 7 (228), 269n. 19 (238)

Pae, Sung Moon, 247n. 35 (16)
Page, Glenn, 70
Pali pali, 71
Paper industry, 172–176, 181, 223
Park, Chung Hee, 24–25, 26, 28, 194, 213
Park, Song-Bae, 184
Park, W. H., 247n. 36 (16)
Passenger Vehicle R&D Center, 119
Patents, 38, 213, 234
 of semiconductor chips, 164–165
Patinkin, Mark, 137, 139
Penny, J. C., 138
Perez, Carlota, 257n. 5 (88), 257n. 8, 9 (90)
Perkins, Dwight H., 245n. 12 (8), 246n. 17, 19 (9), 246n. 21 (10), 249n. 26 (30)
Philips, 165, 168

Pirated products. *See* Imitation
Pitt, Martyn, 259n. 26, 27 (99), 261n. 34 (128)
Pohang Iron and Steel Company, 65
Pohang University of Science and Technology, 65, 120
Porter, Michael, 16, 60, 268n. 22 (215)
Private sector. *See* Firms
Production capability
 in advanced and catching-up countries, 87–90
 in auto industry, 105–106, 108–109, 115, 124–127
 definition and nature of, 4–5, 206–208
Protectionism
 of Korea, 29
 of North American and Europe, 33, 239–240

RCA, 136
Regional Industrial Technology Institutes, 46
Renault, 117
Research and development (in technology)
 in advanced and catching-up countries, 87, 90, 93
 agencies supporting, 45–47
 in electronics industry, 136, 140–144, 146–147
 future of, 234–236
 government financing of, 52–53
 government regulation of, 47–52, 58, 64, 201–204
  government institutes in, 50–51
  military in, 51–52
  science and technology infrastructure in, 48–49
  universities in, 49–50, 64
 at Hyundai, 119–124, 129
 investment in, 54–56, 212–213

 in semiconductor industry, 151, 154–155, 162
 in small and medium-size enterprises, 184–188
Reverse engineering, 13–14, 38, 206, 212. *See also* Imitation
Rhee, Syngman, 25, 213
Ricardo Engineering, 122, 127
Roberts, Edward B., 262n. 7 (134)
Robinson, S., 249n. 21 (28)
Rodgers, Ronald A., 256n. 61 (77)
Roemer, Michael, 245n. 13 (8), 246n. 15 (8), 246n. 16 (9)
Rollei, 144
Rosenberg, Nathan, 268n. 6 (225), 269n. 22, 23 (238)
Rosenfeld, Stephanie, 250n. 32 (32), 250n. 35 (33), 256n. 58 (76)
Russia, 144
Ryu, Dong-Suk, 180, 181

Saenara, 107
Sakong, Il, 247n. 35 (16), 255n. 48 (72)
Samsung *chaebol*, 15, 27, 28, 106, 151, 152, 179, 211
 in DRAM innovation, 161, 162, 163–164, 165
 in nonmemory semiconductor development, 166–167
 in 64K DRAM development, 153–155, 156
 in 256K DRAM development, 157, 159
 in 1M DRAM development, 160–161
Samsung Electronics, 132, 162, 218
 in developing flat panel displays, 145–146
 in producing microwave ovens, 136–139
 research and development at, 141, 143, 144
Samuelson, Paul, 32

298 INDEX

Sarnoff, David, 167
Schendel, Dan, 257n. 3 (87)
Schnaars, Steven, 11, 231, 268n. 9 (230)
Schumpeter, Joseph, 13
Science and technology (S&T) infrastructure
   development of, 47, 48–49
   in universities, 49–50
   See also Technology
Science Citation Index, 199, 234
Science research centers (SRCs), 50
Secondary education, 61, 62, 63, 227, 240
Segyehwa (total globalization policy), 56–57
Sejong the Great, 75
Semiconductor industry
   development of flat panel displays in, 144–146
   imitation in, 151–152
      of integrated circuits, 152–153
      of 64K DRAM chip, 153–154
      of 256K DRAM chip, 157–160
      of 1M DRAM chip, 160–161
   innovation in, 13, 14, 161–162
      of DRAM technology, 162–166
      of nonmemory devices, 166–167
   production and exports in, 149–151, 167–170
   promoting technological learning in, 211, 212
   research and development in, 49, 51
Semiconductor R&D Laboratory, 156
Semi-knocked-down (SKD) assembly plants, 107, 110
Seoul National University, 65, 141
Seoul Science Park, 48–49
Sharp, 129, 145, 155
Shin, Joon-Shik, 255n. 41 (72)
Shin, Yoo-Keun, 78, 247n. 36 (16), 249n. 13 (27), 256n. 62 (78)
Shinpoong Paper Company, 172–176, 181, 223

Shipbuilding industry, 29, 32, 172, 176–179, 206, 216
Shishido, T., 269n. 15, 16 (236)
Siemens, 234
Signetics, 151
Silla dynasty, 7
Simon, Herbert, 258n. 16 (93)
Small and Medium Enterprise Formation Act (1986), 37
Small and Medium Industries Promotion Corporations, 37, 46, 47
Small and medium-size enterprises (SMEs), 37
   development struggle of, 171–172, 188–189, 197–198, 215
   diffusing technology to, 45–47
   entrepreneurship in, 72
   future of, 228–229, 235–236
   Korea Shipbuilding and Engineering, 176–179
   Korea Steel Pipe, 179–182
   labor unrest in, 76
   Medison, 184–188
   research and development in, 56
   Shinpoong Paper, 172–176
   Wonil Machinery Work, 182–184
Small-batch production, 205, 206, 207, 208
Snodgrass, Donald R., 61, 252n. 4 (62)
Socioculture
   effects of labor unrest on, 76–79, 80–81
   entrepreneurship in, 72–73
   within firms, 73–74, 92
   individual commitment in, 69–72
   mobility and networking in, 74–75
   nationalism in, 75–76
   neo-Confucianism in, 68–69, 80
   in promoting technological learning, 204–205, 219, 240–241, 242
Soete, Luc, 257n. 8, 9 (90)
Sokkuram temple, 7
Song, Byung Nak, 247n. 35 (16), 250n.

37 (33), 254n. 28 (68), 256n. 53 (75)
South America, 42, 43, 66, 238–239
South Korea. *See* Korea
Spin-off Support program, 54
SRS, 179
Ssangyong, 15, 27, 28, 117, 152
Stanford Research Institute, 167
Stauton, Neil, 247n. 34 (16)
Steel industry, 32, 172, 179–182, 216
Steers, Richard M., 247n. 36 (16), 249n. 13 (27)
Subaru, 118
Suh, Changrok, 263n. 3 (152), 264n. 8 (157)
Suh, Sang Chul, 245n. 11 (7)
Sullivan, John, 246n. 21 (10)
Sunkyong, 15, 27
Sun Microsystems, 163
Suppliers. *See* Advanced countries
Swiss Bank, 79
Symbios Logic Inc., 166
Syrquin, M., 249n. 21 (28)
System Control, 165

Tacit knowledge, 111, 135, 153, 154
  nature of, 96–98, 99
  in promoting technological learning, 209, 211, 227–228, 233
Taedok Science Town, 49
T'aehak educational institution, 6–7
Taeha Mechatronics, 187
Taehan Electric Wire Company, 132
Taiwan, 28, 30, 42, 49, 62, 75, 90, 212, 213, 228, 229
Takeuchi, Hirotaka, 97
Tariff Reform Act (1984), 36
Tax incentives
  for corporate research, 52–54, 55–56
  promoting exports, 30–31
Technological capability
  building, 205–208, 210
  definition and elements of, 4–6, 59

See also Technological learning
Technological learning
  in auto, electronics, and semiconductor industries, 168–170
  capability building in, 205–208
  chaebols in promoting, 196–198, 228–229
  crisis in promoting, 215–216, 233–234
  definition and factors of, 6, 193–194, 218–219
  education in promoting, 198–199, 227–228
  at firm level, 96–100
  global environment in, 85–91
  government in promoting, 194–196, 228
  from imitation to innovation, 16, 102–103, 193–194, 208–209
  import-export strategies in promoting, 199–200
  institutional environment in, 91–95
  management in promoting, 213–215, 229–233
  phases in, 209–212
  research in promoting, 201–204, 212–213
  in small and medium-size enterprises, 188–189
  socioculture in promoting, 204–205
  transfer of, 100–102, 216–218, 221–227
Technology
  chaebols in promoting, 27–29, 31–32, 196–198
  diffusion of foreign, 44–47
  duplicative and creative imitation in, 11–13
  education in promoting, 198–199, 228–229
  evolution from imitative to innovative, 14–16
  exports in promoting, 199–200
  at firm level, 95–100

future growth in, 234–236
at global level, 85–91
government in promoting, 21–27, 33–37, 57, 194–196, 228
impact of, on industrial development, 3–4
at institutional level, 91–95
in joint ventures in auto industry, 114–117
labor repression in promoting, 32–33
learning strategies promoting, 205–218, 229–234
research and development promoting, 13–14, 47–56, 200–204
small business in promoting, 37, 184–188
socioculture in promoting, 204–205
transfer of foreign, 29–31, 35–36, 39–44, 100–102, 200–201, 221–227
Technology Development Reserve Fund, 53
Technology policy, 39
investment in, 54–56
nature of, 22–24, 57–58
research and development in, 47–54
technology diffusion in, 44–47
transfer of foreign technology in, 39–44
Technology transfer
benefits of government policy on, 200–201, 202
in Daewoo-GM partnership, 114–117
effects of, on suppliers, 221–224
in promoting technological learning, 216–218, 219
supply side, 39–44
of tacit and explicit knowledge, 100–102
Television industry
development and production in, 51, 131, 143, 218

Korean imitation in, 135–136, 146
Tertiary education, 61, 62, 63–65, 226, 240. *See also* Universities
Texas Instruments, 151, 153, 156, 159, 161, 168
Toshiba, 151, 153, 163, 164, 166, 185, 218
Toyota, 105, 106, 118, 119, 123, 124
Trade, 228
antitrust laws promoting fair, 34–35, 295
Tsukuba, 49
Tu, Wei-Ming, 68
Turnkey plants, 40, 42, 101, 102, 173, 182
Tushman, Michael, 257n. 3 (87)

Ultrasound imaging technology, 184–188
Underwriter's Laboratory, 137
Unemployment, 64
Ungson, Gerardo R., 247n. 36 (16), 249n. 13 (27)
Union Optical, 144
United Kingdom, auto industry in, 108–109, 113, 117
United States, 213
attitudes toward protectionism in, 29, 33, 38, 239–240
auto industry in, 105, 108–109, 113, 117, 118, 123, 124
Ford and Hyundai, 110–112
GM and Daewoo, 114–117
economic and military aid to Korea, 10
electronics industry in, 131, 134, 136, 137, 138–139, 143–144, 145, 146
employee turnover rate in, 74
expenditure for education in, 68
industrialization in, 229, 231, 238
in influencing Korean education, 65–66, 67

research and development in, 234–235
semiconductor industry in, 149, 153, 154–157, 158, 159, 160, 161–162, 163–164, 166–167, 168
in transferring technology, 40–41, 44, 73
in withdrawing armed forces from Korea, 31–32
Universities
education in foreign, 65–67
graduates and enrollments in, 61, 62, 63–65
research and development in, 49–50, 141, 162
as source of technological capability, 93, 198–199, 227
U.S. Food and Drug Administration, 186
Utterback, James, 86, 88, 89, 90, 202, 257n. 1 (87), 266n. 1 (194), 267n. 7 (202)

Venture Business Association, 189
Videocassette recorder technology, 136, 212
Vitelic, 156, 159, 161
Vocational training, 63
Vocational Training Law (1966), 63
Vogel, Ezra, 2, 248n. 7 (25), 248n. 8, 11 (26), 252n. 1 (59), 255n. 31, 32 (69), 255n. 45 (72), 256n. 49 (73), 256n. 54 (75)
Volkswagen, 105, 106, 117

Wade, Robert, 248n. 3 (21)
Wages, status of, 33–34
Watanabe, T., 250n. 31 (32)
Weiss, Andrew, 258n. 20 (96)
Western Electric, 156

Westphal, Larry E., 5, 246n. 20 (10), 251n. 54 (43), 253n. 15 (66)
Whatley, Arthur, 254n. 30 (69)
Winter, Sidney G., 13, 97, 246n. 26 (12), 246n. 29 (12), 257n. 1 (87), 258n. 14 (93), 259n. 23 (97)
Wolff, Edward, 227
Womak, J., 260n. 9 (107)
Won, Jong-Sun, 182
Wonil Machinery Work, 172, 182–184
Woo, Jung-En, 247n. 35 (16)
Woodward, Joan, 267n. 9 (205)
Work ethic
effects of labor disputes on, 76–79, 80–81
effects of social class on, 74–75, 80
entrepreneurial, 72–73
on individual level, 69–72
nationalism and, 75–76
on organizational level, 73–74
World Class Korean Products program, 53
World Trade Organization (WTO), 37, 239
Worthley, Reginald, 254n. 30 (69)
Wyman, Donald L., 268n. 5 (225)

Xerox, 155, 218

Yakushiji, Taizo, 269n. 17 (236)
Yonsei University, 141
Yoon, Bang-Soon L., 254n. 20 (67), 264n. 28 (170)
Yugoslavia, 62

Zaibatsu, 15
Zilog, 154, 156
Zymos Corp., 156
Zytex, 154

ABOUT THE AUTHOR

Linsu Kim, a professor of management at Korea University in Seoul, is also the president of the Science and Technology Policy Institute (STEPI), a brain trust of the Korean government. He has taught at Columbia University, Indiana University, Boston University, and the Korea Advanced Institute of Science and Technology. In addition, he was a research fellow at the Center for Policy Alternatives at MIT, and a senior fellow at the Korea Development Institute. The former editor-in-chief of two leading Korean management journals, he was also president of the Korean Academy of Management. He serves on the editorial boards of five American and British academic journals and is a vice president of the Korean Society for Technology Management and Economics. Professor Kim has published more than fifty academic articles and six books.